METAPHORS OF SELF

Metaphors of Self

the meaning of autobiography

BY JAMES OLNEY

PRINCETON UNIVERSITY PRESS

For my Mother and Father

preface

Leslie Stephen may have overstated the case for autobiography slightly when he said that no man had ever written a dull one. But I wonder if it might not be true to say that for the common reader autobiography, taken by and large, is the most appealing form of literature and, after autobiography, biography; true to say that autobiography is the literature that most immediately and deeply engages our interest and holds it and that in the end seems to mean the most to us because it brings an increased awareness, through an understanding of another life in another time and place, of the nature of our own selves and our share in the human condition. I should imagine that novels and history, not to mention philosophy and scientific studies, would come well behind biography and autobiography in popularity; and that they are popular not simply with readers looking to fill an idle hour with the excitement of recorded gossip, but also and especially with readers who are looking for an order and meaning in life that is not always to be found in experience itself. For its choice of subject, a book about autobiography need offer no apologies. There are, on the other hand, as one could expect, given something as central, as various, and as comprehensive as autobiography, many different ways of coming at the subject. About the way of this book, one might give a word of explanation.

The present study is in no way "definitive"—neither in the sense that it attempts a precise and restrictive definition of autobiography nor in the sense that it tries to deal with all relevant aspects of the subject. I am more interested in why men write autobiographies, and have written them for centuries, and in why, after the lapse of those centuries, we continue to read them, than I am in the history of autobiography

7 writers

or in its form per se. I am interested, in other words, in the philosophy and psychology of autobiography. It is my notion that, though it treats often of specific places and times and individuals, and must do so to make its experience real, autobiography is more universal than it is local, more timeless than historic, and more poetic in its significance than merely personal. "Je pense," Jean Cocteau said, in a phrase that expresses nicely my own idea of autobiography, "que chaque ligne, chaque tache, chaque onde qui s'échappent de nous (et peu importe ce qu'elles représentent) composent notre autoportrait et nous dénoncent." As for fixing the formal limits of autobiography, had I tried to do that, I am afraid that it would have meant parting company not only with Eliot and Montaigne but also, probably, with Jung and Fox and Newman. Strictly speaking, only Darwin and Mill, of the seven writers considered in this book, wrote autobiographies; but then I do not, as I have implied, intend to speak very strictly when it is a question of literary genre. I have felt quite free to move about from century to century, from poetry to autobiography, and from Switzerland to France to England, hardly bothering to notice the time or the place of events, concerned instead with the significance of their record.

Language is a different matter. Except in the instances of Montaigne and Jung—the two "theoretical" autobiographers —I deal only with works originally in English; had it been possible, I would have chosen none but writers of English. Montaigne and Jung, however, especially taken together, offer what one can find in no writer in English: a philosophical and a psychological theory for autobiography that coincides with an actual autobiography (*Essays* and *Memories, Dreams, Reflections*). In any case, fine translations of Jung's works are available in the nearly completed Bollingen/Princeton and Routledge and Kegan Paul publication of the *Collected*

Works, and Donald Frame has provided an excellent modern translation of Montaigne.

Surprisingly little has been written about autobiography at all, and virtually nothing about its philosophical and psychological implications. A complete list of studies would include only a handful of books in English: Anna Robson Burr's early book, *The Autobiography: A Critical and Comparative Study*, published in 1909; formal and historical studies by Roy Pascal (*Design and Truth in Autobiography*), Wayne Shumaker (*English Autobiography: Its Emergence, Materials and Form*), and John N. Morris (*Versions of the Self*); Robert F. Sayre's analysis of three American autobiographies (*The Examined Self*); brief monographs of varying interest by A. M. Clark, J. Lionel Tayler, and Lord Butler; and an entertaining two-volume anthology, compiled with a commentary by E. Stuart Bates, *Inside Out: An Introduction to Autobiography*. One might also mention Georg Misch's *Geschichte der Autobiographie* (translated, in two volumes, as *A History of Autobiography in Antiquity*), a work that is, in the best manner of German scholarship, both exhaustive and exhausting; Wilhelm Dilthey's writings in the theory of history in which he points out, again and again, the central importance of autobiography for understanding human history and culture; and a number of articles published in English in the last few years (by Stephen Spender, Richard Hoggart, Alfred Kazin, Barrett J. Mandel, and Stephen A. Shapiro). And that is all, at least of any consequence. Even to these few sources I have made virtually no reference, and for a very simple reason: I had not read them at the time when I was writing. This book was conceived in its present form and largely written in first draft during two years that I spent "up-country" in Liberia. As anyone who has visited the interior of that country will easily recognize, it was a piece of great good fortune that I could find, for example, Nickalls' edition of Fox's *Journal* without worrying about what might have been said, or was being said, about the *Journal* as autobiography. When I came out of Africa, I read the books and found occasional similarities with what I had said, but nowhere, I think, with quite the same intention nor in the same context. Hence, I have been content to let any similarities remain in this book as what, in a sense, they were for me: confirmation of thoughts I pursued in Suakoko, Bong County, Liberia. Nor, and for the same reason, does it seem to me of much value to go back to my text and mount what would surely be artificial arguments over incidental dissimilarities and disagreements. Only one piece of writing has seemed to me of sufficient interest and relevance to the concerns of this book to cause me (in Chapter V) to resume and extend my discussion: an essay by the French philosopher Georges Gusdorf, published under the title "Conditions et limites de l'autobiographie" in a *Festschrift* for Fritz Neubert (*Formen der Selbstdarstellung: Analekten zu einer Geschichte des literarischen Selbstportraits*).

It is the great virtue of autobiography as I see it—though autobiography is not peculiar in this: poetry, for example, does the same, and so does all art—to offer us understanding that is finally not of someone else but of ourselves. When William James, speaking in that double character of psychologist and philosopher that he carried so well, wrote to Henry Adams that "autobiographies are my particular line of literature, the only books I let myself buy outside of metaphysical treatises," he expressed what I take to be the attitude of the common reader, the point of view of the present book. My interest in autobiography, that is to say—and I believe this would be James's interest as well—is on the one hand psychological-philosophical, on the other hand moral; it is focused in one direction on the relation traceable between lived experience and its written record and in the other direction on what that written record offers to us as readers and as human beings. We shall never have the experience in consciousness that the autobiographer had, and consequently we shall never know what, in his deepest and inaccessible self, he was. But we might, from autobiography, as from drama or poetry, know what man has been, or what forms have proved possible to humanity, which is a knowledge that one seeks with the intention more particularly of knowing what man is. And this knowledge is again, to each of us, necessary for a very particular reason: behind the question "What is man?" lies another, more insistent question—the ultimate and most important question, I should think, for every man: "How shall I live?" If autobiography can advance our understanding of that question, and I think it can, then it is a very valuable literature indeed.

look to A for answers to the question "How shall I live?"

acknowledgments

Excerpts from *Four Quartets* (copyright 1943 by T. S. Eliot) are reprinted by permission of Harcourt Brace Jovanovich, Inc., New York, and Faber and Faber, Ltd., London.

Quotations from *Memories, Dreams, Reflections by C. G. Jung*, recorded and edited by Aniela Jaffé (copyright 1961, 1962, 1963 by Random House, Inc.), are reprinted by permission of Pantheon Books, a division of Random House, Inc., New York, and William Collins, Sons and Co., Ltd., London.

Quotations from *The Collected Works of C. G. Jung* are reprinted by permission of Princeton University Press, Princeton, N.J., and Routledge and Kegan Paul, Ltd., London.

The writing of this book has been rather lonely than otherwise; hence there are no colleagues that it seems necessary to name either for thanks or for exculpation from responsibility for what I have written. Personal obligations incurred in writing the book, on the other hand, have been incalculable; in fact, they are co-extensive with the book's very existence. I mean the debts of gratitude, which I here acknowledge and in part discharge, that I owe to my parents, to my brothers and sisters, to my wife Judith. I must also thank Mrs. Joanna Hitchcock, who has done an ideal job of editing the book, and Mr. William McGuire, Associate Editor of Bollingen Series, who has given expert and sympathetic advice (especially in Chapter 3) beyond anything an author could legitimately expect. Finally, I think of one other obligation that requires recognition: there may be somewhere a publisher as kind, as generous, and as helpful as Mr. Herbert S. Bailey, Jr., the Director of Princeton University Press—but I doubt it. My gratitude to him is consequently great.

contents

METAPHORS OF SELF

Know thyself. Delphic Oracle

I beseech You, God, to show my full self to myself.
St. Augustine

Here we see that solipsism strictly carried out coincides with pure realism. The I in solipsism shrinks to an extensionless point and there remains the reality co-ordinated with it. Ludwig Wittgenstein

We may come to think that nothing exists but a stream of souls, that all knowledge is biography, and with Plotinus that every soul is unique. W. B. Yeats

and in Melodious Accents I
Will sit me down & Cry I, I. William Blake

one : A Theory of Autobiography

my metaphysics . . . my physics

The most fruitful approach to the subject of autobiography, I believe, is to consider it neither as a formal nor as an historical matter, which would be to separate it from the writer's life and his personality, but rather to see it in relation to the vital impulse to order that has always caused man to create and that, in the end, determines both the nature and the form of what he creates. In this view, there is no evolving autobiographical form to trace from a beginning through history to its present state because man has always cast his autobiography and has done it in that form to which his private spirit impelled him, often, however, calling the product not an autobiography but a lifework. If this is so, then the final *a lifework* work, whether it be history or poetry, psychology or theology, political economy or natural science, whether it take the form of personal essay or controversial tract, of lyric poem or scientific treatise, will express and reflect its maker and will do so at every stage of his development in articulating the whole work. To turn the matter around, a man's lifework is his fullest autobiography and, he being what he is and where and when he is, neither the lifework nor the autobiography could be otherwise. When, moreover, a man writes, in addition to his other works, something that is confessedly autobiographical—Mill's *Autobiography*, for example, or Fox's *Journal*, Newman's *Apologia pro vitâ suâ*, Darwin's *Autobiography*—then we may expect to be able to trace therein that creative impulse that was uniquely his: it will be unavoidably there in manner and style and, since autobiography is precisely an attempt to describe a lifework, in matter and content as well. A man's autobiography is thus like a magnifying lens, focusing and intensifying that same peculiar creative vitality that informs all the volumes of his collected works; it is the symptomatic key to all else that he did and, naturally, to all that he was.

But if there is no history of autobiography to trace nor any form that a book must observe in order to be autobiography, there have been, nevertheless, men who have provided, in their psychological and philosophical speculations, in their comments on themselves and on life in general, hints and suggestions that may be seen to add up to a theory that accounts for both the fact and the nature of autobiographical expression. Heraclitus was the first, according to historians of Greek philosophy, to declare that every cosmology begins in self-knowledge; he was the first to elaborate a physiology and a physics and to project a cosmology that consciously reflected himself, that unique man, as its center; he was, in other words, the first theoretical autobiographer. As the cosmologer is, Heraclitus recognized, so will be his cosmology. And it is most relevantly his cosmology: not yours and not mine, not Everyman's, not a machine's, most of all not God's cosmology. A picture of the cosmos, indeed the very idea of "cosmos" (from the Greek word meaning "order" or "universe"), is a man-made thing that depends entirely upon its creator for its distinctive configuration. A world view, about which one hears so much—one is told that it has been lost or is no longer coherent or was more elegant in the sixteenth century—is a vision held not by the world but of the world. With his yearning for order—a yearning greater, I should think, than his desire for knowledge—man explores the universe continually for laws and forms not of his own making, but what, in the end, he always finds is his own face: a sort of ubiquitous, inescapable man-in-the-moon which, if he will, he can recognize as his own mirror-image. Man creates, in fact, by the very act of seeking, that order that he would have. However we take hold of the question of knowledge, we are always brought

4

back, with Heraclitus, to the beginning: knowledge in this state, in this fallen and sinful condition as the scholastic philosophers would say, must always be, can only be, human, individual, and subjective. A theology, a philosophy, a physics or a metaphysics—properly seen, these are all autobiography recorded in other characters and other symbols.

What Heraclitus is best known for in the history of philosophy, however, and the subject on which he is most often quoted, is his notion that the elements are in continual flux and transformation, and so also are men: "Fire lives the death of earth and *aer* lives the death of fire, water lives the death of *aer*, earth that of water."[1] For the human being, too, "It is death to souls to become water, death to water to become earth, but from earth comes water and from water soul" (Frag. 36). Thus Heraclitus argues that the variability or flux is internal as well as external, but he maintains also that there is, in both instances, a balancing opposite to this continuous changeability; there is, he says, an invisible, and, being invisible, greater and more pervasive, harmony behind discord and an integral constancy behind flux whether in the soul or in the cosmos. The suffix with which, in modern European languages, we harmonize the various elements of our bodies of knowledge ("-logy") is etymologically the same word as the one to which Heraclitus gave such philosophical cogency: "logos." This, the principle of harmony, of measure, of proportion underlying all change, transforms human variability from mere chaos and disconnection into significant process; and, since logos is both a universal and an individual principle, it is realized in the cosmos and in the self as teleological change,

---

[1] W.K.C. Guthrie, *A History of Greek Philosophy*, 2 vols. (Cambridge: Cambridge Univ. Press, 1962), I, 453. The authenticity of this view, as coming from Heraclitus, is questioned and rejected by G. S. Kirk, *Heraclitus, The Cosmic Fragments* (Cambridge: Cambridge Univ. Press, 1954), pp. 341-44; but the point remains the same: this *is* what Heraclitus has been best known for.

as variation with a purpose, as, if one may so put it, rhythmic flux. Like the elements, individual man never is but is always becoming:[2] his self, as C. G. Jung will say some twenty-five hundred years after Heraclitus—nor did man change much in the interim—is a process rather than a settled state of being. The order that men seek is never static and out there but always going on, and going on within them, and always coming into being. Only with the coming of death must the self settle its accounts. Hence, the same man, according to Heraclitus, cannot step twice into the same stream, and this is doubly true: for the man and for the stream. But there is a oneness of the self, an integrity or internal harmony that holds together the multiplicity and continual transformations of being, and it is not an "imitation" of the unity of the Logos, nor is it the individual's "piece" of the Logos. In every individual, to the degree that he is individual, the whole principle and essence of the Logos is wholly present, so that in his integrity the whole harmony of the universe is entirely and, as it were, uniquely present or existent. What the Logos demands of the individual is that he should realize his logos, which is also more than his own or private logos—it is the Logos. If one takes these four notions together—the intimate relation of self-knowledge and cosmology; the flux of all the world; the "becomingness" of the self; the identity of logos and Logos— Heraclitus' conclusion is logical and wholly human, the con-

---

[2] After a philological discussion of considerable length and of very great interest on "logos" in fifth-century Greece, Guthrie says of the word as Heraclitus uses it in Fragment 50 ("Listening not to me but to the *Logos* it is wise to agree that all things are one"): "the *Logos* is (a) something which one hears (the commonest meaning), (b) that which regulates all events, *a kind of universal law of becoming*, (c) something with an existence independent of him who gives it verbal expression" (1, 425; italics are mine). G. S. Kirk and J. E. Raven, *The Presocratic Philosophers* (Cambridge: Cambridge Univ. Press, 1966), say the "logos" is "the unifying formula or proportionate method of arrangement of things, what might almost be termed the structural plan of things both individual and in sum" (p. 188).

6

clusion of the philosopher and the artist, the conclusion, more simply, of the autobiographer and the man: "I searched out myself."[3] One can do no better than to give W.K.C. Guthrie's excellent gloss on this primary statement in the literature of self-description:

> The verb . . . has two main meanings: (1) to look for . . . (2) to question, inquire of somebody, find out. . . . Thus by the two words of fr. 101 Heraclitus meant, I suggest, first, "I turned my thoughts within and sought to discover my real self"; secondly, "I asked questions of myself"; thirdly, "I treated the answers like Delphic responses hinting, in a riddling way, at the single truth behind them, and tried to discover the real meaning of my selfhood; for I knew that if I understood my self I would have grasped the *logos* which is the real constitution of everything else as well." (1, 418-19.)

Thus Heraclitus anticipated, in these two words and in his thought generally, the entire history of autobiographical literature: in his characteristically brief comment, one finds set forth and drawn tightly inward the motives and the methods of autobiographers of all times; and in his search, Heraclitus realized the philosophy and psychology of writers about the self from Plato and Plotinus and St. Augustine to C. G. Jung and T. S. Eliot and beyond. And the subject is as inexhaustible as the Logos itself, for, as Heraclitus says in Fragment 45, "You could not discover the limits of the self, even by traveling along every path: so deep a logos does it have."[4]

In this cosmology-cum-autobiography, one might remark, perhaps in a sort of hyperbole, the problem of the One and the

---

[3] The translation is from Kirk and Raven, *Presocratic Philosophers*, p. 212; Guthrie's translation is "I searched myself"; Philip Wheelwright, in *Heraclitus* (Princeton: Princeton Univ. Press, 1959), p. 19, translates it, "I have searched myself."

[4] Taking the hint from Wheelwright (p. 59) that the word traditionally translated "soul" could equally well be rendered as "psyche" or "self," I have adapted freely from the translations of Guthrie (1, 476-77), Kirk-Raven (p. 205), and Wheelwright (p. 58).

7

many is resolved by a simple reverse. For all purposes of organization and understanding, one of the many in the heretofore meaningless created universe becomes, in the formal projection of cosmography-and-autobiography, the creative One of his own coherent, richly meaningful, intensely organized, altogether self-oriented universe. "Man tries to make for himself in the fashion that suits him best," according to a greatly individual cosmographer of the present century, "a simplified and intelligible picture of the world; he then tries to some extent to substitute this cosmos of his for the world of experience, and thus to overcome it. This is what the painter, the poet, the speculative philosopher, and the natural scientist do, each in his own fashion. Each makes this cosmos and its construction the pivot of his emotional life, in order to find in this way the peace and security which he cannot find in the narrow whirlpool of personal experience."[5] It must also be, as one can see from the nature of the picture, that his construct will appeal ultimately not to the intellect of the viewer alone but also to his emotions as a whole man. Does it satisfy my feeling and my need for order? This would seem to be the final question we can ask and must ask, not only of the poem or the theological doctrine, but also of a psychology or a philosophy, a theory of evolution or a formal syllogism. "In language, in religion, in art, in science, man can do no more than to build up his own universe," Ernst Cassirer says, "—a symbolic universe that enables him to understand and interpret, to articulate and organize, to synthesize and universalize his human experience."[6] Perhaps the greatest mystery is that men so often refuse credit for what they have achieved, disclaiming their accomplishment as something objective or scientific or impersonal or divine instead of proclaiming it as their

[5] Albert Einstein, *Ideas and Opinions* (New York: Crown Publishers, 1962), p. 225.
[6] *Essay on Man* (New Haven: Yale Univ. Press, 1944), p. 221.

8

metaphysics or science reconstituted as
A and art

own and emotionally satisfying. In his own Heraclitean, symbolic, and oracular manner, William Blake, who never, the few times he had the chance, refused the credit due him as a creative maker, whether artist or philosopher, remarked, in the margin of Swedenborg's *Wisdom of Angels Concerning Divine Love and Divine Wisdom*, "Man can have no idea of anything greater than Man, as a cup cannot contain more than its capaciousness."[7] Yet philosophy, in disregard of this human truth and imagining its metaphysics to be objective and verifiable, is forever filling its cup to overflowing in the delusion that for once its capacity might surpass its capaciousness; and psychology, calling itself an exact science, perpetually chases its own tail, sending its naked intellect after its back end in the vain hope that this time it may prove a little faster than last time, or may surprise the tail and come upon it unawares. These are both, no doubt, edifying spectacles, but they are not, perhaps, destined for a more vulgar success than that. Montaigne, more realistic than the metaphysician, more practical than the scientist-psychologist, and obviously closer in spirit to Heraclitus than either, gets away with both games by refocusing metaphysics and science and reconstituting them as autobiography and art: "I study myself," he proclaims; "That is my metaphysics, that is my physics."[8]

One is surprised, in reading the history of pre-Socratic Greek thought, to notice how many of these early "philosophers" either were actual doctors or at least seem to have practiced a little medicine on the side, having deduced a medical theory from their general picture of the universe. Thus, Alcmaeon carried the cosmological principle of dualism developed by the Pythagoreans over into medical-physi-

[7] *Poetry and Prose of William Blake*, ed. Geoffrey Keynes (London: Nonesuch Press, 1961), p. 737.
[8] "Of experience," *The Complete Works of Montaigne*, trans. Donald Frame (Stanford: Stanford Univ. Press, 1957), p. 821.

9

ological theory, saying that health is the proper balance of opposites; Philolaus drew an analogy between cosmogony and
embryology (life, whether originating in the universe or in
the womb, is "composed of the hot"), as also did Anaxagoras,
who maintained that all life came from the moist; Empedocles,
with his theory of respiration and the circulation of the blood,
claimed to be sought by many who wished "to hear the word
that heals all manner of illness"; and Diogenes of Apollonia
seems to have written a medical text either in conjunction with
or as a complement to his book on cosmology.[9] For these men,
physics, physiology, and philosophy were intimately related,
if not identical, studies; cosmology, medicine, and ethics were
the inseparable and quintessential human concerns. The models that these philosophers constructed to order and explain
experience, whether on a macrocosmic or a microcosmic plane,
whether projected onto the whole universe, the whole society of man, or the whole human body, whether the experience to be organized was phenomenal or noumenal or both
together—in any case, these models were first of all a reflection
of the internal order of their makers rather than an imitation
of external reality. And so, hesitant as present practitioners in
these fields may be to admit it, are contemporary models and
theories in physics, philosophy, and biology.

That there was some sort of relation, probably indescribable, between life on the largest and life on the smallest scale,
between intelligence in the universe and intelligence in man,
between the elemental processes in nature and the elemental
processes in the human body, suggested itself as an hypothesis
to the early Greeks, as it has to so many thinkers since—as,
indeed, it did also to the nonthinker George Fox, who, because God had opened to him the loving principle underlying
all creation, nearly chose to be a medical practitioner. And

[9] See Kirk and Raven, *Presocratic Philosophers*, esp. pp. 232, 234, 313, 321,
341-42, 393, 429, and 444-45.

10

C. G. Jung was to build a life, a career, and a book on a rock that, he felt, united human medicine with the psyche of the universe. It is as much a theory—but no more—to say that there *is* an analogy between the human body and the processes of nature, or between the human mind and God's mind, as it is to say that there is no analogy or only a specific and partial one. Which of these one chooses to hold depends upon what one is; and what one is, it may seem odd to say, depends largely upon which of these one chooses to hold. "So that it is almost a truism to say that the world is what we perceive it to be. We imagine that our mind is a mirror, that it is more or less accurately reflecting what is happening outside us. On the contrary, our mind itself is the principal element of creation. The world, while I am perceiving it, is being incessantly created for myself in time and space."[10] In his Eastern way, Rabindranath Tagore had little use for Western technology and science, but what he says here is as relevant to the activities of the theoretical scientist as it is to the speculative philosopher. Every natural science, even physics itself as Max Planck has said, is based on an act of faith, and without this faith no science could presume itself into being: a faith, first, that there is a causal order in nature and the universe; a faith, second, that there is some unfailing relation between the formal organization of the human mind and the formal organization of nature; and a faith, therefore, that the human mind is capable of discerning and describing the ordered processes that rule the natural universe. But why should any of these be true, except perhaps the last one *if* the first two are? The only objective evidence for or against these articles of faith is, of course, God's, or the mind's that draws out and lays down the rules for the very natural order that we are supposing or questioning and of which we are but parts, if it exists. If one

[10] Rabindranath Tagore, *Personality* (London: Macmillan & Co., 1917), p. 47.

11

believes in that natural order, in that mind, in that God, one can say, "I know because . . . I believe"; or, "God exists because . . . I am sure he exists"; or, "The universe is an orderly place because . . . I know it is." There one is left with witness not of God but of one's self.

Newman, in his *Development of Christian Doctrine*, maintains that "Reason . . . is subservient to faith,"[11] and he is unquestionably right: for the reason that we discover in the universe, and the reason that we bring to that universe, are both founded alike and together in an act of faith. They are both epiphenomena of autobiography. And if science and theology are based on acts of faith, as they undoubtedly are, so, as W. B. Yeats told his father in a letter, is art; the object of the artist's faith might be differently described, but upon the intensity and quality of that faith will surely depend the value of the artifact. "All our art is but the putting our faith and the evidence of our faith into words or forms and our faith is in ecstasy."[12] And this "will to believe," which is given and chosen, goes a long way toward making what is believed be true: if the scientist, the artist, the worshiper imagine deeply enough and believe intensely enough, and if they build their whole science, art, and worship, those edifices in which they move and have their being, unfalteringly on their belief, then they will find in their experiments, whether in laboratory, poem, or church, the order that they have themselves first created, posited, and believed in. What each is in effect doing, Planck, Yeats, or Newman, is to find, as Stephen Dedalus puts it, "in the world without as actual what was in his world within as possible." It is men of little faith who will not ask and who refuse to knock simply because the way is all sub-

[11] *An Essay on the Development of Christian Doctrine* (London: Longmans, Green, & Co., 1909), p. 336.

[12] *The Letters of W. B. Yeats*, ed. Allan Wade (London: Rupert Hart-Davies, 1954), p. 583.

jective: to them it shall not be given nor the door opened. "On to God," Planck says, is the cry of both natural science and religion.[13] And why not? For the first item in the credo of both is "There is a God."

We can only be said to believe something (e.g., "There is a God") if there is an alternative possibility to that belief (e.g., "There is no God"). Newman, in his *Apologia*, will go even further than Planck and maintain that the statement "There is a God" is a certainty altogether prior to belief: it is a mere matter of consciousness and self-consciousness and is no more than to say, "I exist," to articulate the awareness of being that each of us has and that is beyond question or belief. And I presume that Newman would say the same of the scientist's belief: that his faith in universal causal order is concomitant upon his consciousness of order existing in himself. Hence what the most brilliant scientist finds in the universe is, like the Deity of the simplest believer, predicated on and determined by what he first found or intuited or felt in himself. Whether or not an awareness of self-existence and an awareness of God-existence are coextensive and, as Newman would have them, virtually identical, there can be no doubt that any understanding of God and his universe, or the laws of the natural world, or the structure of human society, must come out of and will inevitably be deeply colored by the nature of the self and the knowledge that one has of that self lying at the center, and being the very heart, of the understanding that one comes to. "I begin," says Yeats, as he spirals in on the *anima hominis* so that he might spiral out on the *Anima Mundi*, "I begin to study the only self that I can know, myself, and to

[13] "Religion and Natural Science," in *A Scientific Autobiography and Other Papers* (London: Williams & Norgate, 1950), p. 187. See also, in the same volume, the "Scientific Autobiography" and "Phantom Problems in Science" and the book entitled *The Universe in the Light of Modern Physics*, 2nd ed. (London: George Allen & Unwin, 1937).

wind the thread upon the pern again."[14] They seem very different things, study of the self and study of the world, yet the two cannot be ultimately separated, as subject and object join and merge in consciousness. One sees, looking out from the subjective center, various objects—shapes and forms, people, movement, expressive gestures—yet even these objects "become" in that study, they only exist or are for that study as they relate to me. Inwardly, on the other hand, one "sees" nothing, but "feels" a subject; there is only subjective consciousness without objective shape, there is only, as Hopkins will call it, "that taste of myself, of *I* and *me* above and in all things."[15] It is to this, "that taste of myself," that one first awakes in the morning, not to the world. In experience as in logic, a sense of the subjective self must always be prior to a sense of the objective world.

According to Montaigne, whenever anyone brought a question to Socrates, who was a sort of personal and philosophic patron saint for Montaigne, it mattered little what the nature of the subject might be, for his method of investigation was invariably the same: "he always brought the inquirer back first of all to give an account of the conditions of his present and past life, which he examined and judged, considering any other learning subordinate to that and superfluous" (*Works*, pp. 376-77). With the same autobiographic logic as his predecessor Heraclitus and his successors Montaigne and Yeats, Socrates saw ethics and cosmography as essentially allied pursuits, both raised up from foundations sunk deep in subjective experience. And what, in Montaigne's description, was Socrates' philosophic sauce for others was the same for himself; so in the *Phaedo*, as he prepares to construct his last model of

[14] "Anima Mundi," in *Mythologies* (New York: Macmillan Co., 1959), p. 364.

[15] *Sermons and Devotional Writings* (London: Oxford Univ. Press, 1959), p. 123.

14

subjective reality and his final picture of what man is, Socrates first gives his fellow inquirers a very brief autobiography. The point of that autobiographical sketch of the philosophic mind, which acts as prelude to Socrates' "myth of earthly paradise," is this: that the philosopher, i.e., man, must carefully guard against being swamped by a chaos of meaningless facts; and that the only way that Socrates himself has discovered to prevent this destructive inundation is to advance a theory, possessed of just as much primary validity as the individual imagination or faith can give it, then to test the theory with every possible objection. The theorizing subject that reaches out in consciousness to organize the objects of the world is, according to Socrates, very valuable—indeed, it is all that we have—but it is also very delicate and fragile, only too likely to suffer mutilation of its distinctive shape and identity by the swarm of external reality; and, if destroyed, it is certainly irreplaceable. "I was worn out with my physical investigations," Socrates says, and then he goes on in simile and metaphor: "It occurred to me that I must guard against the same sort of risk which people run when they watch and study an eclipse of the sun; they really do sometimes injure their eyes, unless they study its reflection in water or some other medium. . . . I was afraid that by observing objects with my eyes and trying to comprehend them with each of my other senses I might blind my soul altogether. So I decided that I must have recourse to theories, and use them in trying to discover the truth about things."[16] For Socrates, theory first of all is the thing: a unitary safeguard, a single, radical and radial energy originating in the subjective center, an aggressive, creative expression of the self, a defense of individual integrity in the face of an otherwise multiple, confusing, swarming, and inimical universe. The billion phenomena that bombard us can, at best,

[16] *The Last Days of Socrates*, trans. Hugh Tredennick (Harmondsworth: Penguin Books, 1959), p. 158.

advance our understanding negatively by proving a particular theory invalid or insufficient. On their own, however, they will never fall together into a pattern nor formulate a rule or a law; without the mind of man, they could never become an explaining, containing, protective, and satisfying theory. Theory is knowledge with meaning, and meaning everywhere depends upon a mind that means: such mind as we know only immediately and subjectively. Knowledge, then, must start there, with the mind and the self, and so also must theory.

But there is theory and there is theory, as Einstein argues: there is the faith that underlies every science and all knowledge, but there must also be faith in that faith, for "even scholars of audacious spirit and fine instinct can be obstructed in the interpretation of facts by philosophical prejudices. The prejudice . . . consists in the faith that facts by themselves can and should yield scientific knowledge without free conceptual construction."[17] This "free conceptual construction" is the only way man has of making the universe stop pounding and washing away at his little light of consciousness; it is the only means he possesses of imposing the order of his own creative shape on chaos. In his free act man creates a significance in the universe that would otherwise not be there. "I have learned," Einstein says in another autobiographical passage,

> something else from the theory of gravitation: No ever so inclusive collection of empirical facts can ever lead to the setting up of such complicated equations. A theory can be tested by experience, but there is no way from experience to the setting up of a theory. Equations of such complexity as are the equations of the gravitational field can be found only through the discovery of a logically simple mathematical condition which determines the equations completely or almost completely. Once one has those sufficiently strong formal conditions,

[17] *Albert Einstein: Philosopher-Scientist*, ed. Paul Arthur Schilpp, 2 vols. (New York: Harper, 1959), I, 49.

man the shape-maker

one requires only little knowledge of facts for the setting up of a theory. (*Einstein: Philosopher-Scientist*, 1, 89.)

Form, which in the language of scholastic philosophy is closely related to soul or essential being, is not of the order of facts but of the order of process: an activity exercised continuously outward from a center. Tracing form back from manifestation to source, one sees it recede into a fine and finer point, and there, where it disappears into its own center, is the spiritual mind of man, a great shape-maker impelled forever to find order in himself and to give it to the universe. The Einsteinian "strong formal conditions," very little different in origin and effect from the relational groupings that determine meaning in symbolic logic, must come all from within, none from without.

The task of the philosopher is to search himself and to find his own Einsteinian equation against chaos, his own Socratic theory to prevent blindness of the soul. Having concluded his autobiography and demonstrated his perspective and method in the *Phaedo*, Socrates offers to recreate the entire universe— i.e., his universe—from theoretical scratch in order to prove to his companions, on the basis of a single, agreed hypothesis, that his soul cannot die though in a very short time he is to drink the hemlock that will end the life in his body. "If you grant my assumption," he says, meaning the assumption of the existence of Ideas, "the existence of absolute Beauty and Goodness and Magnitude and all the rest of them," then

"I hope with their help to explain causation to you, and to find a proof that the soul is immortal."
"Certainly I grant it," said Cebes;

and in a few minutes he, together with his comrades, is altogether satisfied by the construction and fully convinced of Socrates' conclusions about the nature and destiny of man.

17

The elaborate myth of earthly paradise that follows Socrates' little autobiography and his theory about theory, with its imaginative description of the upper and nether earth, with all its physical detail and geographic specification, is what all myths are: an attempt at explaining something about human nature and the human condition. As is characteristic of Socratic, and I should think, of any, philosophy, the myth has simultaneously a psychological motivation and a moral intention. It constitutes an expression of psychic self (self-expression: what it is like to be human) at the same time that it formulates a moral imperative (how we shall, or how we must, act, being as we are and as we find ourselves situated). The myth says nothing, obviously, and intends to say nothing, about an objective, scientifically observable realm. Indeed, like any myth and all human explanation, it never could say anything about such an external realm, looking as it does from within and with human eyes: being a man, and content to be so, Socrates can hardly assume to speak from a godly point of view. "Of course," he admits, "no reasonable man ought to insist that the facts are exactly as I have described them." The point of his myth, however, is that *he* is exactly as his theory and his vision suggest, and he, for the moment, is humanity realized. "But that either this or something very like it is a true account of our souls and their future habitation . . . this, I think, is both a reasonable contention and a belief worth risking; for the risk is a noble one" (*Phaedo*, p. 178). If we agree with all the philosophers, scientists, and artists who tell us that order and meaning are of ultimate importance, then it is not only "noble" but also peculiarly human, this will to believe and this risk we run in maintaining faith in our own creations. The myth of an earthly paradise that each of us makes tells in all ways more about us than about a material universe: it expresses us in our selfhood as it creates us, and it gives us a reason for living as it suggests to us how to live.

18

A THEORY OF AUTOBIOGRAPHY

Having pictured how it is to be human, Socrates takes the final step of the philosopher and concludes by describing how it should be. Awakening to the *donnée* of human life, to a confusing condition, composite of body and soul, to that consciousness that is the real mystery and the ultimate puzzling fact for the philosophic mind, what, for the individual, is right action and wrong action? If one has agreed to Socrates' picture of his soul and has believed in the theory he has spun out of his own deepest consciousness of himself, one must also agree with him and believe that

> There is one way, then, in which a man can be free from all anxiety about the fate of his soul; if in life he has abandoned bodily pleasures and adornments as foreign to his purpose and likely to do more harm than good, and has devoted himself to the pleasures of acquiring knowledge; and so by decking his soul not with a borrowed beauty but with its own—with self-control, and goodness, and courage, and liberality, and truth—has fitted himself to await his journey to the next world.
>
> (*Phaedo*, pp. 178-79.)

When he made that conclusion, Socrates was only a few minutes from his own "journey," and one imagines him finding his interim eternity in "the next world" just as he had himself, from the evidence of himself, believed it intensely into existence.

Perhaps it was the voice of Socrates, or perhaps of Plotinus, or of "that William Blake / Who beat upon the wall / Till Truth obeyed his call," but it was surely the voice of some great man now passed from the earth that Yeats once heard in the night: "One night I heard a voice that said: 'The love of God for every human soul is infinite, for every human soul is unique; no other can satisfy the same need in God'" (*Anima Mundi*, pp. 347-48). This voice, which, as in another case with Yeats, was a "strange voice," but undoubtedly

19

spoke through Yeats's own lips,[18] may, at first hearing, seem
to be engaged in nothing more than mystical chat, but in fact,
listened to more attentively, it insists, like Socrates himself,
upon a moral imperative binding the individual to a life that
he has paradoxically no choice but to choose: his destiny, following the voice, would be to will freely that which, being
uniquely in God's love, he could not refuse. Because the soul
—for which one may read "self"—has its origin in inimitable
and irreproducible love, it has also, if Yeats's voice was right,
unique obligations to fulfill. The individual must, to say it
simply, become himself, and in so doing he realizes God's desire and brings into being the object of God's love. Sir Sarvepalli Radhakrishnan puts the case of this self very neatly in
his *Idealist View of Life*: "The self is a teleological unity," he
says; and, "Each soul has its life's star, its main purpose. . . .
As the unity of a single melody is realized in the passage of
time, the unity of the self is realised in the series of stages,
towards the attainment of ends."[19] If one extremity, i.e., the
beginning, of the bridge that is man's life-span is founded
deep in eternal life and in God's love, then so also, as Socrates
maintains in the *Phaedo*, must be the other extreme: hence
the immortality of the soul and the "teleological unity" of
the self, a stable entity secured at both ends and throughout.

What, however, is of particular interest to us in a consideration of the creative achievements of individual men and the
relationship of those achievements to a life lived, on the one
hand, and an autobiography of that life on the other is not so
much God's intentions for the soul but the isolate uniqueness
that nearly everyone agrees to be the primary quality and con-

---

[18] *Mythologies*, p. 366: "Once, twenty years ago, I seemed to awake from
sleep to find my body rigid, and to hear a strange voice speaking these
words through my lips as through lips of stone: 'We make an image of him
who sleeps, and it is not he who sleeps, and we call it Emmanuel.'"

[19] Sir Sarvepalli Radhakrishnan, *An Idealist View of Life*, 2nd ed. (London: George Allen & Unwin, 1937), p. 268.

20

dition of the individual and his experience. On this one discovers biologists in harmony with poets, and natural scientists
with theologians; the scientific West even meets the spiritual
East on this point. The natural scientist may refer to the "individual" while the poet refers to the "self," the theologian
may attribute uniqueness to "soul" and the biologist to
"genes," but they are all agreed on the essential: that the individual self, because of soul and/or genes, experiences an
unrepeated and unrepeatable being. "The chance that any two
human beings, now living or having lived, have identical sets
of genes is practically zero. . . . The hereditary endowment
which each of us has is strictly his own, not present in any-
body else, unprecedented in the past, and almost certainly not
repeatable in the future. A biologist must assert the absolute
uniqueness of every human individual."[20] The same authors
a little further on in their exposition say much the same thing
as G. M. Hopkins had perceived, with the imagination of the
poet and the insight of the philosopher, and declared (and
found confirmed in Duns Scotus) one hundred years earlier.
In the scientists' words: "Since every individual differs from
any other individual, everyone belongs to his own special race:
but to say that makes the race concept absurd."[21] If it is the
case that every individual moves in the world surrounded and
isolated by his own unique consciousness, an awareness grown
out of a unique heredity and unique experiences; if he is a
being unique in mind and in body, in feeling and intuition—
unique, according to Gestalt psychologists, even in his sensory
complement—then there can hardly be any doubt that the

[20] L. C. Dunn and Theodosius Dobzhansky, *Heredity, Race and Society*,
rev. ed. (New York: New American Library, 1964), p. 56.

[21] *Ibid.*, p. 114. Plotinus considers, in the Fifth *Ennead*, tractate 7 ("Is
there an ideal Archetype of Particular Beings?"), whether each individual
soul is not shaped according to its own distinct "Idea" in the mind of God.
He is inclined to think that it is, which would put him in line with Yeats's
voice; see Plotinus, *The Enneads*, trans. Stephen MacKenna, 2nd ed. rev.
B. S. Page (London: Faber & Faber, 1962), pp. 419-21.

21

structure of the world that each man works out for himself in his deep self-consciousness and projects onto the world, though it may resemble other such structures here and there, will be unique as a whole.

One recognizes in the proverb "out of sight out of mind" that to be absent in sense from someone else is to lose all feeling of the real, present existence of the other. But what about "in sight," and what, anyhow, is it to be "in mind"? "In sight" I can see, can touch, can hear another, but this is subjectively *my* seeing, touching, and hearing, and I can never, by these means, have any sense of what it must be to be the other consciousness. Whatever another person may be to the touch, to the eye and the ear, *I* am and must be the radial center that touches, sees, or hears. I can know my feeling and my being when I touch; I cannot know what it is to be thus touched. I do not know, to put it simply, what my touch is like for another, but I am certain in any case that my touch to myself is not at all the same as another's touch to me; so I assume that my touch to another feels quite different from my touch to me. I cannot live in the skin of that other, nor can he live in my skin. One piece of life I know, the core of life which is the principle of me; another piece of life I assume in logic: between the certainty and the assumption there is nothing but void space acting as a perfect nonconductor of life-energy. Between the known quick of my finger and the supposed quick of another hand, dead space prevents any transfer; at touch, the quick of that other does not become my quick, nor vice versa. Thus there is a final break or sundering, for life and for consciousness, at the finger ends, and however live the tips of the fingers, they can only live, can only know and be conscious of, that particular sundered life that informs them.

"Nothing is more difficult," Newman told a congregation, "than to realize that every man has a distinct soul, that every one of all the millions who live or have lived, is as whole and independent a being in himself, as if there were no one else in the whole world but he."[22] The difficulty, of course, is not in knowing that *I* have a distinct soul: I carry that knowledge around with me as myself and could not be freed of it even if I would. The difficulty is in realizing that every other man has a soul also and that it is equally "whole and independent." The self, being as distinct as religion holds the soul to be (or more distinct, since soul is an aspect of self), is infinitely difficult to get at, to encompass, to know how to deal with: it bears no definition; it squirts like mercury away from observation; it is not known except privately and intuitively; it is, for each of us, only itself, unlike anything else experienced or experienceable. And yet, the man who commits himself to the whole task of the autobiographer intends to make this self the subject of his book and to impart some sense of it to the reader.

No one, not Newman or Yeats, not even Jung, who is largely responsible for developing the concept in modern psychology, has ever given himself so intensely to the question of selfhood as G. M. Hopkins, who wrote, during one of his Ignatian exercises, "I find myself both as man and as myself something most determined and distinctive, at pitch, more distinctive and higher pitched than anything else I see; I find myself with my pleasures and pains, my powers and my experiences, my deserts and guilt, my shame and sense of beauty, my dangers, hopes, fears, and all my fate, more important to myself than anything I see" (*Devotional Writings*, p. 122). This intensely "pitched" selfhood Hopkins poured into everything he created. In his thought and in his poetry, the unique and unmistakable manner enacts the formal distinctiveness of individual self even as Hopkins' argument maintains that separate selfhood is the very motive of creation.

[22] Sermon on "The Individuality of the Soul," *Parochial Sermons* (London: Rivington & Parker, 1842), IV, 93.

23

> Each mortal thing does one thing and the same:
> Deals out that being indoors each one dwells;
> Selves—goes itself; *myself* it speaks and spells;
> Crying *Whát I dó is me: for that I came.*

"Selves"—a verb: the word, the concept, and the manner vie with one another for distinctiveness and they cooperate to make the poem uniquely Hopkinsian. If "Each mortal thing does one thing and the same," it must be that each is "selving" out in its unique way an inclusive "Self" of all things (rather like Heraclitus' Logos); for the line says that all things do the same, i.e., do alike, and that each thing does the same, i.e., does it continuously. Elsewhere, in prose again, Hopkins declares that "Self is the intrinsic oneness of a thing" (*Devotional Writings*, p. 146), and I think that one should hold to this as an essential quality of selfhood; indeed, "oneness" is perhaps *the* essential condition of selfhood. But this raises a corollary question: to what extent is the self a continuous entity? and, is "oneness" absolute?

If a man suffers a sudden and great shock or fright, then, whether or not he acts "out of character," I think most people would agree from experience that for the moment he is not his normal self. Extreme pain and extreme anger can also, in the same way, cause an apparent disjunction of selfhood. The very fact of memory and its peculiar operation, bringing back some things, neglecting other things and other times entirely, seems to argue that selfhood is not continuous; for it brings up one self here and another self there, and they are not the same as one another, nor do they even seem to the same degree selves. I should imagine that for most of us our own past selves are less real to us in experience (except in something like feelings of shame; but then the reality is in the present feeling, not in the experience of the past self) even than the present selves of other individuals: that is to say, not real at all. I can look at a photograph of myself and can recall the time, the place, the

24

circumstances, perhaps the emotions, that surrounded its taking; I might see resemblances to the photograph in the image
that the mirror now brings. But there is no living communion
there. Everyone must at sometime have wondered, as T. S.
Eliot does in *The Use of Poetry and the Use of Criticism*, why
we remember some things and not others; and sometimes one
wonders what will be salvaged by memory from the present
and, if one could know, why that. It is not only the past,
either, that varies in presenting earlier selves to us, but the
present also which is capable or not of perceiving with intensity, and of holding with coherence, selves past and present.
There are unquestionably times when the self is more highly
"pitched" or intensely concentrated, more fully realized or
richly "selved" or self-possessed; in some moments, why or
how one does not know, we succeed in incorporating more of
the energy of the body of the unconscious into the narrow
wedge of consciousness, and the self is defined in those moments of great capability as the relation between consciousness and the unconscious, or as the process of bringing unconscious contents into the area of consciousness and under
the control of awareness and will. These highest peaks of self,
when the largest areas of the vague unconscious are brought to
an intensity of consciousness, when the whole potential of
humanity seems realized in the individual, cannot be analyzed
or explained but only experienced and, if the artist's faith is
justified, perhaps re-experienced in metaphors and symbols:
in autobiography and poetry. Conversely, in great pain and
grief, before consciousness and will again assume control, the
wild chaos of the unconscious may batter the edge of consciousness to a momentary ragged bluntness, as one can do
to the sharp edge of a knife, and make of the self little more
than a bewildered animal. Thus, to take extreme cases, first of
disorder and then of order, one may contrast an experience
of Hopkins with that of Yeats. Hopkins describes a terrible

25

posits the large area of the vague unconscious

moment when, because the fragile self was in temporary collapse, it lacked the power to hold, to arrange, to create an ordered nature: "But we hurried too fast and it knocked me up. We went to the College, the seminary being wanted for the secular priests' retreat: almost no gas, for the retorts are being mended; therefore candles in bottles, things not ready, darkness and despair. In fact being unwell I was quite downcast: nature in all her parcels and faculties gaped and fell apart, *fatiscebat*, like a clod heaving and holding only by strings of root. But this must often be."[23] "*Fatiscebat*"—the self first of all: nature could only imitate and do likewise. Moments of completion, on the other hand, of ecstasy and of seeming transcendence—those highest peaks of selfhood that rise out of the foothills and lowlands indiscernible to memory or to the bare rationalizing intellect—such moments people have called an experience of God. "I am awake and asleep, at my moment of revelation, self-possessed in self-surrender," Yeats said;[24] conscious, one might add, and unconscious, individual self and much more, a realization in time of eternity.

> My fiftieth year had come and gone,
> I sat, a solitary man,
> In a crowded London shop,
> An open book and empty cup
> On the marble table-top.
>
> While on the shop and street I gazed
> My body of a sudden blazed;
> And twenty minutes more or less
> It seemed, so great my happiness,
> That I was blessed and could bless.[25]

[23] *The Journals and Papers of Gerard Manley Hopkins*, ed. Humphry House and Graham Storey, 2nd ed. (London: Oxford Univ. Press, 1959), p. 236.

[24] "A General Introduction for my Work," *Essays and Introductions* (London: Macmillan & Co., 1961), p. 524.

[25] "Vacillation." Cf. a prose description, though it tends toward poetry, of what was apparently the same experience: *Mythologies*, pp. 364-65.

A THEORY OF AUTOBIOGRAPHY

For this experience in wholeness and completion a number of men have given a number of names. Gandhi's phrase, describing what his entire life was about, may be as pertinent as any: "What I want to achieve," he says in his *Story of my Experiments with Truth*, "—what I have been striving and pining to achieve these thirty years—is self-realization, to see God face to face, to attain Moksha."[26] For the realized self, life is a unitary and unifying thing, present totally in every part of the living being. It is present and performing its characteristic activities—characteristic for the individual—as much in the sensory organs as in the brain or the pituitary gland or the heart, and so, in the highest degree, in the whole being. And while it is important to say that "self is the intrinsic oneness of a thing," one must also recognize that this oneness of self, which, to our awareness, may seem to come and go but which, I think, in some sense continues without break, evolves out of the balance, the poise, and the cooperation of opposites—out of the senses playing off intuition, for example, and thought working against and with emotion. Psychologically, the great paired opposites are consciousness and the unconscious; philosophically, they are individuality and humanity.

The great paired opposites

Consciousness goes with, and is inextricably involved in, the here and now; yet consciousness also has the capacity both to remember and to anticipate, to create a mental phantasm of itself earlier and elsewhere, later and elsewhere. How difficult but interesting to think that I am the same as that person with my name of four years ago; how much more difficult but interesting to imagine what person—where and in what circumstances, with what environmental conditions of consciousness —I will be four years hence. One must wonder what there is, if anything, besides the thread of consciousness to connect the various transformations of self. And what should be said about

[26] *The Story of my Experiments with Truth*; also called *Gandhi: An Autobiography* (London: Phoenix Press, 1949), p. xii.

27

breaks in that thread? Is one the same person getting up in the morning as going to bed at night? Newman left among his papers a running record of self-transformations that stands as one of the most interesting and curious documents in all of autobiographical literature. The bemused wonder that Newman shows when he thinks how uniquely strange it is to be himself, to possess his own unsharable bundle of consciousness, but yet to be subject to transformation in time and place must be a common mental phenomenon. The editor of Newman's *Autobiographical Writings* says that this "Autobiography in Miniature" extended, in composition, "over a period of no less than seventy-two years, from 1812, when Newman was eleven years of age, to 1884, when he was eighty-three." This is the entire document:

> John Newman wrote this just before he was going up to Greek on Tuesday, June 10th, 1812, when it only wanted 3 days to his going home, thinking of the time (at home) when looking at this he shall recollect when he did it.
>
> At school now back again.
>
> And now at Alton where he never expected to be, being lately come for the Vacation from Oxford where he dared not hope to be—how quick time passes and how ignorant are we of futurity. April 8th 1819 Thursday.
>
> And now at Oxford but with far different feelings—let the date speak—Friday February 16th 1821—
>
> And now in my rooms at Oriel College, a Tutor, a Parish Priest and Fellow, having suffered much, slowly advancing to what is good and holy, and led on by God's hand blindly, not knowing whither He is taking me. Even so, O Lord. September 7, 1829. Monday morning. ¼ past 10.
>
> And now a Catholic at Maryvale and expecting soon to set out for Rome. May 29, 1846.
>
> And now a Priest and Father of the Oratory, having just received the degree of Doctor from the Holy Father. September 23, 1850.
>
> And now a Cardinal. March 2, 1884.[27]

[27] *Autobiographical Writings*, ed. Henry Tristram (London: Sheed & Ward, 1956), p. 5.

These are the bare bones of a life that was, we know from other sources, almost infinitely rich in awareness; but can one suppose that there was any thread of consciousness connecting the boy at home or at school with the old Cardinal in Birmingham? His imagination could surely never have made the leap forward. Can memory really do the same into the past? Does present, deep consciousness of the self extend, by the power of memory, to transformations under other conditions? Or is the self not rather continuous at a level other than, but involving, consciousness—a being at one time conscious and existent, at another time unconscious and potential? That one should be transformed and different with passing time, yet be continuing and the same, is a phenomenon of obvious and singular importance for the autobiographer and the poet of personal experience. Time carries us away not only from others but from ourselves as well, and we are all continuously dying to our own passing selves.

If all selves are unique and, in their uniqueness, only subjectively experienced (i.e., we may experience other selves, but then only as objects, not as proper selves), and if all selves are constantly evolving, transforming, and becoming different from themselves, then how is it at all possible to comprehend or define the self or to give anyone else any sense of it? For a billion unique and literally incomparable instances, where there is no genus but only differentia, do not lend themselves to a common grouping. It may be that the nearest one can come to definition is to look not straight to the self, which is invisible anyway, but sidewise to an experience of the self, and try to discover or create some similitude for the experience that can reflect or evoke it and that may appeal to another individual's experience of the self. To make the attempt is an act of faith. When Yeats says, "My body of a sudden blazed," that is not what he means; or it is what he means, but not all of it, and only by way of meaning something else. T. S. Eliot refers to "wild thyme unseen," but this herb is not his subject,

29

seeking images — theories & equations for sense-making

A THEORY OF AUTOBIOGRAPHY

nor even his object; it is, in a manner of speaking, a vehicle between the two. Both poets explore the inner reaches of self, especially self as it becomes or feels transcendent and more than individual, and seek images that might make the experience available to the reader. They create, like Socrates or Einstein, theories and equations to satisfy a deep-felt need for order and to express the emotional order that they have sought and so found. Yeats described in a letter the making of one such theory or equation for the subjective reality of emotional experience ("a religious system more or less logically worked out": he later called it *A Vision*), developed out of a need for order and a sense of it within: "One goes on from year to year gradually getting the disorder of one's mind in order and this is the real impulse to create" (*Letters*, p. 627).

metaphors

These order-produced and order-producing, emotion-satisfying theories and equations—all the world views and world pictures, models and hypotheses, myths and cosmologies mentioned earlier—it may be that another, for our purposes better and more comprehensive, name for these would be "metaphors": they are something known and of our making, or at least of our choosing, that we put to stand for, and so to help us understand, something unknown and not of our making; they are that by which the lonely subjective consciousness gives order not only to itself but to as much of objective reality as it is capable of formalizing and of controlling. The focus through which an intensity of self-awareness becomes a coherent vision of all reality, the point through which the individual succeeds in making the universe take on his own order, is metaphor: the formal conjunction of single subject and various objects. In the given, whether it be external reality or internal consciousness, there is nothing to be called meaning: the world means nothing; neither does consciousness per se. Our sense that there is a meaning in something—in a poem, in experience—comes only when the elements that go to make up that thing take on a relation to one another; in other words, the meaning emerges with our perception of a pattern, and there can obviously be no pattern in chronologically or geographically discrete items and elements. We must connect one thing with another and finally assume the whole design of which the element is only a part. Metaphor supplies such a connection, relating this to that in such and such a relevant way. But whence comes the metaphorizing imagination, and how are we able to connect elements so that they establish a pattern? For it is clear that the meaning-pattern is not there in the items or the experiences themselves. Is this not what the individual supplies, the poet in writing, the reader in reading: a pattern of connection? And in supplying it, both extend that knowledge they had before to include the new, connected item or experience *and* the relation between old and new. The reader, like the poet, extends the possibilities of meaning-pattern in himself; he extends, that is, the pattern, or the adequacy of the pattern, which in turn may be taken, as it were, for a metaphor of his self.

Metaphor is essentially a way of knowing. New sensory experiences—or their consequence, emotional experience—must be formulated in the mind before one can grasp and hold them, before one can understand them and add them to the contents of knowledge and the complex of self. To a wholly new sensational or emotional experience, one can give sufficient organization only by relating it to the already known, only by perceiving a relation between this experience and another experience already placed, ordered, and incorporated. This is the psychological basis of the metaphorizing process: to grasp the unknown through the known, or to let the known stand for the unknown and thereby fit that into an organized, patterned body of experiential knowledge. A metaphor, then, through which we stamp our own image on the face of nature,

31

allows us to connect the known of ourselves to the unknown of the world, and, making available new·relational patterns, it simultaneously organizes the self into a new and richer entity; so that the old known self is joined to and transformed into the new, the heretofore unknown, self. Metaphor says very little about what the world is, or is like, but a great deal about what I am, or am like, and about what I am becoming; and in the end it connects me more nearly with the deep reaches of myself than with an objective universe.

This notion of metaphor argues, as a sort of corollary to its essential nature, that none of us could have been born a *tabula rasa*; that if each of us is now a separate, distinct, and more or less defined and coherent personality, he could not have begun as a psychological blank. Were each person born the same psychic *tabula*, which is surely what the phrase suggests, and each *rasa*, then the slate could never be filled except in a random, meaningless, undefined, and patternless way, and it would be impossible for him ever to become a psychological individual even to the degree that he could be distinguished from others. No order, no organization, no individual and subjective definition would be possible: there would be simply an all-powerful, objective swarm and confusion. The atoms, in Virginia Woolf's phrase, would truly fall as they might, without order, without pattern; for experience impinges continuously on us in confusion and disorder, and the pattern that organizes comes from within: the atoms, as Gestalt psychology maintains, are *drawn* into channels, into formal relations, and in formal composite they make, with his creative cooperation, the individual. Without what Hopkins would call the instress of the individual there would be only random chaos, the *tabula* undoubtedly covered entirely, but meaninglessly, with marks. One might say, in a paraphrase of Hopkins' idea, that we create the inscapes of nature, and the validity or sufficiency of that creation depends not upon external and dead objects out there, but upon the intensity of the instress, or the energy, that we bring to beholding and forging them. "What you look hard at," Hopkins says truly, "seems to look hard at you" (*Journals*, p. 204). In the most intense instress relationship, we share our form and our life with the perceived objects: we become, in our creative act, all the objects we behold, and, more importantly, the order of those objects. This individually unique, order-producing capacity must be innate, else where does it come from? Few people, I should imagine, would argue that it is divinely infused at some point after birth. To become what we are not, we can only, then, begin from what we are; but the process of becoming must be an evolution and growth, never a disruption, from that potential and inherent being-in-the-beginning. If one conceives of the self as a circle, then it does not suddenly pop into being complete and full-blown like Athena from the forehead of Zeus. In fact, it does not even, so far at least as we can see, ever *begin*: it first *appears* to human perception as a point minutely small, receding, if we try to follow, infinitely into the past where the possibilities lay in our ancestors; the self is first seen as a potential point to be realized as a circle in the process of our living selves. This circle, at whatever stage we cut it, possesses exactly the same shape, the same essential form and configuration, as the point, theoretical or potential, from which it first appeared. Thus one is never presented with a circle of self completed but with a point-becoming-circle-of-self constantly completing. If this point as it first appears to our view is not "potential personality" or "potential self" or "psychic homunculus"—all phrases that seem excessively shocking to experimental psychologists—then what shall we call it?

It should be apparent, from these comments on the self and its metaphors, that an individual point of view, from which one sees things in order, must be (1) unitary; (2) specifically

33

psychic homunculus?

human; (3) personally unique; and that so also must be the metaphors projected from that view: they are created to express the feeling of subjective self, unitary, human, and unique, rather than to imitate the outer world. Any theory or picture of reality or *Weltanschauung*, any poem or painting or piece of music that one might create, must derive its integrity-coherence from one's own integrity-coherence, for external reality certainly, in its raw state, brings nothing of this singleness or completeness. It will possess and display such unitary wholeness only when we read the order of our own personalities into the face of nature. It is by the power of metaphor that we compact the multifarious world of objects into the emotional configuration of the subject eye and by the same power that, in reverse perspective, we expand the form of the percipient eye to cover the extent of the natural world. One creates from moment to moment and continuously the reality to which one gives a metaphoric name and shape, and that shape is one's own shape. This is *my* universe.

Whether the self is, as traditionally supposed, a substantive that thinks, wills, and knows, or is, as some schools of modern philosophy maintain, the activity of thinking, willing, and knowing—the sum of qualities that we predicate of those activities—seems quite beside the point when one is speaking of metaphoric creation in autobiography and poetry; or the problem is resolved in the paradox of point of view, for it depends on how one looks at it. The self expresses itself by the metaphors it creates and projects, and we know it by those metaphors; but it did not exist as it now does and as it now is before creating its metaphors. We do not see or touch the self, but we do see and touch its metaphors: and thus we "know" the self, activity or agent, represented in the metaphor and the metaphorizing. Hopkins' noun-verb linguistic coinage, also highly metaphoric, is a neatly compact answer to the question: the self, in its metaphors, "Selves—goes itself."

A THEORY OF AUTOBIOGRAPHY

By their metaphors shall you know them. And, what is more surprising perhaps, by the same metaphors, if they are used by an artist, shall you know yourselves. It is only metaphor that thus mediates between the internal and the external, between your experience and my experience, between the artist and us, between conscious mind and total being, between a past and a present self, between, one might say, ourselves formed and ourselves becoming.

To write about the self, as, for example, Jung does in his psychological texts, can really only be to produce autobiography (i.e., the writing of one's own life) of a sort, since self is known solely from the single source and in the single manifestation; "searching nature," as Hopkins says, "I taste *self* but at one tankard, that of my own being" (*Devotional Writings*, p. 123). Hence, self as a concept is defined, if such be a definition, in self as an experience, but only there. What a writer about the self and its life, or an autobiographer, cannot give us, nor is there any reason to desire it, is a view of himself *of course* from without. In a favorite analogy of Max Planck's, even the fastest runner cannot pass himself. What the autobiographer knows, of course, or what he experiences, is all from within: a feeling of his own consciousness and the appearance of others surrounding him and relating to him more or less, in this way or that. An autobiography, if one places it in relation to the life from which it comes, is more than a history of the past and more than a book currently circulating in the world; it is also, intentionally or not, a monument of the self as it is becoming, a metaphor of the self at the summary moment of composition. Because of this, one discovers from certain autobiographies, it comes in the end to the same thing to deny the internal world of the self as to deny the external world of objects. The inductive scientist Darwin and the intuitive mystic Fox both miss the vehicle of full, creative expression, the one because he recognizes no formative, living center to create the

35

metaphor, the other because he denies the reality of the meta-phoric object itself. In the one case there is no projective, order-producing subject; in the other there is no receptive, order-receiving object; and so for neither can the metaphoric bridge be built from subjective self-consciousness to objective reality. Darwin's experience comes, as it were, from a well too shallow and broad for communication, Fox's from a well too deep and narrow. Darwin is at once too much a scientist and too little an artist to regard intuition or feeling as of any sig-nificance in the long, nonhuman development of natural his-tory; and Fox is at once too much a mystic and too little an artist to hold and express his intuition and feeling in the super-ficies of time and place (as, for example, Yeats does: book, tabletop, street, body blazing for twenty minutes). The meta-phors they produce—and there are metaphors in the *Auto-biography* and the *Journal*—are largely or entirely uninten-tional and so express only the self as already formed without creating new and expanding selves.

If autobiography is in one sense history, then one can turn that around and say that history is also autobiography, and in a double sense: the makers of history, or those through whom history is made, could find in their autobiographies the destiny of their time achieved in action and speech; and the writers of history organize the events of which they write according to, and out of, their own private necessities and the state of their own selves. Historians impose, and quite properly, their own metaphors on the human past. History, as almost every-one acknowledges, is not an objective collection of facts but one historian's point of view on the facts: a point of view that, taken as a sum of what he has experienced and under-stands, reveals to us the historian. As readers we go to history, as to philosophy, to autobiography and poetry, to learn more not about other people and the past but about ourselves and the present. "Symbolic memory is the process by which man not only repeats his past experience but also reconstructs this experience. Imagination becomes a necessary element of true recollection. . . . Poetry is one of the forms in which a man may give the verdict on himself and his life."[28] But, as Cassirer continues, "poetry is not the only, and perhaps not the most characteristic, form of symbolic memory." That, as he says, would be autobiography. What one seeks in reading auto- biography is not a date, a name, or a place, but a characteristic way of perceiving, of organizing, and of understanding, an individual way of feeling and expressing that one can some- how relate to oneself. The poet, Eliot says—and this would be true as well for the autobiographer and for the reader of either poetry or autobiography—should have as many interests as possible, for he never knows what will prove valuable and relevant in the typically human act of poetry: "He is per- petually engaged in solving the problem that every man must solve for himself, that of relating every human activity to his own."[29] In the fullest variety of autobiography, which has its being in an eternal now, as in certain kinds of poetry, one dis- covers a creative, patterned construction that operates from and in the present over a past made coherent in the recall of memory. "Allow me," St. Augustine entreats his God in the *Confessions*, "I beseech You, grant me to wind round and round in my present memory the spirals of my errors."[30] In our reconstruction, set moving by the autobiographer's origi- nal construction, we properly desire a knowledge not of him nor of the past, not of an external and distant object, "but," as Cassirer says, speaking of the value of history, "a knowledge

[28] Cassirer, *Essay on Man*, p. 52.
[29] "The Aims of Education," chap. 2; included in *To Criticize the Critic* (London: Faber & Faber, 1965), p. 83.
[30] Book IV, chap. 1, 1. The translation is from Peter Brown, *Augustine of Hippo* (London: Faber & Faber, 1967), p. 164.

37

reader · in response, creates a significant self

of ourselves" (*Essay on Man*, p. 203). We create, in our responsive act, a significant self as surely as the artist, whether autobiographer or poet, does in his original act.

History might well be described as the exercise of an imaginative cultural or racial memory that is quite analogous to, and has the same powers put to the same uses as, personal memory in the act of autobiography or poetry; the memory in either case is fused with the pattern-making creativity of the individual historian cum cultural autobiographer cum poet. This, then, would be what the *Four Quartets* calls the "use of memory": if the most real existence, or deepest consciousness, is composed of a series of timeless moments of ecstasy; if we most fully realize the human condition when we live the entire past in a moment pregnant with the future; and if life is a continually evolving and never broken process—then memory, of a deeper and more comprehensive kind than described earlier, memory that is conscious and supraconscious, personal and racial, such memory as Cassirer calls "symbolic," must be the cohesive power that renders us, as separate individuals and as human beings, single and integral. That existence should be unbroken and that it should be one might be taken as the twofold condition defining deepest personal and racial consciousness; and it is inclusive memory that allows us to move imaginatively beyond the present moment but only through the present moment of recall, when we most fully realize our self, composite of past history and future germens. Cognition, Socrates maintains in the *Phaedo*, is a process of recognition and education an exercise of the memory whereby we recall what we knew in eternity: discovery is rediscovery in the nature of selfhood.

It is not at all my present purpose to try to define a literary form, or to distinguish and classify all the varieties and types of autobiography; indeed, definition of autobiography as a literary genre seems to me virtually impossible, because the

38

of history & A

A THEORY OF AUTOBIOGRAPHY

definition must either include so much as to be no definition, or exclude so much as to deprive us of the most relevant texts. Either way, definition is not particularly desirable or significant. There are, however, as everyone recognizes, different kinds of autobiography, and one might very usefully separate the autobiographers considered in this study into two large and loose groups: the first, gathering together autobiographers of what might be called the single metaphor, would include Fox, Darwin, Mill, and sometimes Newman; the second, composed of autobiographers of the double metaphor, would include Montaigne, Jung, Eliot, and sometimes Newman. Heraclitus, with his simple and complex remark that "Man's character is his daimon," suggests an essential distinction between the two groups of autobiographers. Each of the autobiographers simplex had his daimon, his personal genius and guardian spirit, a dominant faculty or function or tendency that formed a part of his whole self and from which there was no escape, even had he wished it: Mill's daimon was the rational mind and Fox's the intuitive Inner Light, Darwin's was nature as objective fact and Newman's religious conscience. For the autobiographer duplex, on the other hand, the daimon, in every case, can only be described as the self: for Jung, it is the self as a psychological concept and an experienced fact; for Montaigne, the self as a particular individual and a human being; for Eliot—or, more properly, for the voice of the *Quartets*—the self meditating on its own nature. The whole self, as it lives symbolically complete in the metaphors of the *Essays* of Montaigne, the *Quartets* of Eliot, and *Memories, Dreams, Reflections* of Jung, is revealed to be greater than the sum of all its various parts, as those live more or less in the *Journal* of Fox, the *Autobiography* of Mill, and the *Autobiography* of Darwin, even the *Apologia* of Newman.

A. M. Clark, in his little book on autobiography, disputes Samuel Johnson's notion that, because of the intimate proximity of subject and object, autobiography ought logically to be

39

an easy exercise in narrative. "For it is impossible," Clark argues, "for a man to get out of his own skin."[31] This is, of course, true. But is it exactly desirable for any man, and especially the autobiographer, to want out of his own skin? The acceptance of "his own skin," of its being *his* skin, always around him but around nobody else, and acceptance of all the subjectivity that that implies, is probably the most characteristic and distinctive sign of the double autobiographer. Fox and Darwin, Mill and Newman, all, in one way or another, tried to get out of their skins, tried to separate entirely their former from their present selves and to relate the events of a lifetime as if the relation were, or could be, after the fact. For Montaigne and Jung the autobiographic process is not after the fact but a part and a manifestation of the living, and not only a part but, in its symbolic recall and completeness, the whole of the living. In the whole image of the man, in the complex metaphor or the symbol—union of conscious and unconscious, of the individual with humanity—these two succeed, as does Eliot in his poem, in being both inside and outside, beyond because entirely within, living and simultaneously capturing in symbolic form. Montaigne and Jung were serenely agreed with Blake that a cup cannot contain more than its capaciousness and that a man cannot see with eyes other than his own; but in their books they fill the cup to capacity and they see everything as fully as possible, while acknowledging that what they see is only with their eyes—but claiming also, and justifying the claim, that theirs are momentarily and symbolically the eyes of humanity.

It is with no intention of being snide that one might suggest, from the evidence of his life and his *Journal*, that George Fox's development ceased at about age eleven, or perhaps earlier. Once the single light of the Lord had shone in and onto him,

[31] Arthur Melville Clark, *Autobiography: Its Genesis and Phases* (London: Oliver & Boyd, 1935), p. 12.

40

Fox was set for life, and though he performed many actions and provoked many reactions, these were all repetitions, more or less, of his first witness to the light; they were not done from any essentially new basis in personality. One self, or a partial self, came early to Fox, and no expansion or evolution was effected after that. It is interesting and significant that, in their own accounts, Darwin, Mill, and Newman all, like Fox, reached a clearly defined end point in development, a specific date beyond which there was no change but only more of the same; that, in each case, this date came well before the composition of the autobiography; and that, again in each case, it was a partial, not a whole, evolution that ceased —development of scientific, mental, or religious faculties— for each of them was ruled by a partial daimon. Thus Darwin: "I have now mentioned all the books which I have published, and these have been the milestones in my life, so that little remains to be said. I am not conscious of any change in my mind during the last thirty years, excepting in one point presently to be mentioned [the 'curious and lamentable loss of the higher aesthetic tastes']; nor indeed could any change have been expected unless one of general deterioration."[32] Thus Mill: "From this time, what is worth relating of my life will come into a very small compass; for I have no further mental changes to tell of."[33] Thus Newman: "From the time that I became a Catholic, of course I have no further history of my religious opinions to narrate."[34] For Jung or Montaigne or

[32] *Autobiography*, ed. Nora Barlow (London: Collins, 1958), p. 136.

[33] *Autobiography* (New York: Columbia Univ. Press, 1960), p. 156. It may be significant that Mill, when he comes to tell how much his education put him ahead of his contemporaries, refers precisely to "an advantage of a quarter of a century." Mill was about to complete a quarter of a century of his life when he was introduced to Mrs. Taylor: that event may be taken as marking the end of his mental education and the beginning of his emotional cultivation (see the section on Mill below).

[34] *Apologia pro vitâ suâ*, ed. Martin J. Svaglic (Oxford: Clarendon Press, 1967), p. 214.

Eliot, in the metaphors they created for whole self, there would be change and development until the metaphor itself, sustained first by the author's and now by the reader's life, should die. This is, I suppose, partly what Yeats meant, and perhaps he was right, when he said, "It is even possible that being is only possessed completely by the dead" (*Essays and Introductions*, p. 226). The epigram is carefully hedged and it glimmers with characteristic, mystical half-lights, but it seems to suggest something like this: that when being is possessed, embodied, and expressed completely, then it becomes identical with meaning, and meaning exists only in a realm quite beyond the present confused life; but the dead, and especially artists, have full being because they no longer live the daily existence of purposeless accidents but the eternal existence of that which their whole lives meant, and specifically the existence of the purposeful work of art. The poet's being and his immortality is in the "eternal now," not in any experience that might lie behind a poem but in the creative and recreative experiencing of the poem: the artist-and-his-poem, the reader-and-his-poem. This being and these intimations or intuitions of immortality do not stretch over time and are not temporally sustainable; they slip instead through the crevices and interstices of time into that other realm of now and forever: the foreverness of completion.

Autobiography, as one can see in the quotations from Darwin, Mill, and Newman, is, among other things, a point of view on the writer's own past life. There is no doubt that our experience of reality must always be from a point of view, and that that point of view, like what he makes of it, must clearly be unique to the individual: it is *his* point of view. But this is not at all to say that the individual cannot be distinguished from his point of view. When one says that it is his point of view one thereby, in a sense, does make this dis-

42

*A a point of view — but not
the person this
can transcend this
Fat, Darwin, Mill don't*

tinction: it belongs peculiarly to him, is proper to him, but it is not he. For the individual too, the fact that he can understand a point of view as a point of view means that he thereby distinguishes his self from it and so transcends it. For he could not see it as a point of view were he not in some sense outside and beyond its limitations. Thus, while it is true to say that one can see with no other eyes than one's own, it is also true to say that one can, after a manner, see oneself seeing with those eyes: one can take a point of view on the point of view one has taken, and so, like Montaigne, Jung, and Eliot, transcend the point of view through the point of view. For autobiographers of the single metaphor, on the other hand—the metaphor that is implied in the phrase, "his way of seeing things"—there is little or no self-awareness, little or no criticism of the assumed point of view. Or one might say that autobiography is simple when, as is the case with Fox, Darwin, and Mill, if not Newman, one can detach the style from the substance and can handle and dissect it to see what it reveals about its maker. I do not mean of these writers, of course, that the style is not always one and the same, but simply that it does not turn back on itself with self-criticism: there is the felt assumption in each case that this is the way the thing is said, that there is no other way. When the manner really cannot be separated from the matter and when the style is the book and the man, or when the style, doubly metaphoric, mythic, rhythmic, symbolic, is what the book is about, then, as in the *Essays*, the *Quartets*, and the *Memories*, the autobiography is duplex.

Awareness of the nature of self-being is essential to the full autobiographic art; this being so, Descartes' "Cogito, ergo sum" is a preautobiographic statement. Few people would dispute what Descartes said, but a great many people, of course, have disputed what that reveals beyond "sum," and what it tells

beyond the cogito?

about the nature and quality of that being whose existence is indisputable. To realize the quality of such being is an act altogether separate, and different in kind, from the original and mere "cogito." This separate act, which is an act in realization, definition, and transcendence, is what one finds in autobiography, complete or double, and in poetry. The act of autobiography and the act of poetry, both as creation and as recreation, constitute a bringing to consciousness of the nature of one's own existence, transforming the mere fact of existence into a realized quality and a possible meaning. In a certain sense, autobiography and poetry are both definitions of the self at a moment and in a place: and I do not mean, for autobiography, that it is a definition of the writer's self in the past, at the time of action, but in the present, at the time of writing. We know Darwin and J. S. Mill, for example, less by what they did and what they narrate than by the peculiar quality of consciousness that informs the writing about that past action. In the great autobiographers, whether it be autobiography as such or poetry, consciousness of this continuing creation of the self accompanies the creation, and, in the moment after, becomes it: Montaigne is aware of himself describing himself in the past and is aware that this awareness is his present view on reality—and is aware of this awareness too.

St. Augustine also, with his psychological acuity and his self-insight, with his deep awareness of the oneness of being though it appear in different guises, writes the double sort of autobiography. In his reconstruction of the past through the present he sees through and confesses how he had tried, in his cunning awareness, to get around even the Lord and to forestall the very grace for which he yet prayed: "But I, a most wretched youth, most wretched from the very start of my youth, had even sought chastity from you, and had said, 'Give me chastity and continence, but not yet!' For I feared that you

44

Montaigne

a definition of the writer's self... at the time of writing

duplex — a double awareness

would hear me quickly."[35] The phenomenon, I suppose, is not uncommon, but Augustine's awareness of the self and its motives is, and very few people possess his Montaignesque awareness of awareness. The last four books of the *Confessions*—i.e., Book X, a psychological analysis of Augustine's mind at the time of writing the *Confessions,* and Books XI-XIII, an exegesis and allegorical interpretation of the opening verses of Genesis—are often omitted in modern editions of the book on the ground that, as one editor says in justifying the omission, "they do not form an integral part of the biography."[36] Looked at in a different light, however, Augustine is seen in these four books to be performing the characteristic activity of the double autobiographer in the eternal present; for instead of describing the events of a philosopher's life as they happened in the past, he portrays himself acting out the life of a psychologist and a philosopher as that life comes into being and is now. That is, he is doing in these four books the same sort of thing as Jung and Montaigne do in their autobiographical writings and as Eliot does in *Four Quartets.*

Art, both autobiographic and poetic, mediates between the transient world of sensation and feeling, of event and emotion, and a constant, stable realm of pattern and significance. The poet, in his passion for perceiving and holding formal patterns, transforms a myriad passing sensations into the single, apprehensible and meaningful artifact; and like the poet, the autobiographer who draws out of the flux of events a coherent pattern, or who creates a sufficient metaphor for experience, discovers in the particular, and reveals to us, the universal. One might, I think, thus explain Jung's archetypes (a concept de-

---

[35] Book VIII, chap. 7, 17; translation by John K. Ryan (Garden City, N.Y.: Image Books, 1960), p. 194.
[36] Dom Roger Huddleston, *The Confessions of St. Augustine* (London: Fontana Books, 1957), p. 13.

veloped by Jung from varieties of personal experience) and thereby suggest the one psychic foundation of autobiography and poetry: archetypes, like poems, contain not inheritable human experience, for that cannot be transferred or inherited, but open possibilities of response. *The Winter's Tale*, for example, vivid and alive as Shakespeare made it in images, is only potential until we, as viewers and psychological participants, complete it from our experience. We bring not the same but other experiences, not the same but other selves, and yet find them "imaged" in the play; and, in response to the play, we make and re-make ourselves, for everyone knows how it is to be new and different from the experience of a poem or a poet. One goes to Shakespeare, to Marvell or Keats or Eliot, and finds there, time after time, new and inexhaustible accesses of being. Their works, like the archetypes, are the efforts and the achieved meanings of humanity precipitated into objective forms that remain there for us as perpetual possibilities for realization, but not as experience to grasp per se. Again, Jung maintains that we dream ultimately only about ourselves and that the figures in our dreams are really images of our own unconscious, or our own total personality. A dream, then, is like a complex metaphor for the process of self as it is at the given moment of dreaming, and this could stand almost equally well as a description of a great deal of dramatic literature where, in all the parts together and in their total, complex relation, but in no single part alone, we find the artist's complete personality. Like any play that realizes and projects the motives and tendencies that are in tense interaction within the total self of the playwright—*Antigone*, say, or *On Baile's Strand*, or *King Lear*—a dream is the projected drama of our whole selves. All of them, archetypes, dreams, and poems, are formal, expressive metaphors patiently biding their time until we bring energy to them, and in the conjunction, the two, formal metaphor and vital energy, joined as self-expression, are

46

transported into eternity. "I add that 'will or energy is eternal delight.' . . . It has, as it were, thrust up its arms towards those angels who have, as Villiers de L'Isle-Adam quotes from Saint Thomas Aquinas, returned into themselves in an eternal moment."[37] Thus the metaphor of art, signifying completion and performing it.

The artist, we say, is "imaginative": he imagines, he makes images, and in them he forges the metaphoric bond that joins the known being to the unknown phenomena. He bodies his meaning forth, he bodies himself as he is at that moment, in expressive images or in imagistic metaphors. His metaphor is a bridge outward from the center to the farthest circumference possible, a bridge that bears his own form and image, a thrust of subjective self into external reality. "If it be true," Yeats said, and Jung and Eliot would have understood him very well, "that God is a circle whose centre is everywhere, the saint goes to the centre, the poet and artist to the ring where everything comes round again" (*Essays and Introductions*, p. 287). Different as the poet and his reader may be in their particular and individuated selves, they are both, as we are all, the outer edge, the human ring, of the circle: on that certainty art erects its conjunctive metaphors. And art, which cannot perhaps tell us what it is to be that other person, the artist, can let us know what it is to be human and to be ourselves. The projected metaphor of twofold autobiographic art thus resolves the dilemma, so consistently frustrating, that lies at the very heart of individual experience. It embraces at once, for the author and his reader, the intellect and natural phenomena, conscious subject and relational objects. The symbolic entity does not indeed explain or justify but offers instead an embodiment in the form of an epitome of the totality and complexity of experience, understood and meaningful.

[37] Yeats, *Explorations*, selected by Mrs. W. B. Yeats (London: Macmillan & Co., 1962), p. 449.

"Thus symbolism, *including the symbolic transference by which it is effected,* is merely one exemplification of the fact that a unity of experience arises out of the confluence of many components."[38] The symbolizing process is of such a nature that it includes consciousness of itself within its operation. This, Yeats would say, is the artist's way—not out of the circle, for that is no longer necessary, but an infinite expansion outward of the circumference of the circle to include in reference the entire phenomenal world and a concentration of the circle to a point of infinite profundity and of life-giving and life-directing significance.

Happiness, as Mill discovered, is not in itself a sufficient motive or goal for living, especially as one will never, in any case, achieve happiness by aiming for it directly; acquisition, of whatever sort, according to all the authors we are dealing with, and achievement in the world are no more satisfactory, nor are family, career, book, or office. What man ultimately seeks is more entirely centered in the self, and has been variously described: it is "a condition of complete simplicity," Eliot says, "(costing not less than everything)" and going "beyond any meaning / We can assign to happiness"; it is "*moksha,*" Gandhi claims, "self-realization" and freedom from birth and death; Yeats calls it completion or ecstasy or tragic joy—the moment when the universe is mine, organized and infused with meaning by my creative act and when paradoxically I have surrendered to a pattern that is not me; it is a meaningful, symbolic life, Jung says, or individuation, becoming what I am by being what I was intended to be; it is simply, for Montaigne, to live the life that God has given and to be oneself; "*sadhana,*" Rabindranath Tagore calls it, "the Realisation of Life," or "*dharma,*" each man's destiny,

[38] Alfred North Whitehead, *Symbolism* (Cambridge: Cambridge Univ. Press, 1928), p. 101. The italics are mine.

"the essence of his nature, the real meaning of his self."[39] To be a Roman Catholic seems now, looking back on his life, to have been Newman's destiny, and to be the first Quaker Fox's; to find himself and the ideal of the whole individual in Harriet Taylor was the fate Mill appears to have been born for, and Darwin to discover the law of evolution. One returns to Heraclitus, for his saying that "Man's character is his daimon" was made true in these men's lives. To create, to realize, and to recognize one's own daimon, and then to embrace it as in the myth of human love related by Aristophanes in the *Symposium,* would seem to be what each of us was made for—his symbolic life and his highest good. The artist's destiny, in autobiography and poetry, is to go yet further; to live the life and at the same time to embrace the wholeness of that life as his daimon and to embody it again in his creation. For "we artists," Yeats boasts proudly, "are the servants not of any cause but of mere naked life, and above all of that life in its nobler forms, where joy and sorrow are one, Artificers of the Great Moment" (*Essays and Introductions,* p. 260).

Newman, referring to the Ancient Saints and the early Church Fathers, says, "Dogma and proof are in them at the same time hagiography."[40] This seems to me the equivalent of saying—and this is the point of the present remarks—that all dogma and proof, i.e., formulations and facts of religious belief, are founded deep in autobiography; that all philosophy, indeed, and all knowledge is real only in autobiography. Cosmology, one might also say, is no more than (but as much as) psychology writ large; history is autobiography enacted on a grand scale; and the poetic-autobiographic metaphor, being both imitation and creation of the self, is sufficient expression

[39] *Sadhana: The Realisation of Life* (London: Macmillan & Co., 1926), p. 75.

[40] "The Last Years of St. Chrysostom," *Historical Sketches,* 3 vols. (London: Basil Montague Pickering, 1872-73), III, 227.

for psychology, history, philosophy, and cosmology. From all the writers in this book, as men and as autobiographers, whether of the single or of the double metaphor, one takes, in Eliot's phrase

> What they had to leave us—a symbol:
> A symbol perfected in death.

Any autobiography, the image of a life, is such a symbol. And the greatest of these writers—the greatest at least in making metaphors: Montaigne, Jung, and Eliot—perfected the symbol in life as well as in death. They perfected it in their art. Montaigne, achieving his eternity with a symbolic flair denied to lesser men, died at the supremely significant moment of the raising of the Host during a mass that was being said in his bedroom: as Christ, who was symbolic man, entered into time in the elements of the mass, Montaigne, who was also, in his degree, symbolic man, left time for the eternity he had created. He became in his very life and in his death, as Yeats says every true artist is, an Artificer of the Great Moment. If these men succeeded in creating symbolic images in their autobiographies, then one cannot doubt that it is because they lived symbolic lives and that they continue to live them in their autobiographies; and in consequence their books mean more to us in the reading, much more, than the account of an isolated life without pattern, a fact without relation or rhythm, an experience without revelation. What they have left us, as *Essays*, as *Memories, Dreams, Reflections*, as *Quartets*, is metaphors for our selves.

two : Montaigne

a book consubstantial with its author

"Montaigne," a recent commentator has said, "is not our contemporary, did not live as we do and was not educated as we are. He was a sixteenth-century man, and his problems, concerns and patterns of thought are those of his century. . . . We must warn against the false modernism involved in making Montaigne into a founding father of the United Nations, an eighteenth-century *philosophe*, or a nineteenth-century pessimist."[1] One would scarcely have thought of making Montaigne into any of these particular and ill-assorted things, but might he not be modern—even "our contemporary"—without our having to indulge in "false modernism"? It is true that Montaigne lived and died within the limits of the sixteenth century, but does his book, his record of a sixteenth-century life, not extend itself out beyond that century to the ancients in one direction, to us and to times yet to be in the other, and so remain forever "contemporary"? To protest too much that Montaigne is a man of his own time and not of ours will inevitably produce the troublesome question: why, then, in our time, so distant from his, do we continue to read and reread Montaigne? Surely it is not (especially for the Montaignesque common reader) because we wish to recreate or to relive the history of Montaigne's age, whether that history be political, economic, theological, or even intellectual or cultural. Nor is it—equally surely—to exercise ourselves in sixteenth-century French.[2] It is not even, I think—though this may seem to go

[1] F. P. Bowman, *Montaigne: Essays* (London: Edward Arnold, 1965), p. 7.
[2] In fact, there will be little exercise in French of any kind in our treatment of Montaigne: quotations are from the easily accessible and excellent translation by Donald Frame, *The Complete Works of Montaigne* (Stanford, Calif.: Stanford University Press, 1957).

against the grain of Montaigne's proclaimed intention—in order to know better Montaigne the man. He does say, again and again, to the point where some readers may tire of hearing it, that he intends to portray himself, he plans to capture one man as he really is, he wishes to describe Michel de Montaigne whole and entire in his book. While this is undoubtedly his intention, however, or a large part of it, there is no logical necessity for the reader to share intention with Montaigne. The question is not why Montaigne wrote the book but why we read it and how, therefore, we had best go about the reading.

To return to Montaigne as a contemporary: his "problems" and "concerns"—whether it be a question of the proper way to face death, or of *ejaculatio praecox*, the validity of human knowledge, or the fickle frailty of women—were not peculiar to the sixteenth century, as we can see both from his copious quotations of the ancients and from our modern experience. Of course the sixteenth century did think about these things; but so, in their various ways, did Socrates and Plutarch, Juvenal and Martial; so, undoubtedly, did the Dark Ages that came between Montaigne and his ancient authors; and so, certainly, do we. There is no question, surely, that Montaigne's subjects (I mean the ones on which we *do* reread him, not the minor exercises—"Of the battle of Dreux," for example—that most readers would agree to let drop) are timeless and hence as much modern as not. And yet it is not his subjects or even his thought that make Montaigne peculiarly available to us in the twentieth century and that make him uniquely valuable in a discussion of autobiography and art. Though the later essays in particular are extraordinarily attractive in the quality of their philosophy, what draws and holds our attention is less Montaigne's thought than his practice and the implications of that practice; it is the bent of his character, his special viewpoint, the way he thinks that speaks so much to us and that, across four centuries, brings him closer to us and our temper than many writers who are much nearer in time. What we come away with after a reading of Montaigne has less to do with him and his century (which should not, however, be an encouragement to misread him) than with ourselves and our immediate present, not to say our future. As Montaigne made himself in making his book—and in revisions remade both together—so the reader creates and recreates himself (not Montaigne) in his response to the *Essays*. We go with Montaigne into himself and—fortuitous paradox—find there ourselves. As Montaigne, portraying the way of his life, discovers how to live, so we can follow his portrait in humanity to rediscover the way (which may properly be quite different from Montaigne's way) for ourselves. Or, perhaps more accurately, we should say that Montaigne is leading the moral life in the very search for it, and that, following his search, searching too, we likewise come finally to realize that the search *is* the moral life and the way, therefore, the end. This, I think, is why we reread the *Essays*—and there can be no better reason—and each time find them almost infinitely rich and continuously new. One wonders, then, if it is "false modernism" to make Montaigne thus into an alter ego and to use him for our own purposes rather than his.

Because Montaigne is so appealing and excellent as man and as writer, it would, in fact, be very easy, but it would also be disastrous, to be misled into pursuing Montaigne's plan and his purposes when one should rightly be pursuing one's own. It would be the most natural thing in the world to give this chapter over to him in quotation or simply to quote one of the fine essays from beginning to end; but the natural in this case would hardly be so blessed as Montaigne regularly finds it. To make him as useful as possible in a discussion of autobiographic literature, we should adopt the Montaignesque way but not his substance: we should willingly surrender the whole portrait of Montaigne and any effort to deal with him adequately on his own generous and extensive ground, gathering what may seem a meager crop from such a large offering of the self. At least, however, we do have Montaigne's example: "For I do not see the whole of anything," he says:

> Of a hundred members and faces that each thing has, I take one, sometimes only to lick it, sometimes to brush the surface, sometimes to pinch it to the bone. I give it a stab, not as wide but as deep as I know how. . . . Scattering a word here, there another, samples separated from their context, dispersed, without a plan and without a promise, I am not bound to make something of them or to adhere to them myself without varying when I please and giving myself up to doubt and uncertainty and my ruling quality, which is ignorance.
>
> ("Of Democritus and Heraclitus," p. 219.)

A genial and admirable, typically Montaignesque confession. Of the more than a hundred members and faces that he presents to us, and that he changes and interchanges as he likes, let us stab at three: Montaigne's modernity, his sanity, and his artistry. These points of access are naturally wrapped up in one another and all together in Montaigne's character as effects are in secondary causes and secondary causes in the First Principle. Coming at one will involve continually turning around the other two, for behind all three and moving them is the expansive and cheerful personality that we call Montaigne.

Before touching Montaigne at these three points, however, it will be well to describe the making of his book—that process and product that Montaigne in one place calls "the essay of my natural faculties" ("Of books," p. 296). The first publication of the *Essays* in 1580 was in two "Books." After several editions, Montaigne re-presented his *Essays* in 1588, with many revisions and additions to the first two books and with an entirely new Book III. In the first two books of this edition of 1588 (labeled the fifth edition) there are two layers of composition and of personality: the original of 1580 and earlier, and the new achievement of 1580 to 1588. To complicate the text a little more and to make it reflect faithfully the unending changes in his personality, Montaigne revised this edition of 1588—all three books—not by restructuring or rewriting individual essays but by adding copious afterthoughts, illuminations, and clarifications (ranging from a word to more than a printed page in length) in the margin of his personal copy of the 1588 edition. This private copy of the *Essays* that Montaigne left thick with marginalia at his death is the *Exemplaire de Bordeaux*, kept in the library of that city, from which all modern editions derive and of which a photocopy was made and published in 1912, edited by Fortunat Strowski. Thus these marginal additions have become, as Montaigne intended they should, an integral part of the essays of his natural faculties. We can view, then, three layers of personality in Books I and II and two layers in Book III. The convention in publishing the *Essays* is to signify the different layers as *a* (the original composition), *b* (revisions appearing in 1588), and *c* (revisions left in marginal manuscript at Montaigne's death). With these three different strata of composition and character before him, the reader has the unique opportunity of watching Montaigne, as it were, communicating with himself across a period of eight or ten years and not only with one earlier self but often with two. "I have grown seven or eight years older since I began: not without some new acquisitions" ("Of the resemblance of children to fathers," p. 574). Montaigne was to grow twelve years older yet after writing this, certainly with more new acquisitions, and the plan of the *Essays* is such that the acquisitions find their mirror in the book just as the original finds there its faithful reflection. Montaigne's vision, his revision, and his re-revision cooperate together to compose the complex portrait of a complex and yet, in the best

55

sense, a simple man—in Eliot's phrase, "the complete consort dancing together." "Aucun manuscrit, en effet, non pas même celui des *Pensées* de Pascal," Strowski says of the Bordeaux copy, "ne révèle avec une plus fidèle précision le mouvement de la pensée de son auteur; aucun ne se rattache plus étroitement à tout le développement intellectuel d'un homme—et cet homme est Montaigne."[3]

It is interesting and relevant to remark that for all the revisions in the *Essays* there are virtually no excisions. Deletion in the *Essays* would betoken something very like repentance in life for things said and done, and repentance, as Montaigne says in his essay on the subject, violates the logic of selfhood. The *a* level is the best expression of which the *a* Montaigne was capable; he did not repent of it at the time, or he would not have published it. For the *c* Montaigne—different in time, in place, and in being—to try to repent for the expression of another man would be foolish and meaningless if not exactly immoral and criminal. Montaigne describes his book as having "built itself up with diverse interruptions and intervals, as occasions sometimes detain me elsewhere [away from his library where he composed] for several months. Moreover, I do not correct my first imaginings by my second— well, yes, perhaps a word or so, but only to vary, not to delete" ("Of the resemblance," p. 574). What Montaigne is up to here, and indeed throughout the *Essays*, is rather like the activity of Myso ("Myso, one of the Seven Sages, of a Timonian and Democritic humor, when he was asked what he was laughing at to himself, answered: 'At the fact that I am laughing to myself'" ["Of the art of discussion," p. 709]), for his admission that he does sometimes vary but not delete is itself a *c* addition to the remark that he did not correct his first imaginings. It would be difficult to say, for either Myso

[3] *Reproduction en Phototypie . . . des Essais de Montaigne* (Paris: Hachette, 1921), p. 6.

56

or Montaigne, where this self-sustaining activity might start or stop. Though Myso presumably, sometime and somehow, stopped laughing at the fact that he was laughing, Montaigne's visionary and revisionary working spin in endless circles in his book of *Essays*. "My book," he claims in another *c* insertion, "is always one. Except that at each new edition, so that the buyer may not come off completely empty-handed, I allow myself to add, since it is only an ill-fitted patchwork, some extra ornaments" ("Of vanity," p. 736). Evolution of self is in Montaigne an ever-widening circle of experience not an erasing or a crossing-over of the record. Anyway, who is to say which reading and meaning might be better—certainly, according to Montaigne, the author is not qualified to judge himself at an earlier stage. "Myself now and myself a while ago are indeed two; but when better, I simply cannot say. It would be fine to be old if we traveled only toward improvement" ("Of vanity," p. 736). But self-completion as we view it in the *Essays* is circular and momentary rather than linear and continuous. Hence the later portrait incorporates and extends the earlier portrait; it does not deny or annul it, and the *c* insertions should not be considered as intrusions into an earlier personality but completions of a later one. It is indisputable that many of the richest and most important passages in Montaigne are *c* insertions, instances of the later Montaigne; with a longer perspective and a larger, more mature vision, they discover a pattern of something like meaning in what otherwise might remain only recorded experience.

Montaigne's *Essays* represent a sort of paradigm of philosophy becoming modern in subject and in style, and they are not content to hint at the secondary, fringe qualities of what we take to be modern but go right to the heart and center of it. In any author, subject and style are likely to be intimately related, but in Montaigne, both by design and in performance, the two are quite inseparable, indistinguishable one from the other. This is not said in the sense in which we say, for example, that Jane Austen's prose is the perfect vehicle for her vision or that Byron chooses an appropriate style for the matter of *Don Juan*: in Montaigne it goes much deeper; the identification begins at a much earlier point. Montaigne takes for his subject his complete but constantly changing self: whatever the title of individual pieces (titles that are often irrelevant to Montaigne's intention and practice), the book is *Essays* in thinking, in feeling, and in being, *Essays* trying or testing the nature of reality as subjectively, privately experienced, *Essays* that record Montaigne's experiments in living and his alone. "Le style," the French proverb says, "c'est l'homme," and since Montaigne takes "l'homme" for his subject, the terms are endlessly intertwined and bound up together in the essential process of self-realization and self-projection: Montaigne's subject is his self, his self is his style, and his style and his subject are one. "In modeling this figure upon myself," Montaigne declares (in another *c* insertion), "I have had to fashion and compose myself so often to bring myself out, that the model itself has to some extent grown firm and taken shape. . . . I have no more made my book than my book has made me—a book consubstantial with its author, concerned with my own self, an integral part of my life" ("Of giving the lie," p. 504). Montaigne thus lands, not half-heartedly or half-way but with both feet and right in the center, on the subject that has preoccupied modern philosophy, modern poetry, modern psychology—and, as Alfred North Whitehead points out in *Science and the Modern World*, even modern theology:

> Modern philosophy is tinged with subjectivism, as against the objective attitude of the ancients. The same change is to be seen in religion. In the early history of the Christian Church, the theological interest centered in discussion on the nature of God,

the meaning of Incarnation, and apocalyptic forecasts of the ultimate fate of the world. At the Reformation, the Church was torn asunder by dissension as to the individual experiences of believers in respect to justification. The individual subject of experience had been substituted for the total drama of reality. Luther asked, "How am I justified?"; modern philosophers have asked, "How do I have knowledge?" The emphasis lies upon the subject of experience.[4]

Montaigne does not precisely "substitute," and so push the "total drama of reality" out of the realm of philosophy, but in the view that he gives us the "subject of experience"—the self or the "I"—is the only subject realistically accessible to human study. Individual experience becomes the only source of knowledge that is at all sure, and that too is dangerously touchy and uncertain ("Truly Protagoras was telling us some good ones, making man the measure of all things, who never even knew his own"; *Sebond*, p. 418); some coherent sense and statement of that self is the *sine qua non* for any modern, i.e., Montaignesque, philosophic construct. In the theatre of the individual, "the total drama of reality" is enacted for Montaigne, and the viewpoint of his modern philosophy constitutes not so much a substitution as an identification, not so much a turning aside from the study of reality as a sharpened refocusing inward before outward, or outward only through the inward.

How, one might ask, does Montaigne come to spring thus full-blown, with a single leap and unaided, into modern subjectivity? The full answer is there to be followed in the *Essays*. "In fine," Montaigne says of his book in his last and greatest essay, "all this fricassee that I am scribbling here is nothing but a record of the essays of my life" ("Of experience," p. 826). His essence as an autobiographer and his value in a discussion of autobiographic art may well lie in this: that

[4] *Science and the Modern World* (New York: Macmillan Co., 1928), p. 201.

Montaigne's philosophy is one of enactment rather than precept.

Whitehead, in the passage quoted from *Science and the Modern World*, suggests that according to the tactics of modern philosophy the question of how we know must be taken as prior to the question of what we know. One way of defining Montaigne's effort is to say that he tries to make us see that this must be so. The epistemological questions that Montaigne raises (primarily in the *Apology for Raymond Sebond*) —raises and brilliantly illuminates but never, of course, attempts to answer, unless by the very example of his questioning—are fundamental: situated as human beings, composed of diseased body and fickle soul, of erring senses and unstable reason, how can we know anything and, in fact, how do we know that there is anything to know? Sebond's purpose, Montaigne says in his odd *Apology*—which ends up less an apology for Sebond than an investigation of how far the human senses and human reason can lead us in a search for valid and verifiable knowledge—"is bold and courageous, for he undertakes by human and natural reasons to establish and prove against all atheists all the articles of the Christian religion" (p. 320). This, as Montaigne soon lets us know, is more than "bold and courageous": it is misguided, wrong-headed, presumptuous, and destined inevitably to fail, and to fail ignominiously. The fact is, and Montaigne demonstrates it at length in this same essay, that "human and natural reasons" are incapable of establishing and proving anything that we can call truth even in the human realm, let alone in the divine. What all philosophies grant to be sadly true of the senses—that there is no way for them to step beyond themselves so as to judge their own evidence—is equally true for reason also, and hence what we receive from faulty senses remains unchecked and uncorrected since reason itself is variable, baseless, and uncertain, always tripping up in trying to stretch beyond its limits. If it were not so desperate and so frustrating, it would be comic to consider that all the great knowledge and all the divine truth promulgated by all the learned men (which would include poor Sebond) are nothing more than the crazy product of these two jokers, senses and reason, working together to our confusion.

And where does this place man in the scheme of creation? A little below the animals would be Montaigne's answer. It is a fact, he says, putting man in the place he has made for himself, that in all the so-called human virtues we are equalled or surpassed by the animals that we complacently suppose we master: there are brute animals that reason better than we do, show greater love for their kind, are more magnanimous and compassionate, more faithful and grateful and steadfast. And when it comes to beauty, worse and worse: on the outside we most resemble the apes, and "for the inside and vital parts, it is the hog" (p. 356). When we think of man naked—well, then at least, we must acknowledge that in one thing his reason has done man good service: "I think we had more reason than any other animal to cover ourselves" (p. 356). Montaigne leaves a little room for human pride, however, for animals do not, he says, surpass us in everything: with "our fine reason" we can claim as "our share inconstancy, irresolution, uncertainty, grief, superstition, worry over things to come, even after our life, ambition, avarice, jealousy, envy, unruly, frantic, and untamable appetites, war, falsehood, disloyalty, detraction, and curiosity" (p. 358). What a sideshow it is; and what is more wonderful than anything—more wonderful even than all the "asininities of human wisdom" (p. 408) proclaimed by the learned men and believed by their dung-eating disciples—is that this creature, this doubly wretched man, with an imagination bent to sin and a body only too ready to comply, is arrogant and vain!

Like the fools that we are ("To learn that we have said or done a foolish thing, that is nothing; we must learn that we

61

are nothing but fools, a far broader and more important lesson"; "Of experience," p. 822), we go on in presumption and vanity, more inconstant than the phenomena we would attempt to order, yet bravely absolute from moment to inconstant moment in our confident assertions, positive that each newest belief (which tomorrow we will have forgotten, or rejected, or will perhaps not even understand), from the five hundred or thousand that we have held, is "the certain and infallible one." Acting the part of the witty and expert skeptic, Montaigne shuffles together some twenty-five or thirty absolutist and absolutely contradictory assertions about the nature of divinity, to the end that the reader may observe them destroying one another and to demonstrate that there is nothing, as Montaigne says and his quotations bear him out, so idiotic that it has not been seriously maintained by some philosopher or other. Montaigne goes about his destructive work in *Sebond* with a certain grim delight, his manner being no less bright and bouncy than his matter is dark and pessimistic; but well before the end the Pyrrhonistic joke turns noticeably bitter in the mouth.

We begin to feel a need for escape in the essay, a need felt, I think, both by the reader and by Montaigne for a way out of the brilliant trap laid and closed by skeptic mockery. If the purpose of philosophy is to teach us or help us to live cheerfully, tranquilly, and well (and Montaigne says that that is indeed its purpose), then this will hardly qualify as the whole of a philosophy. We cannot call Pyrrhonism a philosophy; it is not even a base for a philosophy. It is merely, in Montaigne's hands, a method, a way of pushing aside something that is false, something that is rigid and inflexible, something that is not only dead itself but inimical to life in the searcher. I think we can hear in Montaigne's essay, even while the business of leveling the chattering authorities goes on, the voice of the human spirit crying out for something else, something more.

This is why, for example, there is a curiously positive note in the very rhythms and images, if not in the rational statement, of such a seemingly pessimistic view of the human condition as the following: "Finally, there is no existence that is constant, either of our being or of that of objects. And we, and our judgment, and all mortal things go on flowing and rolling unceasingly. Thus nothing certain can be established about one thing by another, both the judging and the judged being in continual change and motion" (p. 455). It is not simply the energy of destruction that activates this passage but something more hopeful, something more positive, as if already Montaigne were beginning a movement away from the vast dark left by Pyrrhonism and toward what at least seems to be a tiny light at the end of the long tunnel.

When skepticism has done its job—and it does it well—then Montaigne can start to lay a base for a philosophy, not in a statement (like the old destroyed bases), but in a question that neither Pyrrhonism nor anything else can refute. The skeptic demonstration shows us that as far as human beings are concerned, the Archimedean point from which to move the world does not exist. But what if one is not trying to move the world but only to ask it a question? And not expecting an answer but finding something, and perhaps everything, of value in the mere asking? Though we are forced to surrender every other outpost of knowledge, there remains one certainty (but only one) on which we can stand while we formulate the question: this is what William James calls the "one indefectibly certain truth . . . that the present phenomenon of consciousness exists."[5] This may not be much, but it is everything. Granted our fickle variability and inconstancy, granted an inconsistency in us so extreme that we possess nothing to call a "self," a coherent and knowable entity—

[5] *Essays on Faith and Morals*, ed. Ralph Barton Perry (New York: Longmans, Green, & Co., 1943), pp. 45-46.

yet there is a subject for study, if not for knowledge. The Pyrrhonists are clever enough to hunt out even those who deny the possibility of knowledge, for if you say, "I know nothing," they respond with, "To know that you know nothing is to claim to know something." But Montaigne is one cleverer than his erstwhile companions in the skeptic method: "This idea," he explains of the difficulty even of doubting or not knowing, "is more firmly grasped in the form of interrogation: 'What do I know?' The words I bear as a motto, inscribed over a pair of scales" (*Sebond*, p. 393). Slipping through the epistemological needle-eye with a question where a statement, even a negative one, would be too broad to pass, Montaigne issues on the other side to pursue the quest without end, the quest that may give answers but no Answer, discoveries but no Discovery, truths but no Truth.

> I put forward formless and unresolved notions, as do those who publish doubtful questions to debate in the schools, not to establish the truth but to seek it.
>
> I set forth notions that are human and my own . . . matter of opinion, not matter of faith; what I reason out according to me, not what I believe according to God; as children set forth their essays to be instructed, not to instruct. . . . For we are born to quest after truth; to possess it belongs to a greater power. . . . The world is but a school of inquiry. . . . Wonder is the foundation of all philosophy, inquiry its progress, ignorance its end.
>
> There is no end to our researches; our end is in the other world.[6]

Actually, by shifting the focus of philosophical inquiry onto the "I" and his epistemological question, Montaigne succeeds, so far as this world and human beings are concerned, in making the way and the end identical. As a tactical and temperamental necessity, he gives over the expectation of finding

[6] "Of prayer," p. 229; "Of prayer," p. 234; "Of the art of discussion," p. 708; "Of cripples," p. 788; "Of experience," p. 817.

"truth, knowledge, and certainty," but in humorously and endlessly pursuing his question he performs the philosophical function: he lives cheerfully, tranquilly, and well in seeking a mode of living.

It is the given condition of life for each of us to go on "flowing and rolling unceasingly," watching all things flash by smudged and clouded windows of observation, unable to grasp the least of them in sure judgment. One thing only is constant in the process, one thing only accompanies unceasingly the flow and roll: consciousness. But the self and consciousness are inseparable, for coherent self is the result of the process of consciousness. The two go on simultaneously, or, more truly, they go on without regard to limits of time and space: the self comes into existence as it becomes conscious or aware of itself, and self-awareness comes about and advances only as it has an object, the self, to be aware of. Since he must forever roll anyway, Montaigne chooses to roll where rolling is best, and he mounts the drama of all reality on a new stage, an epitome stage of the self, on which one might view the "total drama" in summary and symbolic form: "The world always looks straight ahead; as for me, I turn my gaze inward, I fix it there and keep it busy. Everyone looks in front of him; as for me, I look inside of me; I have no business but with myself; I continually observe myself, I take stock of myself, I taste myself. Others always go elsewhere, if they stop to think about it; they always go forward; as for me, I roll about in myself."[7]

All passes; nothing stays. Rather than trying frantically and futilely to change the conditions of existence, Montaigne accommodates his efforts to the necessities of those conditions.

---

[7] "Of presumption," p. 499. In the original the last clause goes: "moy je me roulle en moy mesme" (*Oeuvres Complètes de Montaigne*, textes établis par Albert Thibaudet et Maurice Rat [Paris: Bibliothèque de la Pléiade, 1962], p. 641). Of course, the effect of sound is lost in translation: the "m" phrases of the original roll off the tongue and around the word at the center that they seem to enact: "roulle."

Whatever we would be, we are human; let us then, Montaigne urges, be human. To Seneca's "O what a vile and abject thing is man if he does not raise himself above humanity!" Montaigne, in the conclusion of his *Sebond*, responds ironically, "That is a good statement and a useful desire, but equally absurd. For to make the handful bigger than the hand, the armful bigger than the arm, and to hope to straddle more than the reach of our legs, is impossible and unnatural. Nor can man raise himself above himself and humanity; for he can see only with his own eyes, and seize only with his own grasp" (p. 457). "Impossible and unnatural"—it is nature herself that "possibilizes" for us; we exist only under and through natural conditions pre-established and given. To accept what we cannot anyway change comes to seem in Montaigne the only right, the only practical and intelligent, the only possible response. "We must learn to endure what we cannot avoid" ("Of experience," p. 835). The problem of how to face death, an example of what we cannot avoid, was a constant preoccupation and torment in the earlier essays; in the last essay Montaigne can say with Edgar in *King Lear*, and say it with mature conviction and assurance, "Men must endure / Their going hence, even as their coming hither: / Ripeness is all." Montaigne turns away from the "impossible and unnatural" of the central essay ("To try to kick against natural necessity," he says later, "is to imitate the folly of Ctesiphon, who undertook a kicking match with his mule; "Of experience," p. 835), to embrace the "natural and therefore necessary and just" of the last essay (where he envisions Caesar and Alexander "in the thick of their great tasks, so fully enjoying natural and therefore necessary and just pleasures"); in this turn and step, Montaigne discovers himself and his "natural faculties" and finds freedom in accepting what is anyhow necessary. "Is it not an error to consider some actions less worthy because they are necessary? No, they will not knock it out of my head that the marriage of pleasure with necessity, with whom, says an ancient, the gods always conspire, is a very suitable one" ("Of experience," p. 855).

The whole duty of man lies in the making of the self according to its own natural laws and necessities: to say that this is an exclusively modern philosophy would not be quite just (the Greeks, after all, are said to have thought of everything first, and in this particular idea they had the assistance of the Delphic oracle: "Know thyself"). But to found, in the Montaignesque way, all philosophy in autobiography; to plunge into subjectivity as wholly and intensely as Montaigne does; to refuse any other subject than the self as completely as he does—this symbolizes the historical tendency of philosophic concerns since the Reformation. Montaigne, of course, is timeless. But if we would fix him in an age, then it would be as reasonable to call him our contemporary as to confine him to the limits of the sixteenth century where we cannot get at him.

It would scarcely be in place, and I trust it will not seem necessary, as it is also not possible, to offer here a formal definition of "sanity" simply in order to say and maintain that Montaigne seems the sanest of writers and thinkers. Sanity is obviously not something that one can take hold of or prove, but there may be signs of sanity to which one can point and on which one can hope for agreement. To make peace, as we have already suggested Montaigne does, with what one cannot alter might be one such sign (contrast Swift, in Yeats's verse, raging against the condition he could never change, "Swift beating on his breast in sibylline frenzy blind / Because the heart in his blood-sodden breast had dragged him down into mankind"). Another sure sign, perhaps the surest and most comprehensive, would be a balanced vision and estimate of the wholeness of experience. The writer who strikes us as morally and intellectually healthy is the one who refuses to throw the whole of himself on a part or fragment without comprehending the entire context that includes the part. Or, in the reverse case, we regard that writer as obsessive or unbalanced who pursues a partial or fragmented truth (and it may well be, in itself, a truth), but who fails to perceive it as a way to an end and a part of a whole, who fails to relate his piece of understanding to a complete intellectual and moral body: at that point of failure he is less than totally healthy, or less than entirely sane, for the reader.

Montaigne, of course, denies that he sees "the whole of anything," and this may, in a sense, be true here and there: first, because "anything" may apply to the ostensible subjects of his titles ("Of fear," "Of friendship," or *Apology for Raymond Sebond*!), where he never intends to offer more than formal courtesy to the subject; second, because, when he deals with his real subject—himself—he has a subject that is always changing, always coming into being, never fully realized or wholly there. If, on the other hand, we look not at one essay or one stab at the subject but at the whole volume of *Essays*, then, in the sense suggested, Montaigne is as free of obsession as any writer who ever lived. Whether or not he sees it steadily (and one could well argue that he does see it steadily in the complete body of *Essays*, in spite of his often deliberate inconsistency), there is no question, I think, but that Montaigne sees life whole. If we read in conjunction an early, a middle, and a late essay—"That our happiness must not be judged until after our death," *Apology for Raymond Sebond*, and "Of experience," for example—it becomes apparent that Montaigne's sanity, like every quality and every virtue in his life and work, was something achieved, a state at which he eventually arrived and within which he lived. The earlier essays are stations on the way, but to be seen as such only from the terminus of the last essays. The balance, maturity, and serenity of these last essays seem inevitable—yet could hardly have been foreseen from the early ones. It is, for example, very much a partial, fragmentary thing that Montaigne does in *Sebond* (at least if we take it unqualified by *b* and *c* insertions). The slashing denunciations in that essay of human pretensions, the humiliating likenesses drawn between humans and the lowest beasts, the insistence on humanity's insignificance and stupidity, its baseness and foulness and corruption—these assaults on the creature man are undoubtedly effective, necessary perhaps, and often amusing. But though it is learned, the essay's violent energy strikes one as unbalanced and immature in its single-minded narrowness and exclusive concentration on the negative and the destructive. When writing *Sebond*, Montaigne was of course also writing other, very different things, and this essay is no doubt an essential part of the whole portrait of the evolving person; but if we consider characteristic essays of Book III ("On some verses of Virgil," for example, or "Of repentance" and "Of experience"), and compare them with *Sebond*, I think it would be fair to say that Montaigne would never, if he had not already done it earlier, have added this essential essay to the whole portrait, at least not in anything like the way we have it. But the achievement in wholeness did come over the course of twenty years and more than a hundred essays.

"Both kings and philosophers," Montaigne casually remarks in the last essay, "defecate, and ladies too." This simple, perhaps obvious fact that Montaigne acknowledges with typical calm is one that has, at least momentarily, unbalanced some powerful minds (cf. Swift again). Lest the reader think the subject of no consequence, however, or out of place in an essay "Of experience," Montaigne proceeds to draw the question back to himself, the focal subject of experience: we should not, he has learned from experience, "subject ourselves . . . to any concern for a particularly comfortable place and seat for this function"; on the other hand, "Of all natural functions that is the one that I can least willingly endure to have interrupted. I have seen many soldiers inconvenienced by the irregularity of their bowels; mine and I never fail the moment of our assignation, which is when I jump out of bed" (pp. 831-32). Very deliberately, Montaigne determined that there would be no part of life too high or too low, too plain or too obscure, too refined or too coarse to come to his attention and to go into his portrait. His book was to be a portrait of a man, and whatever might be natural to a man would be "therefore necessary and just" in the portrait. There is a place for everything in the economy of nature and it is an aspect of Montaigne's sanity that he saw nature whole and insisted that everything should be in its place. Of the learned idiots that cannot enjoy human pleasures in their season and take them naturally as in themselves they are, Montaigne says: "Won't they try to square the circle while perched on their wives! I hate to have people order us to keep our minds in the clouds while our bodies are at table. I would not have the mind nailed down to it nor wallowing at it, but attending to it; sitting at it, not lying down at it" ("Of experience," p. 850). It is the obsessive and the insane who insist with their blind certainty (and often, as Yeats observed, with "passionate intensity") that there is but one way and one truth and that they have it and it is good for all. "Obstinacy and heat of opinion is the surest proof of stupidity. Is there anything," Montaigne blandly asks, "so certain, resolute, disdainful, contemplative, grave, and serious as an ass?" ("Of the art of discussion," p. 717). There are as many ways and as many truths as there have been and are individual selves, and the mark of health and sanity is to retain an openness and flexibility before the myriad possibilities of life. "All the glory that I aspire to in my life is to have lived it tranquilly—tranquilly not according to Metrodorus or Arcesilaus or Aristippus, but according to me. Since philosophy has not been able to find a way to tranquillity that is suitable to all, let everyone seek it individually" ("Of glory," p. 471).

And it is the whole individual—body, mind, and soul—who shall seek the way for his whole self, not a part for itself in denial of the rest. It is the natural condition that all parts are united in the human composite, so "let us bind it together again by mutual services. Let the mind arouse and quicken the heaviness of the body, and the body check and make fast the lightness of the mind" ("Of experience," p. 855). Montaigne fully approves the notion that sages, like all men, should submit "mildly and contentedly to the laws of human nature, and of Venus and Bacchus" ("Of experience," p. 851). It is a natural necessity in the human state, and denying it will change nothing, that body should give expression and access to the soul and the soul inform and enliven the body. It is primarily with the learned philosophers, the glorifiers of mind and soul alone, that Montaigne does battle on behalf of human wholeness. Indeed, he maintains that the body and the soul are ironically well met and fairly joined in the human composite, for if the senses are deceived by external phenomena and in turn deceive the mind and the soul, these latter two are not at all behindhand in the ways of lying and deception. The senses and the soul carry on a merry game of deceit and falsehood, competing to see which shall overlay the other. Montaigne finds it an easy thing to prove to the reader that the pleasures of the soul are no more than illusions, and the pleasures of the body perhaps not even so much. ("I, who boast of embracing the pleasures of life so assiduously and so particularly, find in them, when I look at them thus minutely, virtually nothing but wind. But what of it? We are all wind"; "Of experience," p. 849.) He can prove it—that is, until the reader is sufficiently convinced—and then comes time for him to turn back on himself and his gulled reader with what we all know from common and vulgar experience: that the pleasures of the table, the bottle, and the bed, or the pleasures of the book, the library, and the cloister are real and valuable, whatever the learnedly perverse philosopher or brutishly ignorant lout may say or offer to prove to the contrary.

Only why, Montaigne demands, should we, as philosophers, insist on ascribing "real" pleasure to the soul and only to the soul? Through what conduits has the soul its pure and airy life except the senses of the body? The soul must realize itself through the senses, "else," as Donne says, "a great Prince in prison lies." A great Prince the soul may well be, but powerless and pathetic if the gates are closed on him and he receives nothing from without to sustain life. "The greatest benefit that good health gives me"—and good health was perhaps the finest gift life could make, according to Montaigne—"is sensual pleasure; let us stick to the first pleasure that is present and known" ("Of experience," p. 847). Bodily ecstasy—the physical organism luxuriating in its own abounding, excellent health—is something the ascetic philosophers may scorn, but it is no less real or valuable for that; and it is no less generous, Montaigne says, in sharing its good with the soul, even though heretic puritans deny the value or validity of the senses.

> Our masters are wrong in that, seeking the causes of the extraordinary flights of the soul, they have attributed some to a divine ecstasy, to love, to warlike fierceness, to poetry, to wine, but have not assigned a proper share to health—an ebullient, vigorous, full, lazy health, such as in the past my green years and security supplied me with now and then. The blaze of gaiety kindles in the mind vivid, bright flashes beyond our natural capacity, and some of the lustiest, if not the most extravagant, enthusiasms. ("On some verses of Virgil," p. 641.)

Few philosophers could make so much of such a common subject as Montaigne does here of good health—but few philosophers have had Montaigne's wholeness of vision, his excellent health of mind, his essential and profound sanity of spirit. "Greatness of soul," he says, "is not so much pressing upward and forward as knowing how to set oneself in order and circumscribe oneself. . . . There is nothing so beautiful and legitimate as to play the man well and properly, no knowledge so hard to acquire as the knowledge of how to live this life well and naturally; and the most barbarous of our maladies is to despise our being" ("Of experience," p. 852).

As his philosophy does not deny the real fact of the gross body and refuses to despise it for its nature, so Montaigne's humor does not disdain coarse language and the crude joke, or despise them for their vulgarity. In themselves, he maintains, they are natural and refer to natural facts, and so in this portrait of whole man and his natural faculties "we must leave that vain squeamishness about words to women" ("Of ancient customs," p. 217). To weight his picture of mind and spirit with some healthy earthiness, therefore, Montaigne tells the story of Diogenes: "For Diogenes, practicing masturbation in public, expressed the wish in the presence of bystanders that he could satisfy his stomach that way by rubbing it." He drops in an old saw on the mistake of marrying your mistress: "It is the old saying: 'Shit in your hat and then put it on your head.'" He describes for us several sudden deaths in the toilet. He tells of one lady who, apparently, died from an overactive imagination: "I know that one gentleman, having entertained a goodly company at his house, three or four days later boasted, as a sort of joke (for there was nothing in it), that he had made them eat cat in a pie; at which one lady in the party was so horrified that she fell into a violent stomach disorder and fever, and it was impossible to save her." He passes on a story about Aesop: "Aesop, that great man, saw his master pissing as he walked. 'What next?' he said. 'Shall we have to shit as we run?'" He criticizes the arrogant way doctors treat their helpless patients: they prescribe "for us colicky folk (so disdainfully do they take advantage of our misery), pulverized

73

rat turds, and other such monkey tricks." And he discourses on the will, which, he says, is not all-powerful, as we can see from the fact that it cannot control "the unruly liberty of this member, obtruding so importunately when we have no use for it, and failing so importunately when we have the most use for it," and as we can see too from its failure to control other organs as well:

> The organs that serve to discharge the stomach have their own dilatations and compressions, beyond and against our plans, just like those that are destined to discharge the kidneys. To vindicate the omnipotence of our will, Saint Augustine alleges that he knew a man who commanded his behind to produce as many farts as he wanted, and his commentator Vives goes him one better with another example of his own time, of farts arranged to suit the tone of verses pronounced to their accompaniment; but all this does not really argue any pure obedience in this organ; for is there any that is ordinarily more indiscreet or tumultuous? Besides, I know one so turbulent and unruly, that for forty years it has kept its master farting with a constant and unremitting wind and compulsion, and is thus taking him to his death. And would God I knew only from the history books how many times our stomach, by refusing one single fart, brings us to the gates of a very anguished death; and that the Emperor who gave us liberty to fart anywhere had given us the power to.[8]

Montaigne, as in this passage, does not mind the joke coming back on himself; nearly every joke, in fact, is, one way or another, told against himself. There is one instance, written when he ruefully considered himself an old man: it seems, he says, that nearly all nations have been ashamed of the act of generation; "Perhaps we are right to blame ourselves for making such a stupid production as man, to call the action shameful, and

---

[8] *Sebond*, p. 441; "On some verses of Virgil," p. 649; "We should meddle soberly with judging divine ordinances," p. 161; "Of the power of the imagination," p. 74; "Of experience," p. 856; "Of the resemblance of children to fathers," p. 584; "Of the power of the imagination," pp. 72-73.

shameful the parts that are used for it. (At present mine are truly shameful and pitiful)."[9] What might be repulsive or disgusting or perverse in another writer seldom is in Montaigne because of the healthy good humor of his manner and because of his deliberate care to see the detail as a part of the whole picture and not to emphasize any one detail beyond its value—but also not to miss or deny any natural detail either.

"I rarely repent," Montaigne says in the essay on repentance: an excellent companion-piece to the essay on experience; "my conscience is content with itself—not as the conscience of an angel or a horse, but as the conscience of a man" ("Of repentance," p. 612). Were it not content with itself, it would not be his conscience. As soon as the conscience could see the fault and activate repentance, it would be seeing in the way of another, superior conscience. "Repentance": if the word means anything (there is some real question about that for Montaigne), then the idea is literally mad. In "repeated, planned, and premeditated, constitutional sins, or even professional or vocational sins"—as against "impetuous, prompt, and sudden sins: let us leave them aside" (pp. 616-17)—the whole being, the whole man, as he has evolved to that point, is involved. For that whole being—the result of which being was the "sin"—repentance is meaningless or impossible. He has been, and, so long as he is the same person, continues to be, moved toward the sin rather than toward repentance. Only if he were, or were to become, another being could he repent, but then another being cannot repent the sins of the original one. Moreover, Montaigne argues, how can one speak of repenting for being the person that one has no choice but to be under the individually inbuilt laws of nature? Perhaps, like vengeance, repentance is the Lord's; in any case, it is not properly man's portion. Montaigne insists always on the necessity of understanding a single action in the context of whole

9 "On some verses of Virgil," p. 669.

being, which saves him from the insanity of self-contempt
and from rejection of the experience that has brought him into
present existence. There is comfort and consolation in the
realization that the personal reality now is, and that the experience leading to that reality could not have been otherwise.
"In all affairs, when they are past, however they have turned
out, I have little regret. For this idea takes away the pain: that
they were bound to happen thus, and now they are in the great
stream of the universe and in the chain of Stoical causes. Your
fancy, by wish or imagination, cannot change a single point
without overturning the whole order of things, and the past
and the future" (pp. 618-19). For old age (which "creeps up
on us naturally and imperceptibly" in this essay) to take pride
in its sour incapacity and to call that incapacity repentance
for the vigorous, better, healthier, and happier days of youth
is simply vicious, a disavowal born of weakness, not of natural
strength or true chastity. Of youth and age, Montaigne can
say—and convincingly, for his book proves the depth, the fullness, the reality of his knowledge—"I know them both; I have
a right to speak." Other men may bring other testimony,
which, as it multiplies variety, is all to the good; but no man
can confute Montaigne's experience and his witness: in nature's will he finds his peace. "My bodily state has run its
course," he says in a beautifully serene passage, "with each
thing in due season. I have seen the grass, the flower, and the
fruit; now I see the dryness—happily, since it is naturally"
(p. 620).

Perhaps the sanest aspect all through Montaigne's achievement is his insistence that philosophy has an end and a purpose and that this end is to promote the fullest possible life
at every point for the individual person according to his needs
and his way. "The simple peasants are good men, and good
men the philosophers" ("Of vain subtleties," p. 227), and
either should teach us by his example the great and simple les-

son: to live under nature—one's own and general nature—according to the common experience and the vulgar performance, for "we are all," Montaigne says, looking back on his earlier self in the *Sebond*, "of the common herd": "et nous sommes tous du vulgaire." Montaigne's worry about facing death—the nearly continuous, and thus almost obsessive, concern of the earlier essays—dissolves in the last essays into a serenity that neither the thought of death nor anything else seems to touch. "If a man has any good in him," Montaigne advises, "let him show it in his conduct" ("Of the resemblance," p. 596). Philosophy should show itself in the ordinary business of life and not only or specially in the face of death (except, as Montaigne eventually says, as that *is* a part of ordinary life); philosophy should think about being itself at the dinner table rather than on the operating table, in the marriage bed rather than exclusively on the death bed. "We are great fools. 'He has spent his life in idleness,' we say; 'I have done nothing today.' What, have you not lived? That is not only the fundamental but the most illustrious of your occupations. . . . Our great and glorious masterpiece is to live appropriately. All other things, ruling, hoarding, building, are only little appendages and props, at most" ("Of experience," pp. 850-51). Toward the end of the essay "Of experience," as he begins to draw everything together for a breathtaking and very moving last experiment in truth, Montaigne brings forth what must be taken, in this conclusive position, as a summary of his growth in self and his response to life—and the hallmark of this great statement is the sense that it conveys in every phrase and sentence of a full, various, mature, and cheerful sanity:

> As for me, then, I love life and cultivate it just as God has been pleased to grant it to us. I do not go about wishing that it should lack the need to eat and drink, and it would seem to me no less excusable a failing to wish that need to be doubled.

... Nor do I wish that we should sustain ourselves by merely putting into our mouths a little of that drug by which Epimenides took away his appetite and kept himself alive; nor that we should beget children insensibly with our fingers or our heels, but rather, with due respect, that we could also beget them voluptuously with our fingers and heels; nor that the body should be without desire and without titillation. Those are ungrateful and unfair complaints. I accept with all my heart and with gratitude what nature has done for me, and I am pleased with myself and proud of myself that I do. We wrong that great and all-powerful Giver by refusing his gift, nullifying it, and disfiguring it. Himself all good, he has made all things good. (Pp. 854-55.)

There is to be remarked, between a passage like this one from the final essay and any random passage from an early essay, a very distinct stylistic difference. An interesting question to consider, in turning to Montaigne's artistry, is how much we would read or remember of him if he had not lived to publish his third volume of essays, and also, or especially, if he had not annotated all three volumes. Held up against essays of Book III, those of Books I and II are by and large quite unremarkable—artificial and conventional—in effort and accomplishment. This one would never say of the last essays; nor, significantly, would one say it of the later insertions into those stiff, lightweight, early pieces. Indeed, these illuminating interjections of the later Montaigne often carry, in one or two sentences, more weight than all the remainder of the original essay. Not that the early essays are not sprightly and breezy and pleasant; but it is the journalistic breeziness of a twice-weekly column of charm, the sort of breeziness that goes with (and would, perhaps, disguise) a thinness of substance. At best, such early pieces as "Of thumbs" and "Of ancient customs" are minor exercises, postprandial airings of the spirit, flickerings of the imagination; but they add up to very little, being for the most part as insignificant as they are ingenious, the "chimeras and fantastic monsters" ("Of idleness," p. 21), Montaigne says, born of his idleness in retirement. What is insignificant fooling here, however, becomes, by some essential transformation, the rich and vital humor of the last essays, the natural records and results of a life, and, in spite of Montaigne's demurrers, or perhaps because of them, there is the sense at the end that he has come to something which, with all the insights of his marginalia, his thoughts and afterthoughts, will satisfy him as truth—the truth of himself, and that is as far as he ever supposed a human could reach anyhow.

How much does this transformation have to do with Montaigne's developing artistry and how much with his changing philosophy? Style, as suggested earlier, is a fundamental matter in Montaigne, for he really does make himself with his book— the two being identical, or, in his own phrase, "consubstantial," processes. What one can trace from the early essays to the late is a changing, evolving personality which finds consubstantial expression only in a changing, evolving style. "Profound joy," Montaigne wrote in the margin of "We taste nothing pure," "has more of seriousness than gaiety about it; extreme and full contentment, more soberness than sprightliness" (p. 510). The context suggests that Montaigne means simply that all emotions are mixed, none are pure; but the remark applies equally well as description of the achieved state of self and book, style and man in the late essays: no longer bouncy, sprightly, gay, brilliantly negative, they become sober, contented, serious, profoundly joyous, weighted toward the positive. The last essays are, at one and the same time, more cheerful and more serious, more spirited and more steady, more positive and more profound than the early ones—and these are qualities both of the spirit and of the word in Montaigne. Criticizing Ficino for not treating of a natural and vigorous subject (physical love) in a natural and vigorous language and Aristotle for adopting a mode of expression that conceals his matter instead of revealing it, Montaigne names his own stylistic authority—an authority that he reverences in literature as in life: "I do not recognize in Aristotle most of my ordinary actions: they have been covered and dressed up in another robe for the use of the school. God grant that these men may be doing the right thing! If I were of the trade, I would naturalize art as much as they artify nature" ("On some verses," p. 666).

If Montaigne was not of the trade, then no man has ever been, and being of that philosopher-writer-artist trade, but before all living man, he naturalized art as he said he would, making it the mirror of *his* nature. "I present myself standing and lying down, front and rear, on the right and the left, and in all my natural postures" ("Of the art of discussion," p. 721). In a humorous fit against his writings—praying God and the philosophers to stop him from scribbling more—Montaigne describes his essays as the "excrements of an aged mind, now hard, now loose, and always undigested" ("Of vanity," p. 721). In one mood, one view, one posture this may be so, in another it will be quite different; but always the language and rhythms are adapted to the momentary spirit of their maker. "The speech I love is a simple, natural speech, the same on paper as in the mouth; a speech succulent and sinewy, brief and compressed, not so much dainty and well-combed as vehement and brusque" ("Of the education of children," p. 127). It will be apparent that, for all the number of times that Montaigne invokes the word "natural" to describe his own style, there is a certain self-consciousness about this; the quality pointed to is not affectation but a very obvious awareness of choosing language that will be expressive of the writer's personality. On the other hand, the defense of this might be that this is, after all, the most natural of things: Montaigne was deeply self-conscious, profoundly aware of the state and nature of his own self, and his self-consciousness properly carries over into the texture, tendency, and viewpoint of his expression. "As for the rest," he observes, "my language has no ease or polish; it is harsh and disdainful, with a free and unruly disposition. And I like it that way, if not by judgment, then by inclination" ("Of presumption," p. 484). Not only does Montaigne's personal, quirky style leap out from every page of his *Essays*, but its author never neglects an opportunity of telling the reader about this personal manner: in a style marked generally by fits and starts, by frequent reverses and returns on himself, by caprice and quibble, Montaigne describes his capricious style. "I have naturally a humorous and familiar style, but of a form all my own . . . compact, disorderly, abrupt, individual" ("A consideration upon Cicero," p. 186).

The foregoing descriptions by Montaigne of his own writing are, of course, autobiography, at least in a sense, but there is also something there that is not adequately described by the word "autobiography" (i.e., the writing of one's own life). While unquestionably an autobiographer in the simple sense, Montaigne is also what one might call a theoretical autobiographer or an "auto-autobiographer"—the writer who tells the story of himself telling the story of himself. It is as if Montaigne were to look in a mirror and describe the image of himself looking in a mirror describing . . . and so on to an infinite replication in consciousness of images of himself within images of himself. One seems to hear from the pages of the *Essays* the laughter of Myso faintly echoing back again as Montaigne makes his life the subject of his autobiographical art, and then steps outside the ring, being now both inside and outside the process, to make his art the subject of both his life and his art. This is very like what we find in certain of the novels of Henry James, where awareness is of the essence: the characters, projections of the author's mind and embodiments of his meaning, watch one another and watch them-

81

selves, and the reader, intently watching, is aware always of the supremely conscious intelligence of James watching his watchers. In a well-known passage from one of these Montaignesque dances of awareness (*What Maisie Knew*), the state of reciprocal consciousness reaches a point where, James tells us, "there was an extraordinary mute passage between her vision of this vision of his, his vision of her vision, and her vision of his vision of her vision."[10] It is a bit dizzying to try to encircle with one's own consciousness the double, triple, quadruple consciousness of the two characters—and even quintuple, since there is James's consciousness to include also. The last circle of the work, of course, is the total theatre of the artist's creative mind, and we imagine him surrounding even that while the dialogue of consciousness evolves within. Montaigne dramatizes the evolving process in *Essays*, James in novels and tales. "I cannot," Montaigne both boasts and complains,

> keep my subject still. It goes along befuddled and staggering, with a natural drunkenness. I take it in this condition, just as it is at the moment I give my attention to it. I do not portray being: I portray passing. . . . My history needs to be adapted to the moment. I may presently change, not only by chance, but also by intention. This is a record of various and changeable occurrences, and of irresolute and, when it so befalls, contradictory ideas: whether I am different myself, or whether I take hold of my subjects in different circumstances and aspects. So, all in all, I may indeed contradict myself now and then; but truth, as Demades said, I do not contradict. If my mind could gain a firm footing, I would not make essays, I would make decisions; but it is always in apprenticeship and on trial.
>
> I set forth a humble and inglorious life; that does not matter. You can tie up all moral philosophy with a common and private life just as well as with a life of richer stuff. Each man bears the entire form of man's estate.

[10] *What Maisie Knew* (New York: Charles Scribner's Sons, 1922), p. 182.

Authors communicate with the people by some extrinsic mark; I am the first to do so by my entire being, as Michel de Montaigne, not as a grammarian or a poet or a jurist. If the world complains that I speak too much of myself, I complain that it does not even think of itself.

("Of repentance," pp. 610-11.)

Montaigne is the writer who tells us everything about himself—we know this is so because he tells us that he tells us everything. He is said to be the man that we know as well as ourselves and better than our friends. Can this be so, and in what sense? Surely it goes directly against our normal understanding. The editor of the Pléiade *Montaigne* glosses a passage ("Les effects diroyent plus de la Fortune que de moy") with this note: "Il s'agit ici des actions. Montaigne nous fait comprendre ici pourquoi il n'a pas écrit des Mémoires, mais des Essais" (p. 360). This is an interesting and useful distinction; to make it tells us much about Montaigne's practice. The effect of his art—and the reason why he does not describe actions or deeds but tries instead to capture mental and spiritual quality in a manner and a style, in anecdote and argument— is to make the reader identify with Montaigne's essential self, not in the life but in the autobiographical art, so that we do not respond to what he did in the past but to what he is in the present of his book. As with any work of art, we tend to live into the experience of the *Essays* and come to identify that experience with our own, which would only be possible if Montaigne were creating a coherent, artistic portrait, valid for the reach of humanity, rather than a record of events true only for one man. Whereas our lives and those of our friends may be incoherent as experienced, in order to draw our response Montaigne's portrait, though it be of inconsistent and variable spirit, must be coherent in capturing that inconsistency and unified in its portrayal of that essential quality of human nature. In fact, what we find realized in the *Essays* is much more

83

akin to the spiritual quest of the *Four Quartets* (a quest presented in rhythms, metaphors, and motifs more than in statement) than it is to the memoirs of a public man listing the dates, places, persons, and events of a lifetime rich in action—and, it may be, compensatorily impoverished in spirit. Nor is Montaigne a moralist concerned with the ideal and possessed of a Mosaic tablet of laws to be handed down; he is rather the artist engaged in the real who describes the philosopher enacting the pursuit of himself. "Others form man," he says; "I tell of him, and portray a very particular one" ("Of repentance," p. 610). And, as he says in another place, his has been the queerest preoccupation in the world: "And then, finding myself entirely destitute and void of any other matter, I presented myself to myself for argument and subject. It is the only book in the world of its kind, a book with a wild and eccentric plan" ("Of the affection of fathers for their children," p. 278). Montaigne is the only man who ever made himself the entire subject of his book—the only one, that is, except for all poets, and other artists, and the occasional figure like Jung or Newman who does it under cover of another discipline such as psychology or religion or philosophy.

What, in fact, do we know of Montaigne from his portrait? He gives a myriad details: he could eat nearly anything, but could not tolerate beer; he dressed in black and white; he had an astonishingly weak memory ("if I were to live a long time, I do not doubt that I would forget my own name"); he loved poetry, but could not write it, and after poetry, biography; he hated hypocrisy and, more than any other vice, cruelty; he had a rather low opinion of women intellectually; he was below medium height; he lost his virginity at such an early age that, looking back, he could not recall the event (or was this only weak memory again?); he suffered sometimes from prematurity in sexual congress but, in the same encounters, he retained sense and discretion ("a little excitement, but no folly"); he could not "make a child except before going to sleep, or make one standing up"; he was overscrupulous in keeping promises; he was a good horseman; and a hundred other details. To recognize these details, however, and to add them together is hardly to know Montaigne in the sense that we know a friend. Yet, if we do not know Montaigne as we know a friend, we do come to know him in a way that is strikingly analogous to the way in which we know ourselves: what we experience in the *Essays* is like what we experience as the inner processes that go to make up the self. Montaigne's subject might, in fact, be said to be this process of the self, inconsistent but evolutionary and imperfectly perfect from moment to moment. Hence all these pieces and details are necessary to the portrait, not so much for themselves as for the pattern they establish and for what their very telling, and the manner of that telling, reveals to us about Montaigne. What we can perceive in the *Essays* is not the substance of a character but a mode of proceeding, and what we finally observe is not the person of Montaigne but a style revealing a set, an attitude, a point of view, a mind-in-operation, a self-in-becoming—all of which, having realized it through our reading, we identify in the end with ourselves.

The artist's defense for not giving us general truth direct, and Montaigne's defense, or one of them, for not even trying, is that the universal is real in the particular, and not otherwise nor elsewhere.[11] The faithful specificity of the artist, nowhere better illustrated than in the rich mental, physical, and moral precision of Montaigne's self-portrait, ensures the reality of

[11] Cf. Fitzgerald on the analogous creative process in fiction: "Begin with an individual, and before you know it you find that you have created a type; begin with a type, and you find that you have created—nothing. This is because we are all queer fish, queerer behind our faces and voices than we want anyone to know or than we know ourselves. . . . There are no types, no plurals. There is a rich boy, and this is his and not his brother's story" (*Babylon Revisited and Other Stories* [New York: Charles Scribner's Sons, 1960], p. 152).

the embodied universal on the one hand, the energy of the reader's emphatic response on the other. In Montaigne's artistic portrait, all the concentric circles of abstractions and universals—that he was "Man," "Frenchman," "Gascon," de Montaigne," for example—live and have their being only in the central particularity, only in *this* man, *this* Frenchman, *this* Gascon, *this* de Montaigne: in the unique, unrepeated and unrepeatable, but artistically viable, existence of Michel Eyquem de Montaigne. Within the self and the portrait, each of the abstractions is made real, so that eventually the first and last circles, the circumference and the center, Man and this man, are one and the same, neither existing, either "impossible and unnatural," without the other. Montaigne's philosophy and his art drive steadily through all the distractions and reversals, intentional and temperamental, toward recognition of shared nature in all men, towards affirmation of the unity implied in a quotation above: "Each man bears the entire form of man's estate: chaque homme porte la forme entiere de l'humaine condition."[12] Each man is, in epitome, the human race; or, as Jung might put it, in biological and psychological terms: the ontogenetic pattern (history and development of an individual organism) repeats, contains, and makes real the phylogenetic pattern (history and development of the race). With this discovery and affirmation, Montaigne's book presents us with what Yeats, borrowing from Dante, calls Unity of Being: union of the individual with the supraindividual; of Michel de Montaigne with the whole body of mankind; of personal self with the collective daimon of nature. The recognition that, simultaneously, each human life is totally singular and unique and that each of us in his experience is also realizing the pattern of human life—a pattern realized an infinite number of times before us, a pattern to be repeated an infinite

[12] Pléiade *Montaigne*, p. 773.

number of times after us—is an immensely liberating one; and it leads to the kind of serenity that one finds in late Montaigne; it leads, again in Yeats's phrase, to the assurance that "nothing can injure us."

The greatness of Montaigne's achievement in autobiography lies in the wholeness and balance of his view of life, in the fidelity of his portrait of the questing spirit, in the stylistic verve which exactly mirrors the process of becoming, in the multifold consciousness and self-consciousness, the profound subjectivity that goes so deep that it becomes transformed into an objective vision of the human condition, a vision finally indistinguishable from revelation of the divine. The conclusion to Montaigne's book and portrait represents the crown of a life, in its circularity single yet many-pointed, leaving us in the end where knowledge begins and where artistic creation concludes: Montaigne calls this last experiment with truth "Of experience." How carefully and consciously he has elaborated and set the crown one may appreciate in the bewildering patchwork of *b* and *c* passages. We see Montaigne completing himself in the completion of his portrait. Hand in hand the two move to the destined and foreseen but unknown end, the man becoming complete as the metaphor describes and defines him, the portrait being finished as the man comes to richest maturity. The final paean is significantly an invocation of experience directed to Apollo, god of artists, of music and song, and of prophecy. In the end we have both the metaphor and the fact of existence, a double creation, both experience and an expressive vehicle of experience, a life consubstantial with a meaning.

It is an absolute perfection and virtually divine to know how to enjoy our being rightfully. We seek other conditions because we do not understand the use of our own, and go outside of ourselves because we do not know what it is like inside. Yet there is no use our mounting on stilts, for on stilts we must still walk on our own legs. And on the loftiest throne in the world we are still sitting only on our own rump.

The most beautiful lives, to my mind, are those that conform to the common human pattern, with order, but without miracle and without eccentricity. Now old age needs to be treated a little more tenderly. Let us commend it to that god who is the protector of health and wisdom, but gay and sociable wisdom:

> Grant me but health, Latona's son,
> And to enjoy the wealth I've won,
> And honored age, with mind entire
> And not unsolaced by the lyre.

three : Jung

my personal myth

Like Montaigne, Jung, in the very process of creating an autobiography that is always challenging and frequently moving, offers us simultaneously an abundance of theory for a "science" of autobiography. Fortunately not content with being a practicing physician, though he was that first of all, and pressed into new researches of the most various sorts by his particular and beloved branch of medicine, Jung must often be called nothing more and nothing less than a speculative metaphysician. Though he regularly rejected that term in everything that comprises his writings in theoretical psychology, Jung's autobiography, standing outside the official canon, leads the reader right to it and leaves him there. In this book, composed at the end of his life, Jung finally offers what he had been so reticent about in his theoretical writings: a comprehensive statement of his profound experience in and his achieved understanding of the human condition.

That Jung, again like Montaigne, derived his knowledge and consequent theory of psychology from primary experience should, no doubt, have been apparent all along. That is to say that although Jung, being the empiricist he always insisted he was, observed and collated varieties of psychological phenomena in the clinic and in consultation with hundreds of patients, yet his complex metaphor for psychic experience—his vision, his "myth" as he calls it in the autobiography—came first and last from experience of and in the self. Jung was a scientist concerned with gathering secondary empirical evidence from his patients; but he was before that a man who had suffered the primary experience which he studied in others. Jung himself stood as both object and subject for his explorations of personality. The scientist merges with the sufferer at every point so that Jung, discussing in one place a mandala drawing of his own while still maintaining a proper anonymity, correctly refers to himself as "a male patient."[1] That he was both doctor and patient, that his knowledge as a doctor came from his experience as a patient—this, of course, we should have known if we have any understanding of the relation between a public career and a private life. It was only, however, with the publication of his autobiographical writings (released, by his request, only after his death and not as part of the *Collected Works*) and with that elaboration of his most private life, that the immediate experiential basis for his projected theory of humanity became evident. Of someone ostensibly very different from himself, Jung says, in passing, "There is no doubt that his activities were founded on a numinous experience, which is, indeed, characteristic of all those who are gripped by an archetype" (*Aion, CW,* ix, pt. 2, par. 141). This is quite precisely the relation obtaining between Jung's private experience and his public construct. He was, as he frequently acknowledges, "gripped by an archetype," his actions dictated by the close grasp of his daimon to "individuation." From a numinous experience (an immediate and ineffable encounter with divinity, quite indistinguishable for Jung from

---

[1] "Concerning Mandala Symbolism," *The Archetypes and the Collective Unconscious, The Collected Works of C. G. Jung,* ix, pt. 1, par. 654. Hereafter *CW* refers to the *Collected Works,* now in the course of publication for the Bollingen Foundation by Princeton University Press and in England by Routledge & Kegan Paul. With a few exceptions for reasons that will be evident, references to *CW* are given by volume and paragraph number.

On Jung as a "male patient," cf. a passage from *Memories, Dreams, Reflections by C. G. Jung,* recorded and edited by Aniela Jaffé (New York: Pantheon, 1963; London: Collins and Routledge & Kegan Paul), p. 145/143: "From my encounters with patients and with psychic phenomena which they have paraded before me in an endless stream of images, I have learned an enormous amount—not just knowledge, but above all insight into my own nature." (Here and elsewhere, the first page reference is to the U.S. edition, the second to the British edition.)

an experience of the completed self), foretelling and resulting in the total being of C. G. Jung, came the multivolume *Collected Works*. Once more Jung seems to echo Montaigne: the book and the man are consubstantial. "My life is what I have done, my scientific work; the one is inseparable from the other. The work is the expression of my inner development; for commitment to the contents of the unconscious forms the man and produces his transformations. My works can be regarded as stations along my life's way" (*Memories*, p. 222/211). The autobiography, standing between the experience and the work, the altogether private and the largely public, partakes of both. In *Memories, Dreams, Reflections* the stream of private images runs for the first time together with the projected career, inclining one to say that this is easily Jung's most interesting creation, his fullest statement and—of this I am certain —his best book.

Personal experience lies cheek by jowl with theory in the book, but excellent as it is in demonstrating the source of his ideas, Jung's autobiography is not quite independent of that full theoretical exposition entitled *Collected Works*. And, though there are various, often sufficient justifications for the fact, it should be admitted that, when his writings are all brought together, Jung is often repetitious and occasionally long-winded. In his good-humored response to an interviewer's reference to "your great array of writings," Jung could offer his reader condolence—but little comfort: "Well, yes. People have to read the books, by golly, in spite of the fact that they are thick! I'm sorry."[2] The particular relation that exists between Jung's writings in autobiography and his writings in psychology—a relation consequent upon the fact that in both cases psyche is both subject and object—enjoins an approach

[2] *Conversations with C. G. Jung*, ed. R. I. Evans (Princeton, N.J.: Van Nostrand Co., 1964), p. 116. The quotation has been slightly revised to conform to the version to be published in a volume of Jung's interviews, forthcoming.

to him somewhat different from that for any other writer considered. It will be both helpful and valid, as we examine Jung's portrait of experience, to "amplify" (Jung's phrase) that experience and expression by continuous reference to theory in his other writings. For example, when Jung describes his own visions or fantasies, one can provide the description with its parallel in developed theory from other books, where Jung expands on the psychological source, nature, meaning, and use of visionary experience. Jung's reference to his career in psychiatry as "the subjective experiment out of which my objective life emerged" (*Memories*, p. 113/115) provides the cue for our approach: "Today I can say that I have never lost touch with my initial experiences. All my works, all my creative activity, has come from those initial fantasies and dreams which began in 1912, almost fifty years ago. Everything that I accomplished in later life was already contained in them, although at first only in the form of emotions and images" (*Memories*, p. 192/184). Jung first experienced what he later studied and then erected into an ordered and systematic psychological structure. His writings in psychology are simply an expression of his own archetypal urge to self-realization. His writings on the nature of human psyche constitute a monument to the process of his becoming. Again, Jung says of the fantasies that streamed unwilled out of his own unconscious: "The years when I was pursuing my inner images were the most important of my life—in them everything essential was decided. . . . It was the *prima materia* for a lifetime's work" (*Memories*, p. 199/191). The unconscious, for one concerned, like Jung, with the operations and effects of the human psyche, supplies the impetus and substance for the working of the conscious mind, and that conscious mind returns to elaborate in theory the process out of which it has evolved. Thus Jung's autobiographical *Reflections* is the conjunctive metaphor between felt experience and projected theory.

As Mill's *Autobiography* constitutes a portrait of rational mind and Newman's *Apologia* a portrait of evolving religious spirit, so Jung's *Memories, Dreams, Reflections*—the title significantly suggests the conscious mind casting back over a totality of experience both conscious and unconscious—intends to be a portrait of psyche. Psyche, for Jung, is an inclusive term, comprehending every nonphysical or a-physical human activity, comprehending specifically both conscious and unconscious activities. But any man who, like Jung, sets out to study psyche possesses for the task only psyche itself. Success in such an attempt may or may not be possible; it is, in any case, clearly not reasonable. The attempt, that is, and any success it may achieve, lie quite beyond reason. "Have you ever," Jung once asked an audience, "heard of a hammer beating itself?"[3] Good question. Readers of Jung's work are at least familiar with the attempt. As may be imagined, it can make for excellent confusion if one tries to distinguish the hammer beating from the hammer beaten. It is rather like a conscious microscope trying to look at itself under itself. Such an instrument might well study other objects similar in nature to itself, but it could hardly get outside being what it is so as to look at itself. While it is the object of magnification it cannot also be the subject; as soon as it assumes the place of subject it can no longer get under the lens as object. This, incidentally, is what eventually leads Jung to the seeming tautology, "I am as I am" (*Memories*, p. 358/329). His autobiography, because there is no way to alter the complete identity of subject and object, says, in effect, "I am I." The

[3] *Analytical Psychology: Its Theory and Practice; The Tavistock Lectures* (New York: Pantheon, 1968; London: Routledge & Kegan Paul), pp. 141-42.

subject is also the predicate of the verb: there are no outside terms for comparison. The "I" is unique; there is none other like it; none other can tell us about it. The problem, then, is how Jung shall communicate an experience of self which includes, and thus transcends, both the merely rational on the one hand and the purely spiritual on the other.[4] Where are the terms that can render both these partials of human experience together in a portrait of whole oneness? The answer Jung found was, in a word, myth; or, in another word, metaphor.

Something should be said, by way of approach to Jung's experiment in autobiographic metaphor, about the special nature of psychology or psychiatry as a scientific pursuit. Psychic experience is, to say the least of it, a very elusive item, and to propose to take that as providing data for a science would seem to require some consideration. "My business," Jung announces—and with, I think, considerable pride—"is merely the natural science of the psyche, and my main concern to establish the facts."[5] The word "merely" might seem to set strict limits to the science Jung professes, but what he in fact proposes throughout his scientific writings is very bold: to take immediate human experience as matter for study and, going one daring step further, to set about this study with, for tools, nothing more than the very experiencing being under study. A psychology of the unconscious like Jung's has no

[4] Cf. *Two Essays on Analytical Psychology*, CW, vii, par. 201: "A psychology that satisfies the intellect alone can never be practical, for the totality of the psyche can never be grasped by intellect alone. Whether we will or no, philosophy keeps breaking through, because the psyche seeks an expression that will embrace its total nature." Jung's work might be called one long "breaking through" of philosophy and symbolic expression.

[5] "The Psychology of the Transference," *The Practice of Psychotherapy*, CW, xvi, par. 537. Cf. *ibid.*, par. 524: "Science comes to a stop at the frontiers of logic, but nature does not—she thrives on ground as yet untrodden by theory." But this is precisely the point: Jungian psychology refuses to halt with science "at the frontiers of logic"; it makes a brave attempt to follow nature every step of the way.

terms outside itself; it has nothing but the purely subjective, similistic "it feels like." In a passage of particular complexity, Jung attempts to come at this central paradox of psychology as a science with the curious demonstration that when psychology fails to meet the ordinary criteria for a science it thereby achieves the status of a science, and when it seems to succeed in being scientifically objective, psychology is no longer worthy of the name of science because it has not taken into consideration all the terms of the experiment.

> As I have said, the psychology of complex phenomena finds itself in an uncomfortable situation compared with other natural sciences because it lacks a base outside its object. It can only translate itself back into its own language, or fashion itself in its own image. The more it extends its field of research and the more complicated its objects become, the more it feels the lack of a point which is distinct from those objects. And once the complexity has reached that of the empirical man, his psychology inevitably merges with the psychic process itself. It can no longer be distinguished from the latter, and so turns into it. But the effect of this is that the process attains to consciousness. In this way, psychology actualizes the unconscious urge to consciousness. It is, in fact, the coming to consciousness of the psychic process, but it is not, in the deeper sense, an explanation of this process, for no explanation of the psychic can be anything other than the living process of the psyche itself. Psychology is doomed to cancel itself out as a science and therein precisely it reaches its scientific goal. Every other science has so to speak an outside; not so psychology, whose object is the inside subject of all science.
>
> ("On the Nature of Psyche," *CW*, VIII, par. 429.)

Whether this should bear, or should even desire, the name of science is extremely doubtful, but Jung's rationale goes something like this:

1. Psychic experience is the most immediate and real—indeed, the only real—experience known to us; psyche is

not an epiphenomenon of the brain or anything else, but a process *sui generis*.[6]

2. The psychologist, like any scientist, is concerned always with empirical data, with observable and recordable phenomena.

3. But the only carrier of life, the only experiencer of psychic phenomena for certain, is the individual with his self-awareness, and his whole experience is necessarily subjective.[7]

2 and 3a. As a corollary to the two foregoing assumptions, Jung claims that science has for centuries made the mis-

---

[6] Cf. "Psychology and Religion," *CW*, xi, par. 16: "It is an almost absurd prejudice to suppose that existence can only be physical. As a matter of fact, the only form of existence of which we have immediate knowledge is psychic. We might well say, on the contrary, that physical existence is a mere inference, since we know of matter only in so far as we perceive psychic images mediated by the senses." Again, "The fact is . . . psyche . . . is the only immediate object of experience" ("On the Psychology of the Trickster-Figure," *CW*, ix, pt. 1, par. 484). Cf. also *Conversations*, p. 68; "On Psychic Energy," *CW*, viii, par. 10; "Concerning the Archetypes and the Anima Concept," *CW*, ix, pt. 1, pars. 17-18; *Aion*, *CW*, ix, pt. 2, par. 268; "The Meaning of Psychology for Modern Man," *CW*, x, par. 315; "Flying Saucers: A Modern Myth," *CW*, x, pars. 655-56.

[7] ". . . in psychology the object of knowledge is at the same time the organ of knowledge, which is true of no other science. It has therefore been doubted in all sincerity whether psychology is possible as a science at all. In keeping with this doubt I suggested years ago that every psychological theory should be criticized in the first instance as a subjective confession" ("A Rejoinder to Dr. Bally," *CW*, x, par. 1025). Cf. *Two Essays*, *CW*, vii, par. 130; *Psychological Types*, *CW*, vi, pars. 621-22; *Symbols of Transformation*, *CW*, v, par. 344; "On the Nature of the Psyche," *CW*, viii, pars. 357 and 421 (where Jung refers to the psychologist's "personal equation" as determinative of his theoretical structure); "The Phenomenology of the Spirit in Fairytales," *CW*, ix, pt. 1, par. 384.

Thus, as Jung insists in various places, the psychologies of Freud and Adler are subjectively conditioned, or are private confessions, just as his own theory is. "I consider my contribution to psychology to be my subjective confession. I admit that I see things in such and such a way. But I expect Freud and Adler to do the same and confess that their ideas are their subjective point of view" (*Analytical Psychology*, p. 140). Cf. also *Two Essays*, *CW*, vii, par. 57; "Freud and Jung: Contrasts," *CW*, iv, pars. 771-75; "The State of Psychotherapy," *CW*, x, pars. 340-41, 352, 353.

take of assuming that it could objectively study external phenomena with subjective psyche; but the psyche, "the real vehicle and begetter of all knowledge" (*Aion, CW*, IX, pt. 2, par. 268), is a subjective worm at the very heart of the supposedly objective observation.

4. Therefore science must take into account the subjective nature of psychic apparatus before its calculations can claim any corrected validity; this must be so in any science (e.g., physics), since every science has for subject the human psyche, but especially in psychology, where psyche is also the object of study.

5. Now the scientist studies himself, becomes acutely aware of his total self as a part of the experiment; that is, he becomes conscious of self as a part of process, and to become conscious of self *is* the psychic process. Thus, "his psychology," as Jung says, "inevitably merges with the psychic process itself." This is the heart of the paradox. Psychology, in fulfilling itself, cancels itself out as science and thereby "reaches its scientific goal."

This, as science, is at least a peculiar affair.

The Jungian therapist, in an encounter with a patient, is as much involved in the therapeutic process, from both sides and all around, as the patient.[8] Psychotherapeutic treatment, according to Jung (his insistence here is a mark of his medical tact and human sophistication), must always be an individual matter: a one-to-one, changing and evolving relationship. The

---

[8] "I am unsystematic very much by intention. To my mind, in dealing with individuals, only individual understanding will do. . . . The crucial point is that I confront the patient as one human being to another. Analysis is a dialogue demanding two partners. Analyst and patient sit facing one another, eye to eye" (*Memories*, p. 131/131). Several times Jung mentions bringing his own dreams into the analytic confrontation, he too being thus under analysis. Cf. also "The State of Psychotherapy Today," *CW*, X, pars. 337-39, 357-58; "A Study in the Process of Individuation," *CW*, IX, pt. 1, par. 528; "The Practical Use of Dream Analysis," *CW*, XVI, par. 317.

therapist treats neither a symptom nor a disease but a sick and individual patient. Every time he establishes this coequal relation with a patient, the doctor is first of all obeying the maxim, "Physician, heal thyself." He becomes, in effect, his own patient, the object of his own analysis and treatment; he pursues again—and this seems to be what psychology amounts to for Jung—the individuating urge of his own psyche. As psychic process and psychological science become identical, the individual fulfills and transcends the end of his science.

Jung's is doubtless a great and salutary example. But a science? I think, frankly, we take a large step forward in understanding if we admit that it is not. Jung went on into his eighties healing and completing himself again and again in innumerable encounters, in relation with patients, in relation with whatever other psychic entities he came up against (what he called "a discussion between two psychic systems . . . two human beings confronting one another in their totality"; "The State of Psychotherapy Today," *CW*, x, par. 333). His was the continuing evolution of a great creative personality; but this is surely the first time, and then only through hopelessly complex paradox, that such process has been urged upon us as science (unless, perhaps, we consider as sciences two of Jung's favorite studies—namely, alchemy and astrology). Moreover, every new turn of the screw of self was unique and individual. The unique and individual—Jung knew this well enough—is never matter for science. History finds the unique interesting; religion calls it miracle; but science regards it either as mistaken observation or as an unaccountable exception, therefore negligible. In an age reverencing science, tactics may have demanded that Jung call himself empiricist, phenomenologist, scientist.[9] But a science which is necessarily

9 Near the end of *Psychology and Alchemy* (*CW*, xii, par. 564), Jung refers to the "scientific term . . . 'individuation'" and, in the same paragraph, defines this as "the centralizing processes in the unconscious that

new and different each time it is practiced, a science which cancels "itself out as a science and therein precisely . . . reaches its scientific goal," a science which is really a question of the scientist continuously and publicly making his soul anew under unique and unrepeatable circumstances—such a "science" might better bear another name. If the objection be made that these remarks are misdirected, that they concern Jung's practice of psychotherapy (never intended as science) rather than his theory of psychic structure (always considered as science), then just there lies the joker: his science and his self were identical. The healer, the sufferer, and the theoretician were all one.

The relation of all this to Jung's creative work, specifically his published writings, should be clear. Becoming ever more conscious of the psychic process (for that is what he is doing throughout the *Collected Works*), Jung is following the path to which he himself gave a name: individuation. Consider in this way such characteristic landmarks as the following works —examples of what Jung calls "stations along my life's way":

The Psychology of Dementia Praecox, 1907
The Analysis of Dreams, 1909
Symbols of Transformation, 1912
The Relations Between the Ego and the Unconscious, 1916
On Psychic Energy, 1928
Archetypes of the Collective Unconscious, 1934
A Concept of the Collective Unconscious, 1936
Psychology and Religion, 1938
Conscious, Unconscious, and Individuation, 1939
Psychology and Alchemy, 1935-36
On the Nature of the Psyche, 1947

---

go to form the personality." Surely it is not too bold to say that this "scientific term," having to do with the unknown and unknowable, must be part of a very private "science."

Concerning Mandala Symbolism, 1950
Aion: Researches into the Phenomenology of the Self, 1951
Answer to Job, 1952
Synchronicity: An Acausal Connecting Principle, 1952
Flying Saucers: A Modern Myth, 1958

This is the public record of a full and rich private life. It would be surprising in the extreme if a psychologist, of whatever persuasion, could go to these works and find there solid grounding in a science of psychology. But, on the other hand, anyone who should want to follow, for his own understanding, the edifying spectacle of Jung's psychic evolution—his annexing, for the creative consciousness of the race, greater and greater areas of the living unconscious—will find it traced out exactly in these mirrors of psychic process. Jung's great effort—and this certainly takes nothing away from it—was, after all, a single effort, a lone experiment in life, not, therefore, viable as scientific method or scientific statement.

Science, of course, is many things, depending largely upon who, at the moment, is being scientific. To clarify our comments on Jung, let us advance a couple of general and fairly obvious propositions on the matter, making no greater claim for their validity than (1) that they are relatively true; and (2) that we can thus get ahead in the discussion of Jung. First, then, science deals with abstractions, averages, ideals, possibilities, and probabilities. It operates over the surface of life where these logically derived conceptions can be skimmed off the living substance and studied by the rational intellect apart. Life, however, stays behind in the separator; it is improbable and impossible, a miracle when considered under the laws of cause and effect. It does not exist as or in an abstraction, an average, or an ideal. Life *is*—is concrete, singular, real, and neither possible nor probable but simply existent. These latter, it seems obvious to remark, are not the terms of science but the terms of art. Second, science—qua science—depends up-on the rational intellect for its inductive procedure, for its passage from particular observations to general formulation. That which is not available to the observation and formulation of conscious mind or its extension (e.g., mechanical recording devices) is not matter for science. Since, for science, observed phenomena must follow a general law demonstrable in re-peatable experiments understood or formed by the mind di-recting the experiment, anything which bypasses or transcends the rational faculty, or which stands apart from it, will fall to the part of human concerns other than science.

Psyche is clearly a transcendent phenomenon. It includes in its operation not only the two subordinate functions of sensa-tion and thinking (pre-eminently the scientific functions) as Jung outlines them, but also the functions of intuition and feeling. And more than this, psyche is not coterminous with consciousness, but includes equally within itself the uncon-scious out of which consciousness has, with difficulty, histori-cally separated itself and out of which it continues to separate itself. Ego-consciousness, the sense of an "I" that is separated, defined, and directed, is, according to Jung's perception, a late phenomenon in individual and human history, and it impor-tantly constitutes only one part, a compensatory half, of the total psychic system. It is almost always true, for a variety of reasons, and it is always a mistake, that we attach too great a value to one or the other of these antagonistic psychic twins. In the Western world it happens just now that, because of his-torical and cultural necessities, ego consciousness is grossly overvalued. "Nowadays most people identify themselves al-most exclusively with their consciousness, and imagine that they are only what they know about themselves" (*Memories*, p. 300/278). This overvaluation of conscious intellect results, Jung claims, in an individual and group dissociation of per-sonality, a split between consciousness and its vital source, the

101

underlying, amorphous and ill-defined, but closely felt and powerfully operative unconscious. The East, on the other hand (as a sort of balance and compensation for Western excess?), turns steadily away from the bright light of objective, external, natural, and transient reality—the mediator for which is ego-consciousness—to contemplation of subjective, internal, spiritual, and eternal, black night, the realm of the great unconscious. In either case, the point is that in the land of psyche there are two mansions and in either there are many rooms; but a part, merely because it is overvalued, does not thereby become a capable and worthy ruler of the whole, neither of the single mansion nor of the entire land. For Western man specifically, the lesson is that total psyche is too great a thing to be directed from the straight and close chamber of conscious will. Likewise—and this is important for a writer concerned with depth psychology—psychic experience as a whole is inaccessible to the grasp of rational intellect. We do not *know*, but rather *are*, psychic life. "Reason sets the boundaries far too narrowly for us, and would have us accept only the known—and that too with limitations—and live in a known framework, just as if we were sure how far life actually extends. . . . The more the critical reason dominates, the more impoverished life becomes. . . . Overvalued reason has this in common with political absolutism: under its dominion the individual is pauperized" (*Memories*, p. 302/280). If, as claimed, the subject/object of Jung's writings is really his own deep and devious psyche, then the earlier question returns: how, with nothing but human terms, shall he communicate his single and complex experience to the reader? How, having surrendered as inadequate the abstractive language of rational intellect, shall he make the reader feel "what it must be to be" that transcendent psychic entity, C. G. Jung?

This complexity and doubleness of psyche quite undermines the possibility of rational, scientific communication about experience, but this is only another way of saying that Jung's total achievement should be otherwise considered. "The psyche cannot leap beyond itself," Jung says, and then, sounding very much like Montaigne, or like anyone impelled to metaphoric transformation rather than rational discourse, "Being a part, man cannot grasp the whole. He is at its mercy" (*Memories*, pp. 350/322 and 354/325). The "mercy" of the whole allows him not to know but to be. It is as if man, incapable of a transverse spread of consciousness, incapable of reaching others here and there his equals, were forced to a vertical descent or ascent. Unable to go out of himself to right or to left, he can only transcend what he is by realizing the pattern from above or, which is the same thing, by tracing out the ground plan which exists *in potentia* when he is born. Each individual, the sum of a unique heritage and a body of experiences known to him alone, is, as a living being, absolutely incomparable: nothing other than his own experience can tell him about himself. He is left communicating only with the deep reaches of himself, where he will certainly meet no other minds, but perhaps *an*other mind, unknown and the same, unconscious and the source of his being. But just this, to Jung, is the intention and goal of the human life that moves us. We come to psychic awareness by realizing, not in our intellects but in our lives, a pattern greater than any of us or all of us. "That gives peace," Jung says, "when people feel that they are living the symbolic life, that they are actors in the Divine drama. That gives the only meaning to human life; everything else is banal and you can dismiss it. A career, the producing of children, are all *maya* compared to that one thing, that your life is meaningful."[10] The individual, living and not knowing,

[10] *The Symbolic Life*, Guild Lectures, no. 80 (London: Guild of Pastoral Psychology, 1954), p. 15; to be included in *CW*, xviii, forthcoming.

103

gathers up in himself and simultaneously creates the mythic pattern of the race which alone, for Jung, gives individual life meaning; and meaning, as Jung says, is everything.

Merely because we cannot grasp or hold the psyche with our reason does not mean that it is therefore uncommunicative. It tells us all sorts of things—unfortunately (or fortunately, depending on one's view), in a language we are not used to understanding: the symbolic language of myths, dreams, fantasies, visions. We have to accept the fact that this is how the unconscious talks, and make of it what we can. According to Jung, what we are able to make of it means the difference between psychic life and psychic death, between creative order and mere chaos. These symbolic modes—and this is the source of life for us—unite us with something outside our personal selves. "A dream," for example, Jung says, "is nothing but a lucky idea that comes to us from the dark, all-unifying world of the psyche" ("The Meaning of Psychology for Modern Man," *CW*, x, par. 305). Like myth, which Jung claims constitutes a statement about the nature of psyche[11] rather than "some kind of explanatory allegory of astronomical, meteorological, or vegetative processes" ("On Psychic Energy," *CW*, VIII, par. 71), and like poetry, the dream comes to us trailing symbolic clouds of glory from the inclusive, suprapersonal psyche which is its home; it is

> an inner vision . . . a little hidden door in the innermost and most secret recesses of the soul, opening into that cosmic night which was psyche long before there was any ego-consciousness, and which will remain psyche no matter how far our ego-consciousness extends. For all ego-consciousness is isolated. . . . All consciousness separates; but in dreams we put on the likeness

---

[11] ". . . dogma, like mythology in general, expresses the quintessence of inner experience and thus formulates the operative principles of the objective psyche, i.e., the collective unconscious" (*Aion, CW*, IX, pt. 2, par. 271); "So the statements of every religion, of many poets, etc., are statements about the inner mythological process . . ." (*Conversations*, p. 48).

of that more universal, truer, more eternal man dwelling in the darkness of primordial night. There he is still the whole, and the whole is in him, indistinguishable from nature and bare of all egohood.   (*CW*, x, par. 304.)

The writer who would "put on the likeness of that . . . more eternal man," who would capture the whole psychic experience and not just a part, simply reverses the symbolic language which the psyche, in statements about itself, demonstrates to us is its own proper language. "The need for mythic statements is satisfied when we frame a view of the world which adequately explains the meaning of human existence in the cosmos, a view which springs from our psychic wholeness" (*Memories*, p. 340/313). This metaphor we frame gathers and emits energy in both directions; it is at once a projection of psyche onto the face of the universe, and a satisfaction of psychic experience, a macrocosm contained in the full image of itself. "For it is not that 'God' is a myth, but that myth is the revelation of a divine life in man. It is not we who invent myth, rather it speaks to us as a Word of God" (*Memories*, p. 340/313). Thus we tell the story of Christ's Incarnation— about ourselves. Every man's life is "the self-realization of God in human form" (*Memories*, p. 328/302), a continuing process which happens to us, a recurrent incarnation in which we cooperate. And we do not invent that story about our divinity out of our conscious minds; it comes to us as the voice of our eternal other, existing in the darkness of "cosmic night."

Jung's is such a story, a myth about divine spirit in human form, about God-in-man. Living a myth, must he not write a myth? "An autobiography is so difficult to write because we possess no standards, no objective foundation, from which to judge ourselves. . . . I do not know what I really am like. . . . I am a man. But what is it to be that? Like every other being, I am a splinter of the Infinite deity, but I cannot contrast myself with any animal, any plant or any stone. Only a mythical being has a range greater than man's" (*Memories*, pp. 3-4/17). That mythic being, which Jung assumes with the robes of metaphoric expression, is the individual become divine, man become the Platonic Idea of Man, or, as Jung variously calls this completed composite, the Original Man, the Anthropos, androgynous Adam, Christ.[12] He is the individual completed in pattern and thus become more than individual.

This process—the psyche realizing itself, becoming aware of itself—goes on as much in the *Collected Works of C. G. Jung* as in *Memories, Dreams, Reflections*. Both project metaphors of Jung's moment-to-moment becoming. As a psychologist, Jung maintains that this is all that is possible, really; that absolute truth is humanly unattainable, psychologically meaningless. Those like Jung (poets, for example) who are engaged with the more-than-rational, with the intellectually or cognitively inexplicable, with the experiences of the total psyche and total man, necessarily have recourse to the language of psyche itself, that is, to myth and metaphor. Lacking an Archimedean point outside themselves for judgment, they are forced to abandon discursive language; they cannot explain nor give ultimate reasons nor propose absolute, supra-individual truths.[13] They can only (which is much) translate

[12] Cf. Jung's description of "the Anthropos idea that stands for man's wholeness, that is, the conception of a unitary being who existed before man and at the same time represents man's goal" (*Psychology and Alchemy*, *CW*, xii, par. 210). On Christ's life as such a representative and symbolic figuration, see "Answer to Job," *CW*, xi, par. 648; for "androgynous Adam" and "Original Man" see *Psychology and Alchemy*, *CW*, xii, *passim*; and cf. the similar references to Adam Kadmon, *filius philosophorum*, primordial man, etc., *Mysterium Coniunctionis*, *CW*, xiv, *passim*.

[13] "We are dealing with life-processes which, on account of their numinous character, have from time immemorial provided the strongest incentive for the formation of symbols. These processes are steeped in mystery; they pose riddles with which the human mind will long wrestle for a solution, and perhaps in vain. For, in the last analysis, it is exceedingly doubtful whether human reason is a suitable instrument for this purpose. Not for nothing did alchemy style itself an 'art,' feeling—and rightly so—that it was concerned with creative processes that can be truly grasped only by experience, though

psychic experience into symbol and portray psychic being in metaphor, thus attempting to say, about this most subjective experience, *how it is.* "Every attempt at psychological explanation is, at bottom, the creation of a new myth. We merely translate one symbol into another symbol which is better suited to the existing constellation of our individual fate and that of humanity as a whole. Our science, too, is another of these figurative languages. Thus we simply create a new symbol for that same enigma which confronted all ages before us."[14] In effect, the psychologist, like the atomic physicist (the analogy, one of Jung's favorites, turns on the point that both are dealing with "the unknown and invisible"), does not assert absolutely, but instead constructs "a *model* which opens up a promising and useful field of inquiry. A model does not assert that something *is* so, it simply illustrates a particular mode of observation" ("On the Nature of the Psyche," *CW*, VIII, par. 381). While, in Jung's sense, "a model does not assert that something *is* so," and while it argues nothing about metaphysical reality, yet a metaphor, which is nothing other than a model of the psychologist's own psychic working, does portray how the process of psyche *feels.* It projects a subjective point of view, ordering and organizing experience around that wholly personal center. All relates back for coherence and validity, as it would in the vision of an artist, to the subjective center: how fully has it gathered into itself and its images the whole pattern?

---

intellect may give them a name. . . . Experience, not books, is what leads to understanding" (*Psychology and Alchemy, CW*, XII, par. 564). Jungian intellect did, indeed, give a name to these "life-processes," calling them "individuation."

[14] *Psychological Types:* the translation quoted is by Ralph Manheim and occurs on p. 118 of Jolande Jacobi's *Complex / Archetype / Symbol in the Psychology of C. G. Jung*, Bollingen Series LVII (New York: Pantheon, 1959; 2nd printing, Princeton University Press). With some variation in the translation, the passage occurs in par. 428 of *Psychological Types, CW,* VI.

But does Jung really believe all that? Is he serious about the shadow, about anima/animus, about the collective unconscious and the archetypes? The answer, even for his theoretical writings, must be, "It's a myth, you see—a myth intended to convey how it feels to be human, a myth about the subjective experience of *me*." It all hinges on that "really," on the nature of the reality being questioned. Psychically, myths are the most real of facts. "But myth is not fiction: it consists of facts that are continually repeated and can be observed over and over again. It is something that happens to man, and men have mythical fates just as much as the Greek heroes do" ("Answer to Job," *CW*, xi, par. 648). These mythic statements are real enough; they tell how it is with the psyche now and now. To the same sort of question about reality and belief ("Some will ask whether I believe in the actual existence of my circuits of sun and moon"), directed against a similar attempt in metaphor (the fantastic myth called *A Vision*), Yeats gave Jung's answer, only varying the words: "Now that the system stands out clearly in my imagination I regard them [i.e., recurrent historic periods] as stylistic arrangements of experience comparable to the cubes in the drawing of Wyndham Lewis and to the ovoids in the sculpture of Brancusi. They have helped me to hold in a single thought reality and justice." Or better, perhaps, in the choice words of Yeats's ghostly instructors, who brought him from out of the Great Mind and collective unconscious all the substance of *A Vision*, "We have come to give you metaphors for poetry." Just so, Philemon, in Jung's visions the archetypal wise old man and the counterpart of Yeats's instructors, came to give him metaphors—for psychology. And it is all metaphor, as Yeats says, "All metaphor, Malachi, stilts and all." All metaphor—Philemon, instructors, collective unconscious, dreams, alchemy, astrology, sun gods, rebirth, the Uroboros—for psychic experience. "Thus it is that I have now undertaken, in my eighty-third year, to tell my personal myth. I can only make direct statements, only 'tell stories.' Whether or not the stories are 'true' is not the problem. The only question is whether what I tell is *my* fable, *my* truth" (*Memories*, p. 3/17). Are the metaphors, that is to say, adequate to the psychic experience called C. G. Jung? The metaphoric web spins out here to become a most inclusive myth, and Jung is never concerned to return to the center of his pattern simply because he knows that he has never left the center and never can leave it. There is no psychic truth except what is contained at that point and what spreads out from there to put its stamp on all reality.

The personal myth which Jung experienced and then read in everything around him (whether he read it *into* everything around him is an improper question, a metaphysical question addressed to a psychic experience) is a story of humanity, it bears the name "individuation," and, when amplified and extended, it goes like this:

The human child, at birth, is not a *tabula rasa* come to be filled and formed by the marks of a life (here he is like "all warm-blooded animals who have souls like ourselves"; *Memories*, p. 67/74). The child, it is true, like the primitive, has no awareness of individual self; he exists in a state of unconsciousness and of identification with, in Lawrence's phrase, the "circumambient universe." And all unconscious of the fact though he is, the child contains within him the seeds of self— not just any self but a particular and unique, potential and yet-to-be-realized self. "The psyche of the child in its preconscious state is anything but a *tabula rasa*; it is already preformed in a recognizably individual way, and is moreover equipped with all specifically human instincts, as well as with the a priori foundations of the higher functions" (*Memories*,

p. 348/320). He is equipped, that is, by the instincts to become human, and by "the higher functions" (the urge to individuation) to become *this* and no other human.[15]

The common mistake is to identify psyche with ego-consciousness and to suppose that there is no individual there until it is conscious of itself. But consciousness and the unconscious[16] are by no means coeval. Ego, if we take a long view of it, is seen as an epiphenomenon of the total process of psyche, and must therefore not be confused with the self, the end and intention of that process. The self corresponds not to one or the other half engaged in relation but is rather the issue of the meeting of the two, of dark and bright, of the unconscious and consciousness.[17] Further, in both racial and

---

[15] "You see, we are born into a pattern; we are a pattern. We are a structure that is preestablished through the genes. . . . Man has a certain pattern that makes him specifically human, and no man is born without it" (*Conversations*, p. 52). Cf. *ibid.*, pp. 34 and 69; *Two Essays, CW*, vii, par. 235; "On the Nature of the Psyche," *CW*, viii, par. 398; "Psychological Aspects of the Mother Archetype," *CW*, ix, pt. 1, pars. 151-54 ("There *is* an *a priori* factor in all human activities, namely the inborn, preconscious and unconscious individual structure of the psyche. . . . Like every animal, [man] possesses a preformed psyche which breeds true to his species and which, on closer examination, reveals distinct features traceable to family antecedents"); *ibid.*, pars. 136 and 160; "Flying Saucers: A Modern Myth," *CW*, x, par. 646; *Psychology and Alchemy, CW*, xii, par. 36 ("No doubt it is a great nuisance that mankind is not uniform but compounded of individuals whose psychic structure spreads them over a span of at least ten thousand years"); and Jung's preface to *Psyche and Symbol*, ed. Violet S. de Laszlo (Garden City, N.Y.: Doubleday, Anchor Books, 1958), pp. xv-xvi.

[16] Notice the words that force themselves upon us: "consciousness" is a process of becoming; "the unconscious" is an original state which supplies the energy, as it were, "the life instinct" (*Memories*, p. 349/321), for the process and cooperates with it (thus becoming itself a part of the process). One would not ordinarily use "conscious" as a noun, or speak of "the unconsciousness."

[17] "When I say 'self,' then you mustn't think of 'I, myself,' because that is only your empirical self, and this is covered by the term 'ego'; but when it is a matter of 'self,' then it is a matter of personality and is more complete than the ego, because the ego only consists of what you are conscious of, what you know to be yourself" (*Conversations*, p. 60). "The ego is only the subject of my consciousness, while the self is the subject of my total psyche"

individual experience the unconscious is prior to consciousness, and it remains forever an unknowable foundation to consciousness. "Consciousness is both phylogenetically and onto-
genetically a secondary phenomenon. It is time this obvious
fact were grasped at last. Just as the body has an anatomical
prehistory of millions of years, so also does the psychic system.
. . . Consciousness began its evolution from an animal-like state
which seems to us unconscious, and the same process of differentiation is repeated in every child" (*Memories*, p. 348/
320). From this universal beginning in the black unconscious,
which he can never leave behind but always carries with him,
the individual starts his ascent toward a definite end and goal:
himself. The psyche, cut at any point we choose after this
beginning, reveals itself as a continuous process with a story
and a meaning, with a past composed of causes and effects
and a potential future directed toward its goal. "As I worked
with my fantasies, I became aware that the unconscious un-
dergoes or produces change. Only after I had familiarized
myself with alchemy did I realize that the unconscious is a
process and that the psyche is transformed or developed by
the relationship of the ego to the contents of the unconscious"
(*Memories*, p. 209/200).[18] The individual psyche proceeds by

---

(*Psychological Types*, CW, VI, par. 706). This is "that strange self, alien to
the ego, which was ours from the beginning, the trunk from which the ego
grew" ("The Meaning of Psychology for Modern Man," CW, X, par. 318).
In psychological metaphor, "Christ, as a man, corresponds to the ego, and,
as God, to the self" (*Aion*, CW, IX, pt. 2, par. 171). The end of all our becoming, an end we shall never know but which, paradoxically, we always are,
"I have elected to call . . . the 'self,' by which I understand a psychic totality
and at the same time a centre, neither of which coincides with the ego but
includes it, just as a larger circle encloses a smaller one" ("Concerning Rebirth," CW, IX, pt. 1, par. 248). Cf. "The Psychological Aspects of the Kore,"
CW, IX, pt. 1, pars. 314-15; "Psychology and Religion, CW, XI, pars. 66-69;
and *Psychology and Alchemy*, CW, XII, par. 44.

18 On psyche as process, cf. *Aion*, CW, IX, pt. 2, par. 411 ("The formula
presents a symbol of the self, for the self is not just a static quantity or constant form, but is also a dynamic process. . . . The secret of existence, i.e.,

a law peculiar to itself, realizing the pattern exactly as only it can, drawing out the story toward an end which it must feel was predestined. "Through my work with the patients I realized that paranoid ideas and hallucinations contain a germ of meaning. A personality, a life history, a pattern of hopes and desires lie behind the psychosis" (*Memories*, p. 127/127). A psychosis simply reveals a drive of the psyche toward self which has come to ruin, and thus "a general psychology of the personality lies concealed within psychosis. . . . At bottom we discover nothing new and unknown in the mentally ill; rather, we encounter the substratum of our own natures" (*Memories*, p. 127/127). As we can discover the archaic, unconscious past of human civilization in primitive mentality, so in a psychotic (who, like the infant and the primitive, lives altogether in the unconscious; his is a pathological reversion, theirs a natural, necessary state)[19] we come upon a more archaic stage of our own individual human development—that development, here, however, blocked and at standstill. The psychosis, a human failure demonstrating by its very difference the progress of normal psychic growth, suggests that the delicate balance between consciousness and the unconscious has broken down; that the unconscious, immensely older and more pow-

---

the existence of the atom and its components, may well consist in a continually repeated process of rejuvenation, and one comes to similar conclusions in trying to account for the numinosity of the archetypes"); "Answer to Job," *CW*, xi, par. 745 ("Whatever man's wholeness, or the self, may mean *per se*, empirically it is an image of the goal of life spontaneously produced by the unconscious, irrespective of the wishes and fears of the conscious mind. It stands for the goal of the total man, for the realization of his wholeness and individuality. . . . The dynamic of this process is instinct"); also, "The Meaning of Psychology for Modern Man," *CW*, x, pars. 311-12.

[19] Cf. *Symbols of Transformation*, *CW*, v, par. 26: "The supposition that there may also be in psychology a correspondence between ontogenesis and phylogenesis therefore seems justified. If this is so, it would mean that infantile thinking and dream-thinking are simply a recapitulation of earlier evolutionary stages."

erful, has overwhelmed the individual front of consciousness and drawn the fragile ego back down into primeval darkness.

We do not achieve selfhood (one way of naming the goal of the individuation process) by abandoning the unconscious, which would merely leave the psyche with no vital energy, no substance to bring to consciousness, but by constantly transforming its contents from a general and amorphous state into the rich, controlled and defined matter of individual self. Every individual in psychic process extends between consciousness and the unconscious, living simultaneously in both realms. His life, at once individual and general, is the relation, the connection, between the two. Though it seems not to be possessed of anything like ego-personality, delimited and directed by a single will, the unconscious does exhibit "traces" of personality.[20] For one thing, it regularly expresses itself in

[20] "Conscious, Unconscious, and Individuation," *CW*, ix, pt. 1, par. 507. Cf. "Basic Postulates of Analytical Psychology," *CW*, viii, par. 673: "The unconscious perceives, has purposes and intuitions, feels and thinks as does the conscious mind. . . . Only in one respect is there an essential difference between the conscious and the unconscious functioning of the psyche. Though consciousness is intensive and concentrated, it is transitory and is trained upon the immediate present and the immediate field of attention; moreover, it has access only to material that represents one individual's experience stretching over a few decades. . . . But matters stand very differently with the unconscious. It is not concentrated and intensive, but shades off into obscurity; it is highly extensive and can juxtapose the most heterogeneous elements in the most paradoxical way. More than this, it contains, besides an indeterminable number of subliminal perceptions, the accumulated deposits from the lives of our ancestors, who by their very existence have contributed to the differentiation of the species. If it were possible to personify the unconscious, we might think of it as a collective human being combining the characteristics of both sexes, transcending youth and age, birth and death, and, from having at its command a human experience of one or two million years, practically immortal. If such a being existed, it would be exalted above all temporal change; the present would mean neither more nor less to it than any year in the hundredth millennium before Christ; it would be a dreamer of age-old dreams and, owing to its limitless experience, an incomparable prognosticator. It would have lived countless times over again the life of the individual, the family, the tribe, and the

personalistic (which are at the same time, however, "typical") terms and images—"others," who are part and projections of our selves, come to bring us information through dialogue. Continually transforming, never transformed, each man thus exists as two personalities: that one (No. 1) which moves as a separate and ambitious figure in the objective, daylight world of men; that other (No. 2) which remains stable and undifferentiated in the subjective night of the ages. "Somewhere deep in the background I always knew that I was two persons. One was the son of my parents, who went to school. . . . The other was grown up—old, in fact—skeptical, mistrustful, remote from the world of men, but close to nature, the earth, the sun, the moon, the weather, all living creatures, and above all close to the night, to dreams, and to whatever 'God' worked directly in him" (*Memories*, pp. 44-45/55). A personality this No. 2 may be called, but the fact of his typicality, his otherness and general *im*personality, is equally if not more important. Not subject to individual will, coming unbidden from an eternal and boundless world outside the single person, and gathering into his figure the experience of an entire heritage, No. 2 infuses a significance and meaning into the individual life spun out otherwise alone in time and space.[21] "Although

---

nation, and it would possess a living sense of the rhythm of growth, flowering, and decay." This long passage—considerably longer in the original—presents Jung's most effective metaphor for the complicated relation involving (a) consciousness; (b) the personal unconscious; (c) the collective unconscious. Cf. also *Two Essays, CW*, vii, par. 103; "The Practical Use of Dream Analysis," *CW*, xvi, pars. 317, 329, 351-52; *Conversations*, p. 98; *Psychological Types, CW*, vi, pars. 837-43; "Archetypes of the Collective Unconscious," *CW*, ix, pt. 1, pars. 3-7; "The Role of the Unconscious," *CW*, x, pars. 9-13; and "The Meaning of Psychology for Modern Man," *CW*, x, pars. 285-86.

[21] "This is our immortality, the link through which man feels inextinguishably one with the continuity of all life. The life of the psyche is the life of mankind. Welling up from the depths of the unconscious, its springs gush forth from the root of the whole human race, since the individual is,

at that time I doubtless saw no difference as yet between personalities No. 1 and No. 2, and still claimed the world of No. 2 as my own personal world, there was always, deep in the background, the feeling that something other than myself was involved. It was as though a breath of the great world of stars and endless space had touched me, or as if a spirit had invisibly entered the room—the spirit of one who had long been dead and yet was perpetually present in timelessness until far into the future" (*Memories*, p. 66/73). The otherworldly strength of No. 2 is also, however, its this-worldly weakness; like a "dormant or dreaming" personality, it will remain forever unrealized in the human realm (which is the only medium where its realization would be meaningful), except as it becomes integrated into the total psyche through its compensatory relation with No. 1. "I was beginning to realize that No. 2 had no *pied-à-terre*. In him I was lifted beyond the here and now; in him I felt myself a single eye in a thousand-eyed universe, but incapable of moving so much as a pebble upon the earth" (*Memories*, p. 75/82). No. 1 depends upon No. 2 for significance, No. 2 upon No. 1 for the terms of its human existence. This provides a convenient metaphor (the personality of a boy and the personality/impersonality of an ancient man fused in one symbolic life) for the relation between consciousness and the unconscious.[22]

---

biologically speaking, only a twig broken off from the mother and transplanted" (*Symbols of Transformation*, *CW*, v, par. 296). On the phylogenetic/ontogenetic development of psyche, cf. "Conscious, Unconscious, and Individuation," *CW*, ix, pt. 1, par. 518.

[22] "We know that however much individuals differ from one another in the content of their conscious minds, they become all the more alike when regarded from the standpoint of the unconscious. . . . Differences only arise through individuation. . . . The unconscious, on the other hand, is universal: it not only binds individuals together into a nation or a race, but unites them with the men of the past and with their psychology" (*Symbols of Transformation*, *CW*, v, par. 258). Thus the individual returns again and

The two antinomic activities go on in mutual interaction, either balancing one another out or drawing greater and greater reciprocal life the one from the other. The result in either case is psychic process itself, a more or less rich psychic life. So that we may know where it is tending and help it to this end, we can read this process, not, of course, directly (how could we see or photograph intangible, immaterial, imperceptible process itself?) but indirectly through news that it brings of itself. Psyche, less visible even than an electron, allows itself to be studied in an analogous, indirect way: like the invisible electron, which leaves a "condensation trail . . . behind it as it pushes its way through . . . molecules of gas," psyche too seems to leave behind it, for us to read, a trail of images as it pushes through the inertia of self-contentment. These, of course, are the images thrown up in dreams or in visions during moments of lowered consciousness, images produced by and reflecting the psyche itself which we then read into and out of the seemingly objective surface of reality. The life of the unconscious psyche goes on continuously beneath consciousness; we dream, as it were, all the time, "only our consciousness makes such a noise in the waking state that we no longer hear it."[23] Even in the

---

again to the unconscious as to the source of psychic life: "It is the problem of Antaeus, who could only keep his giant strength through contact with mother earth" (ibid., par. 259). Sexual union figures as a creative reversion to the undifferentiated unconscious, a return to the primal state of identification with all life: "Normal sex life, as a shared experience with apparently similar aims, further strengthens the feeling of unity and identity. . . . Return to that original condition of unconscious oneness is like a return to childhood. . . . It is, in truth, a genuine and incontestable experience of the Divine, whose transcendent force obliterates and consumes everything individual; a real communion with life and the impersonal power of fate" (CW, XVII, par. 330). This is to say, more or less psychologically, much the same thing as Yeats says, more or less mystically: "The marriage bed is the symbol of the solved antinomy, and were more than symbol could a man there lose and keep his identity."

[23] Quoted in Jolande Jacobi, The Psychology of C. G. Jung, 6th ed. (New

waking state, moreover, we can slip into the daydream or the fantasy, and can suddenly sense and "see" in symbolic images the process of the unconscious going on. Thus it is that, in therapy, interpretation of such semiconscious experiences must involve a contextual series. Therapeutic dream-interpretation is the reading of a story in process, the tracing of a pattern with a yesterday and a tomorrow. The pattern will obviously not yield itself through a single point, merely what it is today, but requires that a good many points be placed and connected before its shape and direction are described. Only by some perception of the path as described in the past may we surmise a pattern to be realized in the future. To act as midwife to this embryonic, always potential pattern of individuality is the ideal intention of psychotherapy.

Therapy must adopt a Janus' face and look in both directions, taking them in their proper order: first, toward causes in the past (the mechanical view of psyche as a cause-and-effect process), which have brought personality to its present state; then toward aims in the future (the energic view of psyche as a directed process), which will dictate the shape of personality as it changes.[24] Freud's mistake, the limitation in-

---

Haven: Yale Univ. Press, 1962), p. 71; cf. *Analytical Psychology*, p. 87; *Two Essays*, CW, VII, par. 273; and "Psychology and Religion," CW, XI, par. 53.

[24] Systems of energy in modern physics supply the analogy and terms for Jung's conception of psychic energy; contrasting the mechanistic and energic theories in psychology, he says, "The predominance of one or the other point of view depends less upon the objective behaviour of things than upon the psychological attitude of the investigator and thinker" ("On Psychic Energy," CW, VIII, pars. 2-5); cf. *ibid.*, pars. 42-44, 45 ("What to the causal view is *fact* to the final view is *symbol*, and vice versa"), 93-97; *Two Essays*, CW, VII, par. 210; "The Psychology of the Child Archetype," CW, IX, pt. 1, par. 272; "Conscious, Unconscious, and Individuation," CW, IX, pt. 1, par. 499; *Aion*, CW, IX, pt. 2, par. 279 ("For behind all this looms the vast and unsolved riddle of life itself and of evolution in general, and the question of overriding importance in the end is not the origin of evolution but its goal"); and *Mysterium Coniunctionis*, CW, XIV, par. 53 ("Such [psychic] phenomena, whether historical or individual, cannot be explained

herent in his single-eyed theory (which is necessarily a reflection of personal limitation, since any psychology, being subjectively based, is a mirror for the personality of its founder), was to reduce every present psychic condition to causes in the individual's past, never acknowledging that all psychic process constitutes a teleological chain as well as a causal one. Freud never recognized, or, perhaps, refused to recognize, that psyche has not only come from somewhere; it is also going somewhere. This strictly causal, deterministic approach to psychic experience, an "all-simplifying *reductio ad causam*,"[25] attempts to trace psychic conflict back to its source in complications in infantile sexual experience. Sexuality, "libido" in the Freudian sense and theory, is the single, great, primary form of psychic energy; any other manifestations of psychic energy (religious urgings, for example, or the Adlerian "will to power") are, according to pure psychoanalytic theory,

by causality alone, but must also be considered from the point of view of what happened afterwards. Everything psychic is pregnant with the future.")

This eventually leads to Jung's postulation of "synchronicity," i.e., a state in which physical and psychic events are related not causally but significantly: they are part of a meaning system rather than a cause-effect system. Where synchronicity ("a coincidence in time of two or more causally unrelated events which have the same or a similar meaning"; "Synchronicity," *CW*, VIII, par. 849) obtains, causality is beside the point, and "we must regard them [synchronous events] as creative acts, as the continuous creation of a pattern that exists from all eternity, repeats itself sporadically, and is not derivable from any known antecedents" (*ibid.*, par. 967).

[25] "On Psychic Energy," *CW*, VIII, par. 35. On Freudian "reductive causalism" vs. Jungian "teleological directedness," or the "reductive" and "analytic" as against the "constructive" and "synthetic" interpretations, see *Symbols of Transformation, CW*, V, xxiii; *Psychological Types, CW*, VI, pars. 701-04 and 788; *Two Essays, CW*, VII, pars. 122 and 199; "The Transcendent Function," *CW*, VIII, pars. 146-68; and *Freud and Psychoanalysis, CW*, IV, *passim*. I am aware, naturally, that the version of Freud's views given in the text is drastically oversimplified; I am concerned, however, to present only Jung's myth, not Freud's—and Jung's myth does unquestionably oversimplify Freud's teachings. It would be an interesting exercise to extract Freud's myth from his *Autobiographical Study* and his *Complete Works*: it is assuredly there.

secondary, mere repressions and sublimations of forbidden sexuality; and this bias, too, depends upon the neurotic personality of the founder of psychoanalysis. "There was no mistaking the fact that Freud was emotionally involved in his sexual theory to an extraordinary degree. . . . I had a strong intuition that for him sexuality was a sort of *numinosum*. . . . I can still recall vividly how Freud said to me, 'My dear Jung, promise me never to abandon the sexual theory. That is the most essential thing of all. You see, we must make a dogma of it, an unshakable bulwark' " (*Memories*, p. 150/147). The "sexual theory" finds in adult neurosis a disastrous reversion to childish situations; in present activity it discovers an attempt to return, in a different form and under different conditions, to the point at which the sexual instinct (specifically, a natural but unallowable incestuous desire) was repressed or deflected and from which neurotic conflict stems. Thus libido, from which all psychic life derives, is an enormously powerful, enormously dangerous force.

Having "reduced" or "analyzed" the neurosis to its component elements, the Freudian practitioner leaves it there and calls the patient cured. The limitation of this kind of analysis is twofold: as therapy, it leaves the patient no place to go, for, having traced the neurosis to its roots, it abandons the whole organism without broaching the question of future growth; as theory, it defines libido, and hence psychic energy, in far too narrow a sense. Of course, as the Freudians claim, the psyche is forever returning to its sources in the unconscious; it is forever reverting to the roots of its present condition. But therapy should understand and treat this doubly. We regress to a childish state and to unconscious activity (to be demonstrated and traced by a reductive analysis, the first stage of treatment); but, like Antaeus, we do this in order that we may, with the strength and energy discovered in return to unconscious psychic sources, proceed to a new level of personal development (to be drawn out and pointed toward, as the individual pattern is perceived, by a constructive synthesis, the second stage of treatment). The old mechanistic (causal) and the new energic (final) standpoints are just that: points at which we stand, points from which we subjectively view psychic process, try to understand it and help it on its way. Analysis, through which we can trace the personal psychic story as it has unfolded into the present, is properly not an end in itself but a basis for synthesis, which requires just such a foundation, for synthesis can proceed only after there is some sense of the particular necessities of this individual psyche evolving under its own singular law and pointing toward its own unique end.

> Nor was I fond of deciding on my own what the patient ought to do. I was much more concerned to learn from the patient himself where his natural bent would lead him. In order to find that out, careful analysis of dreams and of other manifestations of the unconscious was necessary. . . .
>
> In many cases of psychiatry, the patient who comes to us has a story that is not told, and which as a rule no one knows of. To my mind, therapy only really begins after the investigation of that wholly personal story. . . .
>
> I am often asked about my psychotherapeutic or analytic method. I cannot reply unequivocally to the question. Therapy is different in every case. . . . The cure ought to grow naturally out of the patient himself. Psychotherapy and analysis are as varied as are human individuals.
>
> (*Memories*, pp. 120/121, 117/118, and 131/130.)

The psychotherapist and the patient, personality confronting personality, bring to life the new and larger self (for each of them) which has been waiting for and advancing toward this and other rebirths since its initial but wholly potential birth in the beginning as an individual human being. It is a generality of psychology of the unconscious that all psychic life be-

120

gins in this way, through the interplay between two balanced, opposed and complementary psychic entities.

Perceiving its own direction and so participating in the making of its own destiny, the psyche advances and is impelled toward selfhood and the goal of its process by the libido-energy which flows from the unconscious to receive individual, differentiated form from the opposite psychic entity—consciousness and its purposeful will. The unconscious is the source of libido-energy; the various instincts, interacting with details of experience, provide the specific forms it takes; it is transformed into energy available to the conscious will through symbols; and individual self, i.e., life in a particular realization, is its eventual intention. Libido now, however, must be conceived in a much broader, more inclusive sense than Freud allows: his metaphor restricts far too severely the variousness of human beings. To understand the great variety of individual psychic experiences, and at the same time the unity of their goal, we should do well to consider this psychic energy as general and undifferentiated, to consider it, indeed, as a life instinct, or, the obverse, as an instinct to life.[26] Psychology should replace talk of specific instinctual energies—thus rebasing all the various psychologies founded on various instincts—with this concept of general psychic energy, which includes, as secondary channelings, all the specific energic manifesta-

[26] "I have therefore suggested that, in view of the psychological use we intend to make of it, we call our hypothetical life-energy 'libido'" ("On Psychic Energy," *CW*, VIII, par. 32). Cf. *Psychological Types*, *CW*, VI, par. 778; *Two Essays*, *CW*, VII, pp. 52-53, n. 6 ("Libido for me means psychic energy, which is equivalent to the intensity with which psychic contents are charged"); *Conversations*, p. 81; "The Role of the Unconscious," *CW*, x, pars. 7-8. Nearly all of *Symbols of Transformation* is an attempt to describe how man has unceasingly visualized libido in images and symbols, all connected by their similar intentions. These expressive images ("not to be understood semiotically, as *signs* for definite things, but as *symbols*"; par. 180) are polyvalent, with eventual reference to the general force of creativity, i.e., the life-instinct. See *CW*, v, esp. pars. 176-89, 193-99, 298, 329.

121

tions, each of which is another particular harnessing of libido power by individual will. The question we should ask now becomes not "what kind of energy is this?" or "where in the complications of childhood did it take a wrong turning?" but rather, "how much energy is there? how is it being transformed? and what is it trying to do?" "I conceived the libido as a psychic analogue of physical energy, hence as a more or less quantitative concept, which therefore should not be defined in qualitative terms. . . . It can appear in various guises. If we conceive of libido as energy, we can take a comprehensive and unified view" (*Memories*, p. 208/199). It will be found that this undifferentiated psychic energy is possessed of a characteristic, inherent instinct, and, since libido, considered as a quantitative rather than a qualitative force, assumes the form of various instincts, this one is an instinct which subsumes all the others. This is, simply, the life instinct, a drive which pushes away from the undifferentiated state toward differentiation and self-creation, toward individual life. This is not to be seen as mere self-preservation, a conservative and uncreative reaction, but as a positive instinct of life to become what it would be: a particular, a certain form and self.

This force flows into the shaping of each of us; we know it immediately as it operates in and transforms ourselves. To understand it or to try to explain it, we elaborate, individually and culturally, all sorts of symbolic figurations. In these more or less conscious attempts of philosophy and mythology, of religion and psychology, of autobiography and poetry to express the subjectively apprehended creative force, we find nothing but the symbols of the psyche reversed. In regarding these figures, we must recognize that what is symbolized is generalized libido, life instinct, rather than a specific formulation of that energy. No matter what the particular image—sun, lake, tree, phallus, hero, whatever—it intends something much more general than itself.

Thus a phallic symbol does not denote the sexual organ, but the libido, and however clearly it appears as such, it does not mean *itself* but is always a symbol of the libido. Symbols are not signs or allegories for something known; they seek rather to express something that is little known or completely unknown. The *tertium comparationis* for all these symbols is the libido, and the unity of meaning lies in the fact that they are all analogies of the same thing. In this realm the fixed meaning of things comes to an end. The sole reality is the libido, whose nature we can only experience through its effect on us.

(*Symbols of Transformation, CW*, v, par. 329.)

In thus putting sex in its place and psychic creativity in its place, the second an instinctual energy plainly supraordinate to the first, we shall better understand the source, the nature, and the purpose of those "numinous" images which appear to us as objective and unwilled facts in moments of lowered consciousness. Symbol-creation, i.e., the transformation of undifferentiated libido-energy into images with the capacity to mediate between the two halves of the psyche, is a function of the unconscious psyche and as such gives us a glimpse into the unknown, into the vast unconscious which surrounds and, unless given controlled release, threatens to inundate the equally valuable but more vulnerable island of consciousness in each of us. In shaping these symbolic images, the unconscious psyche is not the servant but the master of the senses, not the passive creation but the active creator of reality in the external world. Such image-formation is a way of knowing, a means of rendering the external world accessible and useful to the growth of psychic being. "The principle of conscious life is: 'Nihil est in intellectu, quod non prius fuerit in sensu.' But the principle of the unconscious is the autonomy of the psyche itself, reflecting in the play of its images not the world but itself, even though it utilizes the illustrative possibilities offered by the sensible world in order to make its images clear" (*Psychology and Alchemy, CW*, XII, par. 186). Now it becomes apparent that libido is an energy possessed of a direction and something very like a will of its own; that this power, which we feel as objective and quasi-divine, is not used by us but uses us to its own ends; and that, in a happy paradox, these ends turn out to be our ends as well. Libido drives through the individual to become particularized into the self which it desires and which the individual has chosen to be and, considered another way, has no choice but to be. Whether the individual self is a product of its own spinning or the result of an objective process can only be answered by a paradox, which is intended not as an evasion but as a tribute to the complexity of the process. It is neither, either, and both: how one views it must depend upon one's point of view.

It is—to give a metaphoric "local habitation and a name" to the unknown total experience of being human—as if there were, on the one hand, a personal mind and, on the other, a Great Mind, an *anima hominis* and an *Anima Mundi*, a particular realization and a general potentiality, or, once more, a momentary and subjective, personal psyche and an eternal and objective, collective psyche. But the connection here is not really of the order of "on the one hand" and "on the other"; the intimacy of their relation is such that we can only see them as identical. At any given temporal and spatial, i.e., human, point, the *Anima Mundi* becomes real as this particular *anima hominis*, the Great Mind is in and is this personal mind.[27]

---

[27] "The collective unconscious stands for the objective psyche, the personal unconscious for the subjective psyche" (*Two Essays, CW*, VII, p. 66, n. 4). "If this supra-individual psyche exists, everything that is translated into its picture-language would be depersonalized, and if this became conscious would appear to us *sub specie aeternitatis*. Not as my sorrow, but as the sorrow of the world; not a personal isolating pain, but a pain without bitterness that unites all humanity" ("The Structure of the Psyche," *CW*, VIII, par. 316). Cf. *Symbols of Transformation, CW*, V, xxiv (where Jung elaborates a recurrent metaphor: "The psyche is not of today; its ancestry goes back many millions of years. Individual consciousness is only the flower and the fruit of a season, sprung from the perennial rhizome beneath the earth." The rhizome-flower metaphor turns up again in *Memo-*

The profoundest subjectivity, experience of the personal mind through descent into the darkness of the unconscious, is also realization of an objective Other, experience of the Great Mind through ascent to the pattern which controls all human activity. And this removes the sting: the choices we have made personally, if we have followed the dictates of self-becoming, are more than ours, are the choices of life itself.[28] Whence the will and choice leading to selfhood? How shall we separate the realization from the pattern realized? "How," in Yeats's rhetorical question, "How can we know the dancer from the dance?" The rational intellect must remain forever discontented, denied its single and reasonable answer. We can only accept the complex reality and hold the two against one another in balance and in creative image of dancer and dance: life requires them both and requires them equally.

In our lives and only there are the terms joined: we become the living juncture of body and soul, of human acts and divine intention. In the image and pattern of a human life, the marriage of opposites is celebrated.[29] This perspective on hu-

---

ries, p. 4, and in "Freud and Jung: Contrasts," *CW,* IV, par. 769); *Two Essays, CW,* VII, par. 150.

[28] "I should also like the term 'God' in the phrase 'the will of God' to be understood not so much in the Christian sense as in the sense intended by Diotima, when she said: 'Eros, dear Socrates, is a mighty daemon.' The Greek words *daimon* and *daimonion* express a determining power which comes upon man from outside, like providence or fate, though the ethical decision is left to man" (*Aion, CW,* IX, pt. 2, par. 51).

[29] Out of compensatory opposites (consciousness/unconscious) through the transcendent function issues the new being in Jungian rebirth: "The confrontation of the two positions generates a tension charged with energy and creates a living, third thing—not a logical stillbirth in accordance with the principle *tertium non datur* but a movement out of the suspension between opposites, a living birth that leads to a new level of being, a new situation" ("The Transcendent Function," *CW,* VIII, par. 189). This new thing ("a *complexio oppositorum* precisely because there can be no reality without polarity"; *Aion, CW,* IX, pt. 2, par. 423)—for which Christ crucified, flanked by a good and an evil thief, is the supreme symbol in Christendom —is also the oldest of knowledge, a "uniting symbol" that we have always

man life, achieved in and through human experience, constitutes a superhuman vision, a symbolic perception of wholeness transcending human limitations. It exists at one and the same time as participation in the pattern and as comprehension (which can only come from a total view beyond) of the pattern. We embody and thereby doubly realize the pattern. Caught up and confused by the pattern flowing from the Great Mind, but obscurely aware all the while that a pattern is evolving through all the seemingly disconnected activities of a life, in moments of transcendent vision, "One is interwoven into an indescribable whole and yet observes it with complete objectivity" (*Memories*, p. 296/276).[30] We hold, as a human birthright and always in images, a vision of the goal, of the pattern completed, of the "indescribable whole." We have an intuitive image—or, rather, images, for there are many ways of seeing and saying it—of the meaning of a life, a meaning which consists in fitting the single life into a general life and intention which are and are not its own. The image that we hold or are given is a vision of human life raised to a symbolic, a more-than-human significance; or, if we turn it around, it is a picture of our own potential psychic wholeness projected, perhaps, onto one we have known and loved, but what we see in the vision refers us not to the real, changing

carried within us ("Flying Saucers: A Modern Myth," *CW*, x, par. 779). See also *Two Essays*, *CW*, vii, par. 78, and "Answer to Job," *CW*, xi, par. 567.

[30] "And so it is with the hand that guides the crayon or brush, the foot that executes the dance-step, with the eye and the ear, with the word and the thought: a dark impulse is the ultimate arbiter of the pattern, an unconscious *a priori* precipitates itself into plastic form, and one has no inkling that another person's consciousness is being guided by these same principles at the very point where one feels utterly exposed to the boundless subjective vagaries of chance. Over the whole procedure there seems to reign a dim foreknowledge not only of the pattern but of its meaning. Image and meaning are identical; and as the first takes shape, so the latter becomes clear. Actually, the pattern needs no interpretation: it portrays its own meaning" ("On the Nature of the Psyche," *CW*, viii, par. 402).

and decaying, loved being but to an imaged state, a figure of completeness which is the end of all psychic endeavor.

I experienced this objectivity once again later on. That was after the death of my wife. I saw her in a dream which was like a vision. She stood at some distance from me, looking at me squarely. She was in her prime, perhaps about thirty, and wearing the dress which had been made for her many years before by my cousin the medium. It was perhaps the most beautiful thing she had ever worn. Her expression was neither joyful nor sad, but, rather, objectively wise and understanding, without the slightest emotional reaction, as though she were beyond the mist of affects. I knew that it was not she, but a portrait she had made or commissioned for me. It contained the beginning of our relationship, the events of fifty-three years of marriage, and the end of her life also. Face to face with such wholeness one remains speechless, for it can scarcely be comprehended. (*Memories*, p. 296/276.)

Here experience and meaning no longer lie separate. Out of such momentary and visionary insights into "the life of things," out of the brief but then unending times when the unconscious communicates its eternal contents to the temporally engaged conscious mind in images of completion (images which are shaped by the creative psyche on past experiences and then projected by it into future necessities), the individual is given a sense of that path he must choose and follow until he shall, in effect, become the image and the meaning he beheld.

Though in details the life given and enjoined may be tragic, yet the whole, the pattern held and completed, thus being much like a work of art, must be victorious and even, in a suprapersonal way, happy, if the pattern has been continuously affirmed and lived. "Something else, too, came to me from my illness. I might formulate it as an affirmation of things as they are: an unconditional 'yes' to that which is, without subjective protests—acceptance of the conditions of existence as I see them and understand them, acceptance of my own nature as I happen to be" (*Memories*, p. 297/277). It is all foredoomed but chosen from moment to moment; to live one's fate fully is simultaneously a victory for the choosing self and for the foredooming life. "It was only after the illness that I understood how important it is to affirm one's own destiny. . . . Then, to experience defeat is also to experience victory" (*Memories*, p. 297/277). The individual, in such a completion, has done what life destined him to do: he has allowed a meaning to be hammered out painfully in the malleable metal of his own living being. Life, one supposes, must be ever grateful to him through whose experience it flows and becomes real.[31] And the individual—his consolation? "Mean-

---

[31] This is the service that man can render to his creator: in his "realizing" existence to complete the intention and creation of his God. Though as always disavowing metaphysics, Jung, in his "Answer to Job," very nearly identifies God with the objective psyche and, since that is by definition unconscious, he can argue that man's exalted role is to finish creation by bringing to it what God cannot: awareness, consciousness of its existence (cf. Jung's awareness of completing creation in Africa, *Memories*, pp. 255-56/240: "Man, I, in an invisible act of creation put the stamp of perfection on the world by giving it objective existence"). Indeed, Jung says not only that God was unconscious when he created—and, but for man, would have remained so in his creation—but, going one incautious step further, suggests that God was then crazy, "*non compos mentis*" ("Today we would call such a state psychologically 'unconscious,' and in the eyes of the law it would be described as *non compos mentis*"; "Answer to Job," *CW*, xi, par. 638). Whether or not this represents ultimate hubris, Jung seems to want to say that man, being at least potentially *compos mentis* and capable of consciousness, can act as partner with God in bringing the world to fullness of being and conscious existence—a sort of three-cornered "drama of man, world, and God" (*Memories*, p. 256/240). To the subjective human view, Jung says in *Psychology and Alchemy*, "the recent past and the present seem like episodes in a drama that began in the grey mists of antiquity and continues through the centuries into a remote future. This drama is an 'Aurora consurgens'—the dawning of consciousness in mankind" (*CW*, xii, par. 556). And in *Mysterium Coniunctionis* he refers to "that minimal concentration of the psychic factor . . . to speak the word that outweighed the whole of Creation: That is the world, and this is I! That was the first morning of the world, the first sunrise after the primal darkness, when that inchoately conscious complex, the ego, the son of the darkness, know-

ing makes a great many things endurable—perhaps everything" (*Memories*, p. 340/313). Meaning, in contest with
mere personal happiness, is great and shall prevail. Remorse
and repentance for past actions, or disavowal of experience,
can hardly have claim on the self which has been forged in
the encounter between individual choice and impersonal fate.

Because the whole concept of individuation has so many
romantic overtones, it may be that the otherness and the im-
personality of these seminal images, which, in symbolic and
affective form, both contain and forecast self-development,
should be re-emphasized. They are, in a very particular sense,
given to us as human equipment at the moment of birth.
Every man, that is, is born with the peculiarly human, and
not other, instincts. It is not, then, the images or ideas that
are inborn, but the featureless instinct (the depository of libido-energy) and the possibility of forms (pattern of instinctual
behavior) that the instinct may assume. The images ("the
unconscious images of the instincts themselves"), which can
be as various as experience may require ("attuned and adapted
to a definite external situation"),[32] arise from the give and
take between the general life-instinct on the one hand and

---

ingly sundered subject and object, and thus precipitated the world and
itself into definite existence, giving it and itself a voice and a name" (*CW*,
XIV, par. 129).

[32] "The Concept of the Collective Unconscious," *CW*, IX, pt. 1, par. 91,
and "The Undiscovered Self," *CW*, X, par. 547. "There is, nevertheless, an
inborn 'pattern of behaviour' and just such a treasure-house, not indeed of
anticipated, but of accumulated, life-experiences; only, it is not a question
of 'representations' but of sketches, plans, or images which, though not actually 'presented' to the ego, are yet . . . real" ("On the Nature of the Psyche,"
CW, VIII, par. 352). "Because the basic structure of the psyche is everywhere
more or less the same," the psychologist discovers recurrent psychic expressions, experiences, and possibilities: "the human mind possesses general
and typical modes of functioning which correspond to the biological 'pattern of behaviour.' These pre-existent, innate patterns [are] the archetypes"
(*Symbols of Transformation*, *CW*, V, par. 474). "They are forms existing
a priori, or biological norms of psychic activity" ("The Psychological
Aspects of the Kore," *CW*, IX, pt. 1, p. 183, n. 1).

individual experiences on the other, with the creative psyche standing between, where images are formed, to contain and reconcile instinct and experience. The potential forms that achieve real expression in such dream and fantasy images—all products of the unconscious—are inborn, shared, collective; they are not at all for the individual to choose (any more than he chooses his embryonic, inherited body) or to make (to make real, perhaps, through experience, which is one thing; but not to make *ex nihilo*, which is something quite different). In adapting the libido of the unconscious to our uses and necessities,[33] these energies-become-images in fact create us as much as we create them. They *are* us in our basic and human, instinctual nature ("'nature' here means simply that which is, and always was, given"). "Instincts . . . are highly conservative and of extreme antiquity as regards both their dynamism and their form. Their form, when represented to the mind, appears as an *image* which expresses the nature of the instinctive impulse visually and concretely, like a picture. . . . Just as instinct is original and hereditary, so, too, its form is age-old, that is to say, *archetypal*. It is even older and more conservative than the body's form."[34] The archetype "(literally a pre-

[33] "I have called a symbol that converts energy a 'libido analogue.' By this I mean an idea that can give equivalent expression to the libido and canalize it into a form different from the original one. . . . The transformation of libido through the symbol is a process that has been going on ever since the beginnings of humanity and continues still. Symbols were never devised consciously, but were always produced out of the unconscious by way of revelation or intuition" ("On Psychic Energy," *CW*, VIII, par. 92). Cf. *Psychological Types*, *CW*, VI, pars. 746-50 (on the "primordial image" which liberates "psychic energy from its bondage to sheer uncomprehended perception"); *Symbols of Transformation*, *CW*, V, par. 450 (on "the constellated archetype [which] is always the primordial image of the need of the moment"); and "Archetypes of the Collective Unconscious," *CW*, IX, pt. 1, par. 80 (on "the *archetypes of transformation*. They are not personalities, but are typical situations, places, ways and means, that symbolize the kind of transformation in question").

[34] "On the Nature of the Psyche," *CW*, VIII, p. 210, n. 121 and "The Undiscovered Self," *CW*, X, par. 547.

existent form"),[35] like the instinct of which it is a "self-portrait," is a priori and inherent, the *donnée* of human existence.

The archetypes—heritable, evolved deposits of generations and centuries of collective human experience—are a good deal less mysterious and mystical, or, as a concept, outrageous to common sense, than some commentators would have them. They do not constitute a legacy boosting each generation onto the psychic shoulders of the preceding one; nor do they effect a transfer of experience, but rather and simply of the limited possibilities of response to typical human experience. "Endless repetition has engraved these experiences into our psychic constitution, not in the form of images filled with content, but at first only as *forms without content*, representing merely the possibility of a certain type of perception and action" (*CW*, IX, pt. 1, par. 99). The archetypes, taken in composite—this formulation of the concept should shock no one's reason—constitute the human condition. And though we may be said to affirm the human condition, it would be

[35] *CW*, IX, pt. 2, par. 89. "Even dreams are made of collective material to a very high degree, just as, in the mythology and folklore of different peoples, certain motifs repeat themselves in almost identical form. I have called these motifs 'archetypes,' and by this I mean forms or images of a collective nature which occur practically all over the earth as constituents of myths and at the same time as autochthonous, individual products of unconscious origin. The archetypal motifs presumably derive from patterns of the human mind that are transmitted not only by tradition and migration but also by heredity" ("Psychology and Religion," *CW*, XI, par. 88). "The natural man is characterized by unmitigated instinctuality, by his being completely at the mercy of his instincts. The inheritance that opposes this condition consists of mnemonic deposits accruing from all the experience of his ancestors. People are inclined to view this hypothesis with scepticism, thinking that 'inherited ideas' are meant. There is naturally no question of that. It is rather a question of inherited *possibilities* of ideas, 'pathways' gradually traced out through the cumulative experience of our ancestors. To deny the inheritance of these pathways would be tantamount to denying the inheritance of the brain" ("On Psychic Energy," *CW*, VIII, par. 99). Cf. also "A Psychological View of Conscience," *CW*, X, pars. 846-47; "Psychology and Religion," *CW*, XI, pars. 165-66; and *Psychological Types*, *CW*, VI, pars. 512-14.

meaningless to say that we choose it. The terms are given—
and from what source? The present condition, the sum of
possibilities which we discover individually for human existence and activity, is the product of centuries of evolution from
the dark and unconscious, unrecorded because unaware, human past. "I have often been asked where the archetypes or
primordial images come from. It seems to me that their origin
can only be explained by assuming them to be deposits of the
constantly repeated experiences of humanity."[36] Like the human body, given to us at birth to be lived into, the psyche has
changed and adapted and evolved to the present, potential
human state. At any given point of psychic evolution, man is
the result of his own long, collective effort to become aware
—aware of himself, of his humanness, of his relation to a pattern encompassing it all.

Collectively man has made his own terms; individually we
have nothing but those terms to start from, to live into, to
make real. Every individual is the single point at which the
potential becomes the real, at which inheritance reaches out
to become experience.

> And I declare my faith:
> I mock Plotinus' thought
> And cry in Plato's teeth,
> Death and life were not
> Till man made up the whole,
> Made lock, stock and barrel
> Out of his bitter soul,
> Aye, sun and moon and star, all,

---

[36] *Two Essays, CW*, VII, par. 109. See also *Psychological Types, CW*, VI,
par. 659: "These archetypes, whose innermost nature is inaccessible to experience, are the precipitate of the psychic functioning of the whole ancestral
line; the accumulated experiences of organic life in general, a million times
repeated, and condensed into types. In these archetypes, therefore, all experiences are represented which have happened on this planet since primeval
times. . . . The archetype would thus be, to borrow from Kant, the noumenon
of the image which intuition perceives and, in perceiving, creates."

> And further add to that
> That, being dead, we rise,
> Dream and so create
> Translunar Paradise.

What we are given is what we are, but what we are given is also what we have done and been in the long history of evolution. The chicken-and-egg starting point of this cumulative psychic deposit is lost in the metaphysical mist where subjective psyche cannot see[37] (to be defined again and again, however, by self-awareness such as Yeats's in "The Tower"), but for consciousness in the present that hardly matters. If we can find nothing like an objective, absolute origin, we can nevertheless, each of us and subjectively, re-realize the condition as it comes down and in to us. That Yeats in this poem (elsewhere it is otherwise) declares himself a psychic nominalist rather than realist, that he refutes Plato and Plotinus on the question of origins, is beside the point for our understanding of the makeup and characteristic activity of the psyche. Much

[37] The origin of an archetype, which is experienced as "a dynamic image, a fragment of the objective psyche" (*Two Essays, CW*, VII, par. 184), is a vexed question with Jung, though this says nothing against its psychic reality and affectiveness. "I have often been asked where the archetype comes from and whether it is acquired or not. This question cannot be answered directly. Archetypes are, by definition, factors and motifs that arrange the psychic elements into certain images, characterized as archetypal, but in such a way that they can be recognized only from the effects they produce. They exist preconsciously, and presumably they form the structural dominants of the psyche in general. . . . As *a priori* conditioning factors they represent a special, psychological instance of the biological 'pattern of behaviour,' which gives all living organisms their specific qualities. Just as the manifestations of this biological ground plan may change in the course of development, so also can those of the archetype. Empirically considered, however, the archetype did not ever come into existence as a phenomenon of organic life, but entered into the picture with life itself" ("A Psychological Approach to the Trinity," *CW*, XI, p. 149, n. 2). Cf. "Psychological Aspects of the Mother Archetype," *CW*, IX, pt. I, par. 187: "The psyche is part of the inmost mystery of life, and it has its own peculiar structure and form like every other organism. Whether this psychic structure and its elements, the archetypes, ever 'originated' at all is a metaphysical question and therefore unanswerable."

133

more important is the recognition that Yeats in his poem, like Plato and Plotinus in their philosophies, is responding to the felt, experienced condition of humanity, of being a composite of body and soul, of being man and this man. Each of them, as characteristic human response, seeks a metaphor for the experience of himself, a condition known only individually and in the present moment. And, though they reach opposite conclusions, they are, according to the sufficiency of their metaphors, equally right.

The archetypes, when they became real in specific images, are just such expressive and creative metaphors for psychic experience, looking back, for their dynamism and form, to collective experience and forward, for specific content, to individual development. The archetypes, if we view them mechanistically, or causally, seem like the residue of collective human experience; if, however, turning in the other direction, we view them energically, or finally, they seem to direct themselves through us individually toward a positive and foreseen goal.

> Impressive ideas which are hailed as truths have something peculiar about them. Although they come into being at a definite time, they are and have always been timeless; they arise from that realm of creative psychic life out of which the ephemeral mind of the single human being grows like a plant that blossoms, bears fruit and seed, and then withers and dies. Ideas spring from something greater than the personal human being. Man does not make his ideas; we could say that man's ideas make him.[38]

[38] "Freud and Jung: Contrasts," *CW*, iv, par. 769. Cf. *Psychological Types*, *CW*, vi, pars. 732-33: "Accordingly, I use the term idea to express the *meaning* of a primordial image, a meaning that has been abstracted from the *concretism* . . . of the image. . . . In so far, however, as an idea is the formulated meaning of a primordial image by which it was represented symbolically . . . , its essence is not just something derived or developed, but, psychologically speaking, exists *a priori*, as a given possibility for thought-combinations in general."

With the substitution of "idea" for "archetype," it becomes apparent that there is nothing new either about the archetypes themselves or about a human conception of them. Seen thus, they look very like Plato's "Ideas" in psychological modern dress: a creative formulation expressing in human terms the deepest subjective experience of divine spirit infusing the created world. The distinction between Ideas and archetypes, which are quite alike in their affective energy, is metaphysical rather than psychological, hence does not much concern this discussion. A word, however, might be said which will more clearly define the characteristic nature of the archetype by contrasting it with a similar concept. Platonic Ideas are "real" and exist, prior to human experience, in the mind of God. It takes only a subtle shift of viewpoint to conceive of archetypes as prior to individual experience, but as equally the deposit of a collective effort, by which very effort man has given shape to what we call "the mind of God."[39] As they are pre-existent to his own experience, however, the archetypes are real and objective for the individual. The subjectivity/objectivity of our conception of God can never be settled until the whole game is up and we see it from outside, or can be settled only momentarily as we adopt this or that point of view, and understand that what we have is that: one point of view on experience, one metaphor of the self, taken from within and maintained under threat of chaos.

Shaped out of past experience, the archetypes shape our future experience. They show us what man has been and what we are becoming, or what they "want" to become through us.[40] Archetypal images, appearing spontaneously, independ-

[39] "The collective unconscious, being the repository of man's experience and at the same time the prior condition of this experience, is an image of the world which has taken aeons to form" (*Two Essays, CW*, VII, par. 151).

[40] "As a numinous factor, the archetype determines the nature of the configurational process and the course it will follow, with seeming foreknowledge, or as though it were already in possession of the goal to be

ently, and unwilled, useful if we can integrate them into total development, destructive if left altogether autonomous to overwhelm consciousness, arise out of the collective unconscious as formative factors in our individual selves. Coming from the collective unconscious, they have never been a part of individual conscious material now for some reason repressed; collective contents, if they move at all, must move in one direction—toward consciousness—and, as archetypal images, represent the point of conjunction between the unconscious and consciousness.[41] Take, by way of illustration, an archetype that is characteristic in nature and effect: the wise old man which, specifically realized in particular images, appears time after time in dreams, myths, fantasies. This, like every archetype, is predetermined only as to form—wise old man: a force of information in and for the process of self-development—not as to content. Thus we all have it inherently and potentially in us to discover an ancient and new fund of information, and we "image" this information in the

---

circumscribed by the centring process" ("On the Nature of the Psyche," *CW*, VIII, par. 411).

[41] "Modern psychology treats the products of unconscious fantasy-activity as self-portraits of what is going on in the unconscious, or as statements of the unconscious psyche about itself. They fall into two categories. First, fantasies (including dreams) of a personal character. . . . Second, fantasies (including dreams) of an impersonal character. . . . These fantasy-images undoubtedly have their closest analogues in mythological types. We must therefore assume that they correspond to certain *collective* (and not personal) structural elements of the human psyche in general, and, like the morphological elements of the human body, are *inherited*. Although tradition and transmission by migration certainly play a part, there are, as we have said, very many cases that cannot be accounted for in this way and drive us to the hypothesis of 'autochthonous revival.' These cases are so numerous that we are obliged to assume the existence of a collective psychic substratum. I have called this the *collective unconscious*. . . .

"In a state of reduced intensity of consciousness (in dreams, delirium, reveries, visions, etc.). . . . the hitherto unconscious material streams, as though from opened side-sluices, into the field of consciousness" ("The Psychology of the Child Archetype," *CW*, IX, pt. 1, pars. 262-63). See also "The Concept of the Collective Unconscious," *CW*, IX, pt. 1, pars. 88-90.

form, predetermined and universal, of a wise old man. The specific nature of the information, dependent upon personal necessity, and the exact wise figure, dependent upon individual experience, are not determined before the fact.[42] The archetype may be projected onto a suitable person in our experience (for example, a grandfather), or may be personified in such a figure in dreams. In either case, we project the unknown and in itself unknowable archetype onto a real and living, known, substantial person, and so determine the content from personal experience. But—and this is the crucial point for understanding and self-development—this is only a projection.[43] The grandfather is not really the wise old man but only, so far as we are concerned for our own development, a fallible and personal being. The true provenance of this formal image is the unknown part of the self: the unconscious, and, more precisely, the collective unconscious. Psychotherapy would demonstrate that this is so and refer the new-found, old knowledge back to inherent powers, back to the collective and unconscious part of the self. Thus it would point to the vast riches for development to be found, finally, not (as at first they were, or seemed to be) in others, but within the self. The wise old man, who is at first another—an autonomous, objective partner in a colloquy—is at last the same—an un-

[42] Archetypal experiences "demand to be individually shaped in and by each man's life and work. They are images sprung from the life, the joys and sorrows, of our ancestors; and to life they seek to return, not in experience only, but in deed" (*Two Essays*, *CW*, VII, par. 120). Cf. *Conversations*, p. 67; "The Undiscovered Self," *CW*, x, par. 547; *Psychology and Alchemy*, *CW*, XII, pars. 328-29; and "Flying Saucers: A Modern Myth," *CW*, x, par. 624 (which explains that, modern experience being what it is, the activated archetype "that has always expressed order, deliverance, salvation, and wholeness" is projected onto a specific image of a circular and technologically sophisticated nature: i.e., the "flying saucer").

[43] "We can hardly get around the hypothesis that an emotionally charged content is lying ready in the unconscious and springs into projection at a certain moment" ("Concerning the Archetypes and the Anima Concept," *CW*, IX, pt. 1, par. 134).

known half of the self. For self-development each of us stands quite alone: others are not there.

But one step more. Whence comes the archetype, the form of wise old man? It is innate and a priori, inherited from the collective psyche shaped in the experience of father and grandfather. So we are alone until we realize that we are also all of our inheritance, the present moment of our racial past. We are the sum of our ancestors, paradoxically alone and not alone. For strength in the making of self we reach down and back, up and forward, not out to the side; always, as individuals, we must go vertically and not laterally. The archetype speaks to us with the voice of traditional authority and wisdom because it is that inherited, personal but much greater, suprapersonal power of generations now momentarily resident in us. What the wise old man tells us, from within and from the centuries, is to be ourselves and all of ourselves, to be the realized whole which has lain in us, like a psychic homunculus, from birth.

In the wise old man is figured an unknown half of the self, but the total self, too, that largest unknown, has no less its archetype, its own symbolic form. This archetype, the greatest, the most inclusive and affective of them all, realizes itself in a variety of images, all to be taken as conclusive, all meaning and enjoining selfhood. It bears several names (mandala, *imago Dei*, symbol of wholeness, the God within) and a great many image forms (e.g., tower, stone, *lapis philosophorum*, flying saucer, quaternity, squared circle, round fish, Uroboros, Buddha, Christ).[44] Any one of them, bringing news about the

[44] The mandala is "one typical archetypal form. It is what is called *ultimo exquadra circulae*, the square in the circle, or the circle in the square. It is an age-old symbol that goes right back to the pre-history of man. It is all over the earth and it either expresses the Deity or the self; and these two terms are psychologically very much related. . . .

"It is the archetype of inner order. . . . It expresses the fact that there is

self, to and from the self, represents both an achieved state and a functional symbol on the drive to individuation, represents, that is, a summary symbol depicting how far the individual has come and where he must go. Always there, for the individual from birth, for mankind from time immemorial, the archetype of completion is the end of the journey, the goal toward which, if we attend to it, life insistently points. The mandala (using that phrase for any image of psychic wholeness: "The Sanskrit word *mandala* means 'circle'"; *CW*, IX, pt. I, par. 629) is the expression not of one or another of the separable instincts but of the inclusive life-instinct itself: the expressive vehicle of undifferentiated libido, of psychic energy in its ultimate form and significance.[45]

From the beginning I felt the Tower as in some way a place

a center and a periphery, and it tries to embrace the whole. It is the symbol of wholeness. . . .

"It is, we should say, the main archetype" (*Conversations*, pp. 62-63).

"In so far as the mandala encompasses, protects, and defends the psychic totality against outside influences and seeks to unite the inner opposites, it is at the same time a distinct *individuation symbol*. . . . I have defined this spontaneous image as a symbolical representation of the *self*, by which I mean not the ego but the totality composed of the conscious *and* the unconscious" ("Flying Saucers: A Modern Myth," *CW*, X, par. 621). Cf. *ibid.*, pars. 779-80; *Aion, CW*, IX, pt. 2, par. 297 ("in the products of the unconscious the self appears as it were *a priori*, that is, in well-known circle and quaternity symbols which may already have occurred in the earliest dreams of childhood, long before there was any possibility of consciousness or understanding"); and *Psychology and Alchemy, CW*, XII, pars. 40-41, and p. 42, n. 2.

[45] "Since, psychologically speaking, the God-image is a complex of ideas of an archetypal nature, it must necessarily be regarded as representing a certain sum of energy (libido) which appears in projection" (*Symbols of Transformation, CW*, V, par. 89). "It represents the strongest, the most ineluctable urge in every being, namely the urge to realize itself. It is, as it were, an incarnation of *the inability to do otherwise*, equipped with all the powers of nature and instinct. . . . The urge and compulsion to self-realization is a law of nature and thus of invincible power, even though its effect, at the start, is insignificant and improbable" ("The Psychology of the Child Archetype," *CW*, IX, pt. I, par. 289).

of maturation—a maternal womb or a maternal figure in which I could become what I was, what I am and will be. It gave me a feeling as if I were being reborn in stone. It is thus a concretization of the individuation process, a memorial *aere perennius*. During the building work, of course, I never considered these matters. I built the house in sections, always following the concrete needs of the moment. It might also be said that I built it in a kind of dream. Only afterward did I see how all the parts fitted together and that a meaningful form had resulted: a symbol of psychic wholeness.

(*Memories*, p. 225/214.)

Exegi monumentum—the self and its creative symbol. The purpose of life is to live it; a life lived, a personality achieved, constitutes its own memorial, a completed process symbolized outwardly in such metaphors as it has struck off spontaneously in the creation of self: in such significant forms as poem and book, square stone and round tower.[46]

[46] The basic motif of all the various mandala images, Jung says, "is the premonition of a centre of personality, a kind of central point within the psyche, to which everything is related, by which everything is arranged, and which is itself a source of energy. The energy of the central point is manifested in the almost irresistible compulsion and urge to *become what one is*, just as every organism is driven to assume the form that is characteristic of its nature, no matter what the circumstances. This centre is not felt or thought of as the ego but, if one may so express it, as the *self*. Although the centre is represented by an innermost point, it is surrounded by a periphery containing everything that belongs to the self—the paired opposites that make up the total personality. This totality comprises consciousness first of all, then the personal unconscious, and finally an indefinitely large segment of the collective unconscious whose archetypes are common to all mankind" ("Concerning Mandala Symbolism," *CW*, IX, pt. 1, par. 634).

"The self is the hypothetical summation of an indescribable totality, one half of which is constituted by ego-consciousness, the other by the shadow" (*Mysterium Coniunctionis*, *CW*, XIV, p. 107, n. 66).

"The transcendent function does not proceed without aim and purpose, but leads to the revelation of the essential man. . . . The meaning and purpose of the process is the realization, in all its aspects, of the personality originally hidden away in the embryonic germ-plasm; the production and unfolding of the original, potential wholeness. The symbols used by the unconscious to this end are the same as those which mankind has always used to express wholeness, completeness, and perfection: symbols, as a rule, of

The mandala, as in its original Indian elaboration, is a symbol of the divine, creative spirit, whether we consider that divine spirit to speak solely from within human experience or from an objective source outside ourselves.[47] The question is

---

the quaternity and the circle. For these reasons I have termed this the *individuation process*" (*Two Essays, CW*, VII, par. 186).

"Individuation means becoming an 'in-dividual,' and, in so far as 'individuality' embraces our innermost, last, and incomparable uniqueness, it also implies becoming one's own self. We could therefore translate individuation as 'coming to selfhood' or 'self-realization.' . . . in other words, it is a process by which a man becomes the definite, unique being he in fact is" (*Two Essays, CW*, VII, pars. 266-67). Cf. also *Conversations*, p. 96 ("A man or woman becomes that which he or she is from the beginning"); "Archetypes of the Collective Unconscious," *CW*, IX, pt. 1, par. 84 ("this process follows the natural course of life—a life in which the individual becomes what he always was"); and "The Development of Personality," *CW*, XVII, par. 286 ("For in every adult there lurks a child—an eternal child, something that is always becoming, is never completed, and calls for unceasing care, attention, and education").

[47] Is the *imago Dei* a creation, then, of the subjective psyche, or is it objectively real? Jung ordinarily refuses the question, but when he agrees to discuss the matter, he comes out for psychological subjectivity: "I am therefore of the opinion that, in general, psychic energy or libido creates the God-image by making use of archetypal patterns, and that man in consequence worships the psychic force active within him as something divine. We thus arrive at the objectionable conclusion that, from the psychological point of view, the God-image is a real but subjective phenomenon" (*Symbols of Transformation, CW*, V, par. 129). "From the empirical standpoint of analytical psychology, the God-image is the symbolic expression of a particular psychic state or function. . . . Hence, for our psychology . . . God is not even relative, but a function of the unconscious—the manifestation of a dissociated quantum of libido that has activated the God-image" (*Psychological Types, CW*, VI, pars. 412-13). Again: "The ultimate fate of every dogma is that it gradually becomes soulless. Life wants to create new forms, and therefore, when a dogma loses its vitality, it must perforce activate the archetype that has always helped man to express the mystery of the soul. Note that I do not go so far as to say that the archetype actually produces the divine figure. . . . I maintain only that the psychic archetype makes it possible for the divine figure to take form and become accessible to understanding" (*Mysterium Coniunctionis, CW*, XIV, par. 488). Symbols of wholeness Jung describes similarly as "the reactivation of an archaic god-image" (*Two Essays, CW*, VII, par. 248). Cf. also "Answer to Job," *CW*, XI, par. 758, and Jung's foreword to *God and the Unconscious* by Victor White, O.P., *CW*, XI, par. 454.

141

whether we would consider the phenomena of mandala psychologically or metaphysically. Perhaps, as suggested earlier, the mandala is most pregnantly seen in both ways at once: prior to individual experience, it is still the sum of collective experience; individually, it is a priori, collectively, a posteriori.[48] If we merge the two points of view, then self becomes indistinguishable from, though perhaps not identical with, divinity, the two being united in an indivisible, insoluble, and paradoxical image.[49] An individual life is a living of that image:

[48] "The goal of the individuation process is the synthesis of the self. From another point of view the term 'entelechy' might be preferable to 'synthesis.' There is an empirical reason why 'entelechy' is, in certain conditions, more fitting: the symbols of wholeness frequently occur at the beginning of the individuation process, indeed they can often be observed in the first dreams of early infancy. This observation says much for the *a priori* existence of potential wholeness, and on this account the idea of *entelechy* instantly recommends itself. But in so far as the individuation process occurs, empirically speaking, as a synthesis, it looks, paradoxically enough, as if something already existent were being put together. From this point of view, the term 'synthesis' is also applicable" ("The Psychology of the Child Archetype," *CW*, IX, pt. 1, par. 278).

[49] "The self . . . is a God-image, or at least cannot be distinguished from one" (*Aion, CW*, IX, pt. 2, par. 42).

". . . the self can be distinguished only conceptually from what has always been referred to as 'God,' but not practically. Both concepts apparently rest on an identical numinous factor which is a condition of reality" (*Mysterium Coniunctionis, CW*, XIV, par. 778).

"The use of the comparative method shows without a doubt that the quaternity is a more or less direct representation of the God who is manifest in his creation. We might, therefore, conclude that the symbol spontaneously produced in the dreams of modern people means something similar—*the God within*" ("Psychology and Religion," *CW*, XI, par. 101).

"I have called this centre the *self*. Intellectually the self is no more than a psychological concept, a construct that serves to express an unknowable essence which we cannot grasp as such, since by definition it transcends our powers of comprehension. It might equally well be called the 'God within us.' The beginnings of our whole psychic life seem to be inextricably rooted in this point, and all our highest and ultimate purposes seem to be striving towards it. This paradox is unavoidable, as always, when we try to define something that lies beyond the bourn of our understanding" (*Two Essays, CW*, VII, par. 399).

"I know people for whom the encounter with the strange power within

142

eternal and infinite spirit caught and realized in the tangle of time and space. Psychic wholeness gathers up all times, both individual and racial, both human and divine, into the present moment of symbolic containment, into a consciousness of the human condition. All our past is contained in our momentary completion, which points in generative richness to our future. The individual, if he is in fact a total individual, is the fruit of his past, but at the same time the seeds of the future, his psyche and body the bridge stretched between two destinies which are his and more than his: "the enchainment of past and future / Woven in the weakness of the changing body." We cast these images, in our efforts to create and communicate, again and again, and always in the form of "as if" truths, metaphors more or less adequate to the experience of the psychic moment.

In the Tower at Bollingen it is *as if* one lived in many centuries simultaneously. The place will outlive me, and in its location and style it points to things of long ago. There is very little about it to suggest the present. . . . There is nothing to disturb the dead, neither electric light nor telephone. Moreover, my ancestors' souls are sustained by the atmosphere of the house, since I answer for them the questions that their lives once left behind. I carve out rough answers as best I can. I have even drawn them on the walls. It is *as if* a silent, greater family, stretching down the centuries, were peopling the house. There I live in my second personality and see life in the round, as something forever coming into being and passing on.[50]

---

themselves was such an overwhelming experience that they called it 'God.' So experienced, 'God' too is a 'theory' in the most literal sense, a way of looking at the world, an image which the limited human mind creates in order to express an unfathomable and ineffable experience. The experience alone is real, not to be disputed; but the image can be soiled or broken to pieces" ("The Meaning of Psychology for Modern Man," *CW*, x, par. 330). Cf. also *Aion*, *CW*, ix, pt. 2, pars. 303-305.

[50] *Memories*, p. 237/224. The italics, emphasizing Jung's characteristic mode of expression for psychic experience, where everything is subjective, metaphoric, and "as if," are mine.

This "coming into being" of generations is effected only in time, yet it is a pattern "forever" happening, as if destined from before and after time.

For the psychologist, life, in its steady progress from birth to death, has not only its individual but its typical pattern as well. The movement of life characteristically reverses itself at midpoint, as if, establishing the whole pattern by a tension of opposites, youth and age necessarily assume opposed and counterpoised attitudes. It is of the greatest importance for psychotherapy to recognize that the psychology of youth is not the psychology of age, that the aims of age are not the same as but in balanced contrast to the aims of youth. At about the halfway point ("nel mezzo del cammin di nostra vita"—age thirty-five: the division of years is quite exactly Dantesque), the path bends back upon itself and down into the dark and unexplored reaches of unconscious being; hereafter the gaze and goal of life cease to be directed outward on the world, turning back instead toward the center and the inner man.[51] Having extended ourselves for half a life, we do well to begin

[51] "Obviously it is in the youthful period of life that we have most to gain from a thorough recognition of the instinctual side. . . . Proper recognition and appreciation of normal instincts leads the young person into life and entangles him with fate, thus involving him in life's necessities and the consequent sacrifices and efforts through which his character is developed and his experience matured. For the mature person, however, the continued expansion of life is obviously not the right principle, because the descent towards life's afternoon demands simplification, limitation, and intensification—in other words, individual culture" ("On Psychic Energy," *CW*, VIII, par. 113).

Death "is the great perfector, drawing his inexorable line under the balance-sheet of human life. In him alone is wholeness—one way or another—attained. Death is the end of the empirical man and the goal of the spiritual man" ("Flying Saucers: A Modern Myth," *CW*, x, par. 695). Cf. also *Symbols of Transformation*, *CW*, v, par. 680 ("It is as if the libido were not only a ceaseless forward movement, an unending will for life, evolution, creation . . . ; like the sun, the libido also wills its own descent, its own involution. During the first half of life it strives for growth; during the second half, softly at first and then ever more perceptibly, it points towards an altered goal"); and "Psychotherapists or the Clergy," *CW*, XI, par. 509.

to gather and contain those energies in visions of the end: "No longer in Lethean foliage caught / Begin the preparation for your death." This circling in on the individual center should be seen not only as a pattern imposed upon psychic life but equally as possibilities released and made available, for beyond the midpoint the individual is free to live the life of his soul, free as he was not when "caught in that sensual music" (though Yeats, from whom, of course, both "caught" phrases come, puts that midpoint, because of individual experience, considerably after thirty-five). This turn establishes both a new freedom and a new service: freedom from external laws and entanglements, service to the unique law of self.

When the line of life ceases to be a mere extension and expenditure in human time and world space and begins to curve back to describe the circle of a mandala symbol, when the profoundly individual pattern assumes the dimensions of fate and divine intention, when God ("Deus est circulus cuius centrum est ubique, circumferentia vero nusquam"[52]) again becomes embodied as man, as he has an infinite number of times already, then depth psychology has seen and recognized this before: it is the individuation process in classic outline, the typical activity and goal of the second half of life.[53] The life of Christ or

[52] "A Psychological Approach to the Trinity," *CW*, xi, p. 155, n. 6. This quotation, given in various forms (e.g., "God is an infinite circle (or sphere) whose centre is everywhere and the circumference nowhere"; *CW*, ix, pt. 1, par. 572), called sometimes a "definition," sometimes a "saying," sometimes an "old image," and credited indifferently to St. Augustine, an anonymous Church Father, or a nameless Gnostic writer, is easily Jung's favorite phrase for characterizing God. Cf. *Aion*, *CW*, ix, pt. 2, par. 237; "Flying Saucers: A Modern Myth," *CW*, x, par. 622 and again par. 806; "Psychology and Religion," *CW*, xi, par. 92.

[53] For definitions of "individuation"—in which, as will be apparent, Jung is prodigal—see, e.g.: "Conscious, Unconscious, and Individuation," *CW*, ix, pt. 2, par. 490 ("I use the term 'individuation' to denote the process by which a person becomes a psychological 'in-dividual,' that is, a separate, indivisible unity or 'whole'"); *Aion*, *CW*, ix, pt. 2, pars. 408-11 (a schematic rendering of the individuation process); "Answer to Job," *CW*, xi, pars. 755-56; and *Psychological Types*, *CW*, vi, pars. 755-62 ("The more a man's

Buddha—their individuated lives being great symbolic utterances or realizations of psychic wholeness and spiritual completion[54]—stands to the individual as "the image of development of the self." The old ideal of a Christian life as an *imitatio Christi* is valid only if that means living out one's own individual destiny as Christ lived his; it is quite invalid, indeed destructive, if understood to mean a literal imitation in detail of that other life with its essentially different formative law. "Christ is an exemplar who dwells in every Christian as his integral personality" (*Memories*, p. 280/261). Since every man is a "splinter of the infinite deity" (*Memories*, p. 4/17), an incarnation of objective psyche, he mistakes his own nature if he imitates Christ and Christ's way. Properly seen, he *is* Christ. In an image of Christ we project and discover the

---

life is shaped by the collective norm, the greater is his individual immorality").

[54] "*Christ exemplifies the archetype of the self*" (*Aion*, *CW*, IX, pt. 2, par. 70; the italics are Jung's).

"In the world of Christian ideas Christ undoubtedly represents the self. As the apotheosis of individuality, the self has the attributes of uniqueness and of occurring once only in time. But since the psychological self is a transcendent concept, expressing the totality of conscious and unconscious contents, it can only be described in antinomial terms; that is, the above attributes must be supplemented by their opposites if the transcendental situation is to be characterized correctly. . . . As an historical personage Christ is unitemporal and unique; as God, universal and eternal. Likewise the self: as the essence of individuality it is unitemporal and unique; as an archetypal symbol it is a God-image and therefore universal and eternal. . . . Hence individuation is a 'mysterium coniunctionis,' the self being experienced as a nuptial union of opposite halves and depicted as a composite whole in mandalas that are drawn spontaneously by patients" (*ibid.*, pars. 115-17). Cf. the visionary mystical marriage Jung experienced when sick, in which he played a part but a mysterious part: "I cannot tell you how wonderful it was. . . . I do not know exactly what part I played in it. At bottom it was I myself: I was the marriage" (*Memories*, p. 294/274). See also "The Undiscovered Self," *CW*, X, par. 529 ("Christianity holds up before us a symbol whose content is the individual way of life of a man, the Son of Man, and . . . it even regards this individuation process as the incarnation and revelation of God himself"); *Psychology and Alchemy*, *CW*, XII, par. 20; and *Mysterium Coniunctionis*, *CW*, XIV, *passim*, esp. par. 664.

idea of our selves, a symbol of transformation, "an expression of the life-spirit, the *anima mundi* or *filius macrocosmi,* the Anthropos who animates the whole cosmos" (*Memories*, p. 211/201).[55] All reverence, then, to the realized self, through whose experience in individuation God once more enters into time.[56]

The individual-in-becoming circles around his own core of selfhood, drawn in toward that central point which becomes indistinguishable in the end from the divine, order- and meaning-giving "still point of the turning world." The point of reference and direction in the process of individuation is as much human as divine, but as much divine as human.

> The self, I thought, was like the monad which I am, and which is my world. The mandala represents this monad, and corresponds to the microcosmic nature of the psyche. . . .
>
> When I began drawing the mandalas, however, I saw that everything, all the paths I had been following, all the steps I had taken, were leading back to a single point—namely, to

[55] "The demand made by the *imitatio Christi*—that we should follow the ideal and seek to become like it—ought logically to have the result of developing and exalting the inner man. . . . For it is not a question of an imitation that leaves a man unchanged and makes him into a mere artifact, but of realizing the ideal on one's own account—*Deo concedente*—in one's own individual life" (*Psychology and Alchemy, CW,* xii, par. 7). See also "Psychotherapists or the Clergy," *CW,* xi, par. 522: "Are we to understand the 'imitation of Christ' in the sense that we should copy his life and, if I may use the expression, ape his stigmata; or in the deeper sense that we are to live our own proper lives as truly as he lived his in its individual uniqueness?"

[56] "By the 'transcendence of life' I mean those aforementioned experiences of the initiate who takes part in a sacred rite which reveals to him the perpetual continuation of life through transformation and renewal. . . . A living example of the mystery drama representing the permanence as well as the transformation of life is the Mass. . . . The Mass is an extramundane and extratemporal act in which Christ is sacrificed and then resurrected in the transformed substances; and this rite of his sacrificial death is not a repetition of the historical event but the original, unique, and eternal act. The experience of the Mass is therefore a participation in the transcendence of life, which overcomes all bounds of space and time. It is a moment of eternity in time" ("Concerning Rebirth," *CW,* ix, pt. 1, pars. 208-209).

the mid-point. It became increasingly plain to me that the mandala is the center. It is the exponent of all paths. It is the path to the center, to individuation.

During those years, between 1918 and 1920, I began to understand that the goal of psychic development is the self. There is no linear evolution; there is only a circumambulation of the self. Uniform development exists, at the most, only at the beginning; later, everything points toward the center.

(Memories, pp. 196-97/188.)

The individual, his life an arc rounding out the curve of collective human life, sinks finally to quiet in the center of the circle he has described, comes to the destined end which only he could make real. The circumference draws in to a point, and the light of consciousness—that consciousness which has been a partner with God in the creation of the universe, an achievement forever added now to the possibilities of human awareness and response, forever a part of the objective psyche, earned for the collectivity by the effort of individual psyche— sinks back into the surrounding dark from which it originally came in travail, back into the all-enfolding collective unconscious, "safe," now, "safe in the womb of the universe" (*Memories*, p. 293/273).

Thus, or something very like it, the metaphor, the dream, the myth, personal and public, of C. G. Jung. The metaphor, as one sees quite plainly, first proved itself on the pulse of its author. His autobiography, an account of the myth in its personal aspect, he calls *Memories, Dreams, Reflections*. It is, in Wallace Stevens' phrase describing poetry, an "abstraction blooded" by the images grown out of and giving shape to a particular life. But the myth that presses along the artery of those dreams gave vital form in no less a degree to the public theory. The *Collected Works* might equally well—better, one might say—be entitled *Essays; or, The Making of C. G. Jung*. It is not so much an *Opus Scientificum*—for, given the subject,

it never could be that—as it is a large and complex metaphor
for all that he and he alone knew about the process of becoming a self—i.e., his unique self, a heritage and an experience. How could anything like a science ever hope to take its
bearings in Jung's work—unless, going way back, we define
"science" so loosely as to take from it any distinctive meaning? But none of this is to be taken as suggesting that Jung's
work is meaningless or beside the point. Quite the contrary:
his was a mythic, a representative and symbolic life, like Montaigne's. From it we learn of attempts and achievements, hints
captured, directions opened, possibilities realized. It isn't that
Jung was less than a scientist; he was more. He was a man
of a full and rich life who, in his work and writings, discovered
metaphors adequate to the experience of that life. Some ten
or a dozen years before he agreed, apparently somewhat re-
luctantly, to the making of *Memories, Dreams, Reflections*,
Jung himself remarked, apropos of certain writings in which
the reader might discern the implicit outlines of an autobiography:

> Writing a prefatory note to these *diversa* gives me a peculiar
> feeling. A collection of my essays from various times and situa-
> tions of life is rather like a grasshopper with type on its feet
> jumping through the world of ideas, leaving occasional traces
> behind it; and it requires a considerable effort of imagination
> to reconstruct from the zigzag track of these footprints the
> nature of the animal that produced them. I envy no one this
> task, as I myself have a distaste for autobiography. The im-
> mense expanse of possibly recognizable objects in the world
> has lured me forth to those twilit border zones where the figure
> I have meanwhile become steps towards me. The long path I
> have traversed is littered with husks sloughed off, witnesses
> of countless moultings, these *relicta* one calls books. They con-
> ceal as much as they reveal. Every step is a symbol of those to
> follow. He who mounts a flight of steps does not linger on
> them, nor look back at them, even though age invites him to
> linger or slow down his pace. The great wind of the peaks

roars ever more loudly in his ears. His gaze sweeps distances that flee away into the infinite. The last steps are the loveliest and most precious, for they lead to that fullness to reach which the innermost essence of man is born.[57]

Besides their obvious relevance in a consideration of the forms and ways of autobiography, these lines, in their very phrasing, seem to suggest the form, only barely obscured, of a Romantic poet only slightly *manqué*. In the example of his living, taking his own life as the stuff of his art, Jung became an artist of moral experience. We freely admit that Montaigne, another artist of moral experience, was not a scientist; neither was T. S. Eliot. But the admission is irrelevant. We can nonetheless learn much about psychology—*our* psychology—from Montaigne and Eliot, or from Jung. His was a remarkable creative achievement in which, as he made his own soul, the face of humanity took on a new aspect.

[57] A dedication, "To the owner of this book: Dr. Jürg Fierz," which Jung wrote for a bound volume of his own offprints prepared by Fierz, literary editor of the *Weltwoche* (Zurich). It is dated Küsnacht, December 21, 1945. From *C. G. Jung: Letters*, selected and ed. Gerhard Adler and Aniela Jaffé, trans. R.F.C. Hull, Bollingen Series XCV, vol. 1 (Princeton, N.J.: Princeton Univ. Press, and London: Routledge & Kegan Paul, 1973); by permission of the publishers.

four : Autobiography Simplex

et nous sommes tous du vulgaire

Montaigne hardly tires ever of telling his reader that there is nothing grand or impressive or the least unusual about himself; that he is the most ordinary of men, and thus a good subject through whom to study common humanity; or that if he is in any way out of the ordinary, it is only in being entirely concerned with himself and not at all with any other subject. Darwin and Mill too acknowledged, with a charming and disarming frankness, that they were "of the common herd." Any child, Mill maintained, of only ordinary capacities, could do what he had so remarkably done, provided only that the child have a father like James Mill (which would, of course, be rather unlikely). Of himself, in fact, Mill goes so far as to claim that, in respect of most natural gifts, he was "rather below than above par." Darwin, as unforward in his own behalf as Mill, echoes this modest disclaimer when, balancing up his strengths and his weaknesses, he refers in sum to "such moderate abilities as I possess." As for Fox, probably the first principle of his religion was that all men are equal in the Light of God, and spiritual value counted with Fox for everything: social distinctions certainly, but also intellectual distinctions, meant nothing to that spiritual democrat. Newman, because his *Apologia* constituted special pleading about a unique experience, had no occasion to compare his achievements or his endowments with those of other men. But there is no question that he, like his three partners in this chapter, was, in the most important respect, "du vulgaire": for they all, in their particular ways, Newman no less and perhaps rather more intensely than the others, were engaged in the common destiny of every conscious man: living the human condition.

Though it may, I think, be otherwise in the work of art, no man, as Mill remarked, can be all things in his living day; and each of these four men was a single and particular, often extreme, thing. Being very different men one from another, Fox, Darwin, Mill, and Newman saw the universe and created it in very different ways; and in the metaphors they developed to express their visions, we can read in clear outline the personalities of the metaphor-makers. Mill's writings represent a coherent view of life, and they could never have been produced by Newman, both on account of what they say and how they say it; the same is true for Fox and Darwin, or for Fox and Newman, Newman and Darwin, etc. The lifework, in each case, is a coherent projection of the writer's self, a production unified and stamped with the image of the man, his mind and his spirit. The universe, because Darwin *saw* it that way and made it so, *was* a closed mechanical system of cause and effect, and so was he, the creator of this expressive, mechanical metaphor. And the human mind, because Mill so thought it, *was* a sort of syllogistic computer reflecting, in its characteristic operation, a computer-like universe. The fact that Mill and Darwin saw machines acted as a universal fiat: Let there be machines, and there were machines. A cartoon in the *New Yorker* some years ago that showed a computer producing the answer "Cogito ergo sum" has an exact and special relevance for the cases of Mill and Darwin. But Fox saw the universe as like "a great Ring of pure and endless light" and the human soul in the same image: and as he saw it, so must it have been. The truth for Newman was that the world and the human soul are organic processes of becoming, evolving according to laws unique to each, toward realization of the Divine. Of course he was right, for he believed intensely in his belief. And so were they all, because they all did so—being the men they were.

The metaphoric light in which each of these four men saw

his own and all life tells much, naturally, about the individual, and also perhaps something about the human condition itself; and especially this may be true when one takes together these several different, opposed and complementary, views on or metaphors for an experience that is always one and the same though it happens in a unique way to the individual: subjective life. On the one hand, each of the men had his psychological bias and his characteristic direction, each displayed in his makeup and in his work a vision that was unique and personal: Fox looked to his "inward Light" of intuition and Newman to the "Kindly Light" that eventually led him to Rome; Mill was taught to see everything in the clear and unfeeling light of syllogistic logic, and Darwin was by nature predisposed to the common light of day. Over against this personal bias, on the other hand, for each of these writers—as, indeed, also for Montaigne, Jung, and Eliot—there was something else, something impersonal and, as they all felt, objective; as if life were made up of a flow of energy between two poles of value, two related but different and opposed existences that constantly, however, exchange and interchange being. This other field of force and value, all the writers would agree, though they could never agree on the nature of the force, lies outside the individual, yet is realized by and in the existence of the individual. While Fox's light, for example, was inner, it remained, all the same, other; while, for Newman, the lives of the saints were an expression of dogma and doctrine, the formulary of dogma and doctrine, the Church, was a manifest institution; while it was the mind of man that did the thinking, the forms of thought, being prior to experience, were, as Mill maintained, indisputable and immutable; and while Darwin's virtually divine law of evolution comprehended man and realized itself in man, it went far beyond him in bringing nature to her present full and various state. Thus there is an impersonal face, as it were, in the personal metaphors of Fox, Newman, Mill, and

Darwin: the impersonal or suprapersonal visage of human life itself.

For convenience I have occasionally, in the chapter that follows, borrowed descriptive terms from Jung's essay on psychological types. That Jung's theory was something other than entirely original with him is obvious, and in any case he freely acknowledges his indebtedness to medieval pseudosciences for his "scientific" classifications. Astrology and alchemy gave Jung, as they gave Yeats at about the same time, traditional modes and expressions for the division and unification of human experience. Anyhow, it is apparent to everyone that men differ in their responses to the encountered phenomena of life; they differ as night and day, as Darwin and Fox, as Newman and Mill. They differ and are yet a part of the one human community. If we see them opposed on the psychological wheel, they are, nevertheless, all on the same wheel. Out of their lives and autobiographies, therefore, one might hope to construct, ideally and synthetically, a total personality and to imagine a total autobiography. Balancing the mystic against the scientist and the sensationalist thinker against the intuitive feeler, we may achieve some concept of the whole man that can, in turn, be placed against each of these four partials—setting up, in interaction, the two fields of energy, personal and suprapersonal, from which life seems to flow.

Looking back, each of these men created in his autobiography a metaphor that was new for a new self, but that was also determined by the same personal tendencies and temperament as the metaphor of his lifework. With such special gifts as he had—and in the area of his strength, each was very strong indeed: they were almost perfect types—the individual constructed his own universe and lived in it; and reflecting on what he had done and been, he tried to describe it in a piece of writing: Fox in a *Journal* and Darwin in an *Autobiography*, Mill in an *Autobiography* and Newman in an *Apologia pro vitâ suâ.* With more or less awareness, they projected metaphors for the state of their being at the moment of composing. (I think the extent to which they were aware of creating and projecting metaphors is probably progressive in the order given—Fox not at all, Darwin very slightly, Mill somewhat, and Newman greatly aware; which also is a fair judgment on their general awareness and self-awareness as men.) Whether he intended it to be so or not, each of them revealed what he was in the autobiographic moment by the quality of consciousness with which he revealed what he had done in the past. What one discovers in these autobiographical writings is that the man reconstructs his universe and impresses himself on it by the metaphor that he finds appropriate to reconstructing his own history. It would be true to say of these men, I think, that their autobiographies are, in several senses, the most *typical* of their works.

1. Fox: "I'll firk him!"

George Fox, as one can plainly see in "yᵉ great Jornall of my Life, Sufferings, Travills and Imprisonments,"[1] had a

---

[1] *The Journal of George Fox*, ed. Norman Penney, 2 vols. (Cambridge: Cambridge Univ. Press, 1911), II, 347. The textual problem with Fox's *Journal* is a complicated one. Fox did not, in general, keep a running journal or diary. At different times in his life he dictated his memoirs, intending them for eventual publication. A committee of Quakers was formed at his death to edit and publish his papers; Thomas Ellwood led the committee and was responsible for editing the *Journal*. In this first edition of the *Journal* (1694, followed by a second volume composed of letters in 1698), Ellwood collated material from various sources and freely adapted what he put together, smoothing here and correcting there, omitting material in one place and adding his own material in another. This, and revisions of it, was the *Journal* until the present century. In 1911 Norman Penney edited (*verbatim et literatim*) the MS *Journal* in two volumes and in 1925 the MS *Short Journal, Itinerary Journals*, and *Haistwell Diary*. This uniform three-volume edition reproduced most of the source material of Ellwood's original version of George Fox's *Journal*. In 1924 Penney edited a new, abbreviated version of the *Journal* for Cambridge University Press which

difficult passage through the world. Time and again that physical world of men and facts vented its collective wrath on Fox: it beat him with "hands, Bibles, and sticks," it bit, pummeled, and kicked him, abused him with dog-whips and horse-whips, doused him with water and worse, it "firked" him generally —but to no avail. His persecutors were quite unsuccessful in their assault on the leader of the Children of the Light. "I was mazed and dazzled with the blows," Fox says of one such drubbing (*Journal*, p. 44), but in fact it mattered little how his body might be punished, for what his tormentors were after they could never touch, and yet it was always there to sustain Fox in his troubles. The "inward Light," the "openings" of God, the source and surety of Fox's faith, were forever inaccessible to them (unless, as sometimes happened, they looked and found the inner light within themselves; then, instead of seeking to destroy the light in another, they became "convinced" and accepted the quaking profession with George Fox himself). For all its brute strength, the world could never change George Fox by a jot. Not only was he of an extraordinarily strong constitution, and so could survive his trials, but physical pains and pleasures—the relation of the body to its physical environment—seem to have mattered little more than

---

drew material from the Ellwood edition and from the 1911 *Journal* and the *Short Journal*. This edition was reproduced in a popular version in Everyman. In 1952 John L. Nickalls re-edited the *Journal* for Cambridge, drawing upon all earlier sources and editions and including as well some material from Fox's *American Diaries* and other minor sources. At present the only editions still in print are the Everyman (from Penney's edition of 1924), available both in England and the U.S., and, in the U.S. only, a version edited from the Ellwood text by Rufus Jones in 1930, originally called *George Fox: An Autobiography* and now, reissued as a Capricorn paperback, called *The Journals of George Fox*.

All the editions mentioned have been consulted. Nickalls' edition is unquestionably the best and most useful of them all, yet once or twice one would like to refer to passages not included in his text. All references, therefore, except where otherwise noted, will be to this edition by Nickalls of 1952.

nothing to him. Sensation was not his mode. Fox gave no sign of the world's treatment of him; indeed, except in negative ways, he gave little recognition that the world even existed.

To turn from Montaigne and Jung, who may have had their troubles but who always got on with the world somehow, to George Fox is like turning our attention to a quite different species in nature. No longer is the subject large and genial, pre-eminently aware of self and of other selves, twofold and three-dimensional. George Fox is indeed a fascinating and appealing figure, but his appeal is single and partial, evoking a response not from the whole man and from all men, but from one only aspect of the human composite and from a few men alone. There are many explanations and justifications for it, but the fact is that Fox is narrow—very narrow. He only knows, only means one single thing, and that single knowledge and meaning are themselves drastically limited. It will advance one nowhere to try to take Fox as a full and characteristic human being. Fox, a man of a single talent (albeit more valuable to him than all other talents combined), stands at the furthest extreme from the ideal of Renaissance Man. His specific character (specific in every sense: he is like a particular species unto himself) is best suggested not by adjectives that multiply variety but by adjectives that qualify and limit and restrict. He is religious man, but of a particular variety—mystical-religious man. But, again, he is mystical-religious man of a very particular sort, or in a restricted sense—puritanical-mystical-religious man. He is, in short, George Fox. If Montaigne is a man of multifold vision who sees in all directions at once, with a comprehensive, 360-degree vision of the created world and human consciousness of that world, Fox stands as a great cyclops with one eye square in the middle of a flat forehead, an eye incapable of movement, set in a head which cannot rotate; an eye staring always straight east with no knowledge of a north or a south, much less of a west. Or perhaps one could better say that he stares straight up or in, with no awareness of either human variety, the points of the compass, or human frailty, the earthly base on which he stands.

In reading Fox it is well to remember always that he represents a very special, perhaps very alien case. We must understand that he was commanded of the Lord; that the command was made manifest to him in an Inner Voice and Spirit; that this Voice represents mystic awareness of a spiritual power inside and beyond individual self; and that it was at the behest of this Voice that he looked continuously and rigidly in one direction. Fox heard the Voice; he knew the Presence; he did as he had to do. Now it is sometimes true that as we consider Fox's actions in response to the Voice, it seems to us that the Voice came to him with strange injunctions. Yet Fox knew that his part was not to question but, having heard, to do. So, for example, in the passage which is very likely the most famous in the *Journal*, Fox did not hesitate in taking off his shoes and walking into Lichfield.

> I went over hedge and ditch till I came within a mile of Lichfield. When I came into a great field where there were shepherds keeping their sheep, I was commanded of the Lord to pull off my shoes of a sudden; and I stood still, and the word of the Lord was like a fire in me; and being winter, I untied my shoes and put them off; and when I had done I was commanded to give them to the shepherds and was to charge them to let no one have them except they paid for them. And the poor shepherds trembled and were astonished.
>
> So I went about a mile till I came into the town, and as soon as I came within the town the word of the Lord came unto me again to cry, "Woe unto the bloody city of Lichfield!"; so I went up and down the streets crying, "Woe unto the bloody city of Lichfield!" Being market day I went into the market place and went up and down in several places of it and made stands, crying, "Woe unto the bloody city of Lichfield!" and no one touched me nor laid hands on me. As I went down the town there ran like a channel of blood down the streets, and the market place was like a pool of blood.

And so at last some friends and friendly people came to me and said, "Alack, George! where are thy shoes?" and I told them it was no matter; so when I declared what was upon me and cleared myself, I came out of the town in peace about a mile to the shepherds: and there I went to them and took my shoes and gave them some money, but the fire of the Lord was so in my feet and all over me that I did not matter to put my shoes on any more and was at a stand whether I should or no till I felt freedom from the Lord so to do.

And so at last I came to a ditch and washed my feet and put on my shoes. *(Journal, pp. 71-72.)*

Fox goes on to explain why the Voice should have commanded his cry of "Woe" ("But after, I came to see that there were a thousand martyrs in Lichfield in the Emperor Diocletian's time"). His reasoning and explaining are, in fact, weak and unconvincing. But this is hardly the point. The explanations are feeble because they lack any sense of pressure or immediacy or necessity. They do not ring of experience. When Fox describes the Voice, however—which was a motive *before* the event, not a reasoned explanation after—it comes from profound depths of immediate experience.

It was just such immediate and mystic experience that Fox claimed as the base of all his knowledge, a knowledge that was severely narrow but awesomely deep. When he came to Lichfield, no one could have convinced him logically that he should act in that unaccountable way; but the Voice made him know he had to act so. No one could have persuaded him by reason, or by talking of the Emperor Diocletian's or any other time, that his feet ought to be warm if, in experiential fact, they were not warm. But he felt them warm, knew them warm; and then reason had no powers to persuade him that they should be cold. What, one might ask, is "should be" in the face of "is"? What is reason in the face of experience? In such an event, the rational intellect, a single part, after all, of a whole organism, is nowhere, simply bypassed by the direct experience of the entire being. This kind of knowledge, which

159

is had by each of us singly, uniquely, individually, experientially, or it is not had at all, is the only sure knowledge. Logic, reason, abstract persuasion of what should be is, by comparison, pale and wan, bloodless, lifeless. It is only this kind of knowledge of the existent that can effectually move our will. Reason can be refuted; experience cannot. Likewise, there is no rational or logical validation for experience and the mystic has, necessarily and by definition, to depend for his being on a-logical, nonrational, direct experience. Here is Fox's description of how and what he knows, coming as a gracious salvation:

> And when all my hopes in them and in all men were gone, so that I had nothing outwardly to help me, nor could tell what to do, then, Oh then, I heard a voice which said, "There is one, even Christ Jesus, that can speak to thy condition," and when I heard it my heart did leap for joy. Then the Lord did let me see why there was none upon the earth that could speak to my condition, namely, that I might give him all the glory; for all are concluded under sin, and shut up in unbelief as I had been, that Jesus Christ might have the pre-eminence, who enlightens, and gives grace, and faith, and power. Thus, when God doth work who shall let it? And this I knew experimentally.
>
> (*Journal*, p. 11.)[2]

Only when Fox understands that there is "nothing outwardly to help me" and that "there was none upon the earth that could speak to my condition," does he hear the voice which

[2] On the "otherness" of the voice that Fox heard, cf. Jung: "The God-image thrown up by a spontaneous act of creation is a living figure, a being that exists in its own right and therefore confronts its ostensible creator autonomously. As proof of this it may be mentioned that the relation between the creator and the created is a *dialectical* one, and that, as experience shows, man has often been the person who is addressed. From this the naïve-minded person concludes, rightly or wrongly, that the figure produced exists in and for itself, and he is inclined to assume that it was not he who fashioned it, but that it fashioned itself in him—a possibility which no amount of criticism can disprove, since the genesis of this figure is a natural process with a teleological orientation in which the cause anticipates the goal" (*Symbols of Transformation, CW*, v, par. 95).

was always there, within and beyond, to speak to his condition. And this he knew in one way only—the word is of central importance: "experimentally." This he knew, in other words, by all that he was, a conjunction of all that happened to him and all that he happened back with.

Profoundly "convinced" himself, Fox, in turn, set about to convince the world. He brought a certain number of people into the Light and he successfully faced down a number of others who denied the Light, but the world, naturally, for the most part went on its usual, merry way. No matter. Fox continued to testify, in season and out, up and down England, Scotland, Wales, and Ireland, in Holland, and in savage North America and Barbados, to the Inner Voice; and sometimes, through the strength of his very conviction and his voice, he carried the day. "I will not be afraid of thee," one judge told Fox, who always moved quickly to the attack in such encounters, when Fox was brought before the court for refusing to swear an oath; "thou speaks so loud, thy Voice drowns mine and the Court's, I must call for three or four Cryers to drown thy Voice, thou hast good lungs."[3] He had good lungs, no doubt, but his voice was thus strong because through it, Fox was sure, spoke another Voice. The strength of Fox's appeal, however, lay not so much in the message he proclaimed (intellectually a very slight thing, after all) as in the power of his personality—that personality that shone out from the center of his conviction like a lamp of the Lord. He seems to have been living evidence, for those who were prepared to respond, of the transformative power of mystic experience. He had, according to all whom he met, a piercing eye that could terrify the wicked and compel and comfort the devout. His good lungs and his sharp eye, his voice and his vision, were alike ascribed by Fox to his experience of the divine.

[3] *Examination and Trial of Margaret Fell and George Fox . . .* etc., in *Harleian Miscellany*, VI (London, 1745), 261.

Moreover, the commitment between Fox and his God was a reciprocal one. Fox testified to his conviction, and God responded with evidence to show that his servant's conviction was not a delusion. Fox was certain that, with the great openings he had, he could work medical cures for the good of mankind, and he was half inclined to become a doctor. Instead, however, he devoted his curative powers to things of the spirit, and in that realm he worked miraculous cures that might have been considered natural had he pursued the revelations that he claimed in physical medicine. In Coleshill, for example, he cured the King's evil in a girl by laying on of hands and prayer; in Hawkshead he restored to perfect health an eleven-year-old boy, although "all doctors had given him over"; in Arnside he returned to Prophet Myers the use of an arm "which had been lame for a long time"; in Baldock, "to the astonishment of the town and country," he raised up a woman who, her family was sure, "was not a woman for this world"; and in New Jersey in far-off America, when Friend John Jay was thrown from his horse "and broke his neck as they called it, and the people took him up dead," then Fox

took him by the hair of his head, and his head turned like a cloth it was so loose. I threw away my stick and gloves, and took his head in both my hands, and set my knees against the tree and wrested his head and I did perceive it was not broken out that way. And I put my hand under his chin, and behind his head, and wrested his head two or three times with all my strength, and brought it in, and I did perceive his neck began to be stiff, and then he began to rattle, and after to breathe, and the people were amazed, and I bid them have a good heart and be of good faith, and carry him into the house, and then they set him by the fire, and I bid them get him some warm thing to drink and get him to bed. So after he had been in the house awhile, he began to speak, and did not know where he had been. So we bound up his neck warm with a napkin, and the next day we passed on and he with us, pretty well, about sixteen miles to

a meeting at Middletown, and many hundreds of miles afterwards, through the woods and bogs.[4]

Fox details cure after cure of this sort, both in his *Journal* and
in his "Book of Miracles" (which was never published, though
Fox intended it to be, and is now lost; but see *George Fox's
"Book of Miracles*," edited by Henry Cadbury, for its contents). In these miraculous cures, of course, Fox saw not his
own virtue—he would have denied that they were "natural"—
but the beneficent power and a striking evidence of God.

There were also, as signs of God's power working through
George Fox, miracles that were the reverse of cures—viz., the
sufferings and punishments that befell those who persecuted
Quakers and did not leave off until God had made an example
of them. The wretched John Line, who carried some Children
of the Light to jail and then took a false oath against them, was
one such terrible example:

> John Line, constable, died in the year 1682 a sad spectacle to
> behold; he grievously rotted away alive, and so died his wife
> also (being a persecutor) after the same manner or the like ex-
> ample. . . . This John Line did confess that he never prospered
> since he laid hands on the Quakers . . . and wished he had never
> meddled with them, and said he never prospered since . . . and
> said he was sorry he had a hand in persecuting the Quakers, and
> also that he would never meddle with them more, and said he
> thought the hand of the Lord was against him for it.[5]

Even for the miserable John Line, though he was too late in
seeing it, the Light was not entirely obscured.

It is a cardinal point of Fox's belief and Quaker doctrine
that the Inner Light shines potentially within all men; or, in
the expression that Tolstoy, the founder of another private religion, chose as the title for one of his books, *The Kingdom of*

[4] *Journal*, pp. 707, 172, 147, 228, 631-32.
[5] *Short Journal*, p. 80; modernized spelling is adopted from *George Fox's
"Book of Miracles*," p. 146. Cf. also Nickalls, p. 442.

God is Within You. One should search for truth first of all not anywhere else but in life of the most private and isolate sort. Truth for Fox and his descendant Quakers lives not in Scripture, not in history, not in tradition, not in a church visible or invisible, not even in the natural world. Look within, into individual, interior life: there and there only does, or can, the Spirit live. It cannot live in an object (e.g., a crucifix), nor in a building (e.g., a church, in Fox's scornful phrase always referred to as "a steeple-house"), nor in a book (e.g., Scripture: "then they might carry the spirit in their pockets as they did the Scriptures"; *Journal*, p. 36), but only in the life of the individual and his immediate experience. For a mystic of Fox's purifying temper, none of these is likely to sway; the great temptation is the natural world. Nature is the apparent cause of all things. Why, then, not reverence nature as the Spirit? Why not fade away into nature and under natural laws, achieving thereby the desired mystic union? Fox, though at one time sorely tempted by nature, sat quietly until the true Voice came to him to make strong his faith in a personal and supernatural God:

> And one morning, as I was sitting by the fire, a great cloud came over me, and a temptation beset me; but I sat still. And it was said, "All things come by nature"; and the elements and stars came over me so that I was in a manner quite clouded with it. But inasmuch as I sat, still and silent, the people of the house perceived nothing. And as I sat still under it and let it alone, a living hope arose in me, and a true voice, which said, "There is a living God who made all things." And immediately the cloud and temptation vanished away, and life rose over it all, and my heart was glad, and I praised the living God.
>
> (*Journal*, p. 25.)

Thus nature herself is but a secondary cause, an expression of the living spirit, as also are, for example, the Scriptures. God is the beginning and end of all things, not Scripture, nor nature, nor created humanity. Living in that spirit and with the Spirit living in him, Fox records opening after opening after opening from the Lord (the phrase, signifying direct revelation in experience, is familiar to every reader of the *Journal*).

> Now the Lord God hath opened to me by his invisible power how that every man was enlightened by the divine light of Christ; and I saw it shine through all. . . . This I saw in the pure openings of the Light without the help of any man, neither did I then know where to find it in the Scriptures; though afterwards, searching the Scriptures, I found it. For I saw in that Light and Spirit which was before Scripture was given forth. . . .
>
> Now I was sent to turn people from darkness to the light that they might receive Christ Jesus, for to as many as should receive him in his light, I saw that he would give power to become the sons of God, which I had obtained by receiving Christ. And I was to direct people to the Spirit that gave forth the Scriptures, by which they might be led into all truth, and so up to Christ and God, as they had been who gave them forth. (*Journal*, pp. 33-34.)

The Spirit gives life, and in the life the Spirit lives. This is the ultimate union, simultaneous and paradoxical completion of personality and loss of personality. The self is transcended and absorbed in the divine when it discovers that it is but a spark and a manifestation, a momentary and human realization, of the divine.

Few people would claim mystic experience and fewer still would know how to communicate any sense of what it might be like. It is the sort of experience that is, par excellence, nontransferable. What the mystic has experienced, what he knows, is ineffable, literally unspeakable, incommensurate with human language and finite communication. When Fox hears the Voice, it is a sound not shaped by human lips nor to a human ear; when he sees the Light, it shines within him alone. For Fox the cognitive process is entirely a question of the graciously given and the interiorly apprehended, of deductive intuition and a priori feeling. In the *Journal*, the human drama parades itself not across the stage of the world but across the stage of Fox's consciousness in and of the Inner Light. Everything in the outer world is read by him in the light of this inner reality.

The mystic in any case has little use for rational thought, and when it happens that his mysticism is wed to puritanism, as with Fox, he has even less use for sensory experience of the created world. As a Puritan, Fox sought to "purify" belief and practice until they were free of the human smudge and smell, until they were again of the original essence. He was vehemently opposed to set ritual, to religious ornamentation, to the visible and manifest church, because these would all seem to suggest, in contradiction of his direct perception, that the Spirit can live in a physical, material, sensible (hence, dead) thing.[6] Likewise, Fox scorns all art, religious or secular, for art seemed to claim that the Spirit, or a spirit, can be contained in matter. Fox's denunciation of one especially licentious man is climaxed by reference to his known practice of writing poetry: "I was moved to go and speak to one of the wickedest men in the county, one who was a common drunkard, a noted whore-master, and a rhyme-maker; and I reproved him in the dread of the mighty God for his evil courses" (*Journal*, pp. 26-27). His purifying temper carried Fox back, not like any seventeenth-century Anglican divine to the "primitive church," but to that which was before churches, before Scripture, before men, before nature herself. He yearned for the real beginning where there was the Word, where there was God, where there was spirit and only spirit—for "God,"

[6] One might ask where the spirit of George Fox lived if not in a physical, material, sensible thing. The answer suggests the extremity of his view, as well as the unreality of his "philosophy," but I believe we should have to say that in theory Fox did literally deny the body.

"the Word," and "Spirit" are all synonyms in our feeble human attempt to name the unnameable. What Fox revered was something altogether disembodied and pure, something invisible, intangible, inaudible. At least it was this to the external world, but by the interior world of the spirit it could be seen and heard, tasted and even touched.

Whenever Fox speaks in sensory terms, as in fact he does rather often, he is not talking about the ears and eyes with which we apprehend the world. By an interesting psychological process, the senses are all internalized with Fox to become metaphors adapted to the only reality: pure spirit. In the experience at Lichfield, "the word of the Lord was like a fire in me" and "the fire of the Lord was so in my feet" that the cold was impotent to harm Fox. And "when first I set my horse's feet a-top of the Scottish ground I felt the Seed of God to sparkle about me like innumerable sparks of fire, though there is abundance of thick, cloddy earth of hypocrisy and falseness that is a-top, and a briary, brambly nature which is to be burnt up with God's word" (*Journal*, p. 331). The Puritan-mystic transforms the senses to a new object (spirit) and new uses (knowing spirit). To look on outward beauties, Fox says, or to taste the dainties of the world, is perversion; therefore, he adjures in a letter "To Friends in Barbados, Virginia, Maryland, New England, and elsewhere," look and feed interiorly:

> Oh! Friends, You all that have tasted of the *Power* of the *Lord God*, and of his *Truth*, that is pure, and doth not admit of any impurity nor change . . . mind the pure *Power* of the *Lord God* . . . and whatsoever is gotten up through the *Carnal* Reason, and your *Eyes* going from the *Power* of *God* . . . let that be purged out of your *Hearts*. . . . I feel some *Minds*, and some *Bodies* have let in that which hath defiled them, and doth defile them: O *Cleanse, cleanse, cleanse,* and *joyn* to the pure *Immortal Power*; for the *Power* of the *Lord God* will make

167

room for it self, either in cleansing, or in vomiting, or casting out. . . . The *Beesom* of the *Lord* is going forth to sweep, the *Candle* of the *Lord* is lighted to search every corner of your *Houses*; for the *Just* walks in the *Path*, which is a *shining Light*, which admits of no rubbish in it. . . . Keep out the *Lusts* of the *Eye*, the *Lusts* of the *Flesh*, and *Pride* of *Life*, *which is not of the Father*. . . . Therefore all *Friends* and *People*, mind that which first convinced you, that *Power* of *God* which first awakened you, and arise and live in it, that all your *Eyes*, *Minds* and *Hearts* may be kept single and naked to *God*, and to one another; and uncloathed of all that which is contrary, and is got up since: For the *Seed* and the *Life* of *Christ Jesus* reigns and rules, Glory to him for ever.[7]

Fox, one supposes from this letter, had heard about "carnal reason" and about the palate in the mouth and the eyes of the body, but they were as little powerful in their appeal to him as is the inner apprehension of the mystic for the man who has never been touched by that experience.

In each of Fox's attempts to describe the indescribable one feels that the real experience was undoubtedly quite different and unutterably private; that this mode of figurative expression, powerful as it is, is hopelessly inadequate to Fox's desires. To describe a vision of pure spirit must be impossible, but Fox tries, through symbols and metaphors, to render some sense of God's presence and his own vision of God's love. (Because his senses were turned inward, however, I imagine that Fox would not have thought of these as symbols or metaphors: they were instead something like direct spirit-sense experiences.)

And I went back into Nottinghamshire, and there the Lord shewed me that the natures of those things which were hurtful without were within, in the hearts and minds of wicked men.

[7] *A Collection of Many Select and Christian Epistles . . . by that Ancient, Eminent, Faithful Friend and Minister of Christ Jesus, George Fox* (published as vol. II of first edition of the *Journal*; London, 1698), pp. 226-27.

... I saw also that there was an ocean of darkness and death, but an infinite ocean of light and love, which flowed over the ocean of darkness. And in that also I saw the infinite love of God; and I had great openings. . . .

And I saw into that which was without end, and things which cannot be uttered, and of the greatness and infiniteness of the love of God, which cannot be expressed by words. For I had been brought through the very ocean of darkness and death, and through the power and over the power of Satan, by the eternal glorious power of Christ. . . . Then could I say I had been in spiritual Babylon, Sodom, Egypt, and the grave; but by the eternal power of God I was come out of it, and was brought over it and the power of it, into the power of Christ. And I saw the harvest white, and the Seed of God lying thick in the ground, as ever did wheat that was sown outwardly, and none to gather it; and for this I mourned with tears.

(*Journal*, pp. 19-21.)

The Seed of the Spirit, the seed of self transformed, lies within for cultivation, for growth, for harvest. This is the metaphor, or one of them, that Fox discovered for his experience and, although not adequate, it proved again and again usable, coming up finally as the last words in the account that Thomas Ellwood gives of Fox's death: "Diverse Friends came to visit him in his Ilness; unto some of whom he said, 'All is well: The *Seed* of God reigns over all, and over Death it self. And though (*said he*) I am weak in Body; yet the *Power* of *God* is over all, and the *Seed* reigns over all disorderly Spirits.' "[8] This is the final transformation of the finite self in the infinite Light, the last fructification of the Seed in this single life, the complete union and reunion of the individual with the first cause and the final principle. The circle of mystic experience is thus closed when the divine Seed, become the human fruit, becomes again, in death, the seed of life.

This movement through many momentary circles of self-completion to the one perfect and final circle of reunion is,

[8] *Journal*, ed. Ellwood, 1st ed. (London, 1694), pp. 613-14.

for a man of Fox's temperament, simply the abstracted human pattern which realizes the divine intention, a pattern always under the immediate direction of the power of divine love. This, of course, is the single, great subject for all mystics and writers on mysticism: union achieved through love, through God's loving desire that we beseech union with him, and the soul's loving response which ensures that union. The prime mover who lovingly sets creation in motion, being too great, as the author of *The Cloud of Unknowing* tells us, for the fragmentary response of the intellect, is accessible only to a reciprocal "loving power," a response of the total being. "All reasonable creatures," this fourteenth-century mystic says, "angel and man, have in them, each one by himself, one principal working power, the which is called a knowing power, and another principal working power, the which is called a loving power. Of the which two powers, to the first, the which is a knowing power, God who is the maker of them is evermore incomprehensible; but to the second, the which is the loving power, he is, in every man diversely, all comprehensible to the full."[9] Fox was a man of the pure and immaterial spirit, moving in responsive loving power toward the very source of his own movement. "And as I walked towards the gaol," he says of one of his many temporal afflictions, "the word of the Lord came to me saying, 'My love was always to thee, and thou art in my love.' And I was ravished with the sense of the love of God and greatly strengthened in my inward man" (*Journal*, p. 46). This, the center of Fox's life and career, leads to all sorts of consequent actions and reactions, beliefs, and conclusions: it leads to Fox's egalitarianism; to his puritanism; to his personalism in religious practice; and to the world's reaction to Fox and his teaching. It leads, in a word,

---

[9] *The Cloud of Unknowing and Other Treatises*, ed. Dom Justin McCann (Westminster, Md.: Newman Press, 1952), chap. IV, pp. 10-11.

to Quakerism, the religion founded and blooded in Fox's own life.

This first Quaker, confirmed in and by the supernatural, had no use at all for temporal categories. Social, political, economic distinctions just meant nothing to Fox, and this is true everywhere, with high and with low. The only distinction Fox admitted was spiritual, depending upon the degree to which a given man submitted to, recognized, and witnessed the Inner Light shining within all. Fox was as unbending before Cromwell and Charles II, with both of whom he had dealings on behalf of his coreligionists, as he was uncondescending to the lowest of the low.[10] It was Fox's claim—a claim he maintained not for himself uniquely but for every man equally—that he was not a priest of an established church but was instead a prophet-apostle of the Inner Light, not an intermediary

[10] Cf. Fox's abrupt address to Charles II on the subject of persecuted Quakers: "FOR THE KING—Friend, Who art the chief ruler of these dominions, here is a list of some of the sufferings of the people of God, in scorn called Quakers, that have suffered under the changeable powers before thee" (*Journal*, p. 423). The divine threat implied later in this letter is clearly spelled out in an earlier letter to the King:

King Charles,

Thou camest not into this Nation by *Sword*, nor by *Victory* of *War*; but by the *Power* of the *Lord*: Now if thou dost not live in it, thou wilt not prosper. . . . And if thou do not stop *Persecution*, and *Persecutors*, and take away all *Laws*, that do hold up *Persecution* about Religion; but if thou do persist in them, and uphold *Persecution*; that will make thee as *blind*, as them that have gone before thee. For *Persecution* hath always *blinded* those, that have gone into it: And such *God* by his *Power* over-*throws*, and doth his *Valiant Acts* upon; and bringeth Salvation to his *Oppressed* ones. And if thou dost bear the *Sword in vain*, and let *Drunkenness, Oaths, Plays, May-games*, (with *Fidlers, Drums, Trumpets*, to play at them) with such like Abominations and Vanities be encouraged, or go unpunished; as setting up of *May-poles*, with the Image of the *Crown* a top of them, &c. the Nations will quickly turn like Sodom and Gomorrah, and be as bad as the *Old World*; who grieved the Lord, till he overthrew them: And so he will you, if these things be not suddenly prevented.

(This was written by Fox while in jail but, as always, impenitent: *Journal*, ed. Ellwood, 1st ed., p. 225.)

171

between God and man but, like every man, a very temple of the Holy Ghost. In America, Fox effectively confuted a doctor who maintained a spiritual aristocracy by calling in an Indian and demonstrating that the Indian, equally with the doctor or any man, had "the Light and the Spirit" potentially within him.

The Inner Light, resident within every individual, admits no terms of comparison between different men. Fox, because his mystic vision disallowed all worldly distinctions, consistently, and to the extreme discontent of the world as he again and again encountered it, refused all formal, artificial modes of division. In his address to others Fox doggedly pursued his principle of equality: "Moreover when the Lord sent me forth into the world, he forbade me to put off my hat to any, high or low; and I was required to 'thee' and 'thou' all men and women, without any respect to rich or poor, great or small" (*Journal*, p. 36). Adopting the plain dress of a plain people, Fox finally, against his principle, became distinguished by the plain leather breeches in which he always appeared, "so that it was a dreadful thing unto them [the "priests" of the established church] when it was told them, 'The man in leathern breeches is come'" (*Journal*, p. 83). And if he did not want to render homage to society, no more did he want the world to distinguish him by presenting its formal gestures as a mark of respect. Major Ceely, the justice who had arrested Fox and then, seeing him in the prison-yard, removed his hat and spoke civilly ("How do you, Mr. Fox? Your servant, Sir"), got this for abrupt response: "Major Ceely, take heed of hypocrisy and a rotten heart, for when came I to be thy master and thee my servant?" (*Journal*, p. 250).

In every way a Puritan, for whom the Spirit lived subjectively, purely, and privately, Fox disregarded the outer phenomenal world—that part of experience that we ordinarily take as objective, real, and factual—as completely as Darwin

ever did the inner world of individual subjective experience.
It is not that Fox successfully resists the sensory pull and appeal; rather, as a Puritan drawn by the pure and inner vision
from the age of eleven, he is simply blank to the swarm of
the senses, as if that were no reality at all for him.

> When I came to eleven years of age, I knew pureness and
> righteousness; for while I was a child I was taught how to
> walk to be kept pure. . . . For the Lord showed me. . . . that
> I might not eat and drink to make myself wanton but for health,
> using the creatures in their service, as servants in their places,
> to the glory of him that hath created them; they being in their
> covenant, and I being brought up into the covenant, as sancti-
> fied by the Word which was in the beginning, by which all
> things are upheld; wherein is unity with the creation.
>
> (*Journal*, pp. 1-2.)

Fox was as committed to finding an abiding meaning and significance in human existence as Darwin would later be committed to discovering the laws of change and evolution in the
natural creation. And with Fox as with Darwin—the two polar
opposites—the denial of total self discovers its fit punishment
—if, that is, the necessary conclusion to faith and action should
be called punishment. Darwin, obliterating in his discipline
the private half of selfhood, was visited by sickness eventually
traceable to the denied realm of the unconscious psyche; Fox,
acting as if the world itself were unreal, found that world
striking, biting, howling to prove its solid reality. Reversing
Dr. Johnson's famous "refutation" of Bishop Berkeley's philosophy of immaterial spirit,[11] the material world kicked Fox
time after time by way of demonstrating that it existed independently and objectively, outside the consciousness of any

---

[11] Boswell: "I observed, that though we are satisfied his doctrine is not
true, it is impossible to refute it. I never shall forget the alacrity with which
Johnson answered, striking his foot with mighty force against a large stone,
till he rebounded from it, 'I refute it *thus*'" (*Life of Johnson* [London:
Oxford Univ. Press, 1952], p. 333).

necessary perceiving mind. The response made to Fox and his determined followers by the local ruling establishment, in the various guises of priest, magistrate, jailer, and good citizen, was no more and no less than one might expect. "Oh, the blows, punchings, beatings, and imprisonments that we underwent for not putting off our hats to men!" (*Journal*, p. 37). Describing a particular encounter of individual spirit with the massed and unhappy forces of the world, Fox tells how he was set upon, knocked down, kicked and trampled in the steeple-house, beaten out into the streets, thrown down and pounded with sticks and finally left unconscious in a watery ditch until revived and raised up by the Spirit that sustained him: "There I lay a pretty space, and when I recovered myself again, and saw myself lying on a watery common and all the people standing about me, I lay a little still, and the power of the Lord sprang through me, and the eternal refreshings refreshed me, that I stood up again in the eternal power of God and stretched out my arms amongst them all, and said again with a loud voice, 'Strike again, here is my arms and my head and my cheeks.'" The world, of course, ready as it always is to do violence against the strong-lunged individual who stands apart in its despite, did exactly as Fox asked, proving to itself its own reality, but proving nothing to Fox except its real non-existence before the spirit.

> And there was a mason, a rude fellow, a professor called, he gave me a blow with all his might just a-top of my hand, as it was stretched out, with his walking rule-staff. And my hand and arm was so numbed and bruised that I could not draw it in unto me again but it stood out as it was. Then the people cried out, "He hath spoiled his hand, for ever having any use of it more." The skin was struck off my hand and a little blood came, and I looked at it in the love of God, and I was in the love of God to them all that had persecuted me.
>
> And after a while the Lord's power sprang through me again, and through my hand and arm, that in a minute I re-

covered my hand and arm and strength in the face and sight of them all and it was as well as it was before. (*Journal*, p. 128.)

In structure and style the *Journal* is like this throughout: it is Fox's great daybook of openings on the one hand and encounters with a hostile world on the other. These two kinds of experience, the visionary glory within and the harsh reality without, are loosely connected in a simple, chronological, and Biblical style. "And so after, I passed through the country and. . . . I was moved to go from a meeting in Nottinghamshire to a steeplehouse. . . . And I went to Gainsborough. . . . And after, the wicked priest went and raised a slander upon us. . . . And so I passed out of the country in the Lord's power. . . . And after this I went to Warmsworth steeplehouse. . . . And so after I went to another steeplehouse in the afternoon" (*Journal*, pp. 95-97). Seven paragraph beginnings, chosen at random, reveal the logic of the *Journal*: it is composed of moments of the spirit in the world, manifestations of the nontemporal under temporal conditions, strung together in chronological series as paragraphs. Except for this chronological "and so . . . and so . . . and so" arrangement, the *Journal* is structurally a shambles, a patchwork of fits and starts. But this is as it must be. Fox does not appear to us as a cogent and organized reasoner (like Newman, for example, or Mill), whose logic is revealed in the shape of his prose and his book, but as a mystic of momentary insight. As he is, so is his book.

Fox's life was guided by his intuitive/experimental knowledge of the divine. And he was, or claimed to be, intuitive in the more common usage of that word as well: he had the sort of intuition that could foretell what would happen (he records premonitions of both good and evil events which later came to be) or that could reveal in a flash the inner state of another person's heart and soul. He could see a witch and know she was one ("I cast my eye upon an unclean woman and told her she was a witch. . . . and people told me that I had discovered a great thing, for all the country looked upon her to be a witch"), or look on a prostitute and name her sin ("there came in also at another time a woman and stood a little off from me and I cast my eye upon her; and I said she had been an harlot, for I perfectly saw the condition and life of the woman"), and neither the witch nor the harlot could deny the truth of his discernment. "The Lord had given me a spirit of discerning by which I many times saw the states and conditions of people, and would try their spirits." In like manner, the last time he saw James Nayler before that unhappy man took his fateful ride into Bristol,[12] Fox knew that bad days were ahead for the Quakers as well as for Nayler ("And as I parted from him I cast my eyes upon him, and a fear struck in me concerning him"), and his final meeting with Cromwell revealed to Fox that the Protector was soon to be a dead man ("I met

[12] Nayler suffered his terrible fate for going the same way as Fox, only much further. He, too, perceived outer events through the medium of the Inner Light, and scorned the power of the world in that Light; but where Fox merely saw external reality in his own, unusual way, Nayler mistook and misjudged it entirely. He allowed his female followers to address him as "everlasting Son of Righteousness and Prince of Peace," the "fairest of ten thousand," and "only begotten Son of God"; he suffered them to kiss his feet and allowed them to precede him through great rain and mud on his horseback entry into Bristol, singing to him, "Holy, holy, holy, Lord God of Sabaoth, &c." His "crime" being greater than Fox's, the world came down on Nayler much harder. For his exaggerated devotion to the Voice within and his consequent loss of touch with reality—i.e., for his "horrid blasphemy" against the religion professed by the world that ruled—Nayler was pilloried and whipped through the streets of London, had a *B* (for blasphemy) burned into his forehead and a hot iron pierced through his tongue, was made to ride backwards and was whipped again through the streets of Bristol—and then was thrown back into jail. The world successfully broke Nayler; it never could break Fox. Of the event and of its implications for Quakers, Fox says simply, "a little before the time we were set at liberty, James ran out into imaginations, and a company with him; and they raised up a great darkness in the nation. And he came to Bristol and made a disturbance there" (*Journal*, p. 268). The account of Nayler's "horrid blasphemy" is from James Deacon's pamphlet. *The Grand Imposter examined: Or, the Life, Trial, and Examination of James Nayler, the seduced and seducing Quaker; with the Manner of his Riding into Bristol* (London, 1656).

him riding into Hampton-Court Park, and . . . I saw and felt a waft of death go forth against him, and he looked like a dead man").[13] These premonitions and intuitions, Fox believed, were only minor reflections or evidences of his one great intuition of everlasting truth.

Everything that the Fox of the *Journal* is and knows is based on isolated and transcendent moments, each complete in itself but otherwise unrelated to what goes before and after. Perhaps taken at the end, the life and the *Journal* portrait may exhibit a sort of pattern. If so, it would only be in the perception that the life was itself a spiritual moment—or better, a Moment composed not of cause and effect or action and consequence but simply of many, one-after-the-other, discrete and individual moments flowing into one. It is a valuable book that Fox gives us in his *Journal*: a brave and sincere attempt (thus being a mirror for its maker's character) to describe one unique way of living and one special life.

But the truth is that George Fox is not much read today and is probably not very popular with most of those who do happen to read him. I had occasion four or five years ago to discuss Fox's *Journal* as a document in the literature of autobiography with a group of college honors students. They told me, rather to my surprise, for my reaction had been quite different, that they didn't like the *Journal*—they didn't like reading it and they didn't like George Fox. Finally, I suppose, when one thinks about it, the reasons are not very far to seek. First, Fox is disastrously lacking in humor, particularly in the ability to see anything of the ridiculous in himself. He can—and this would be a remarkable achievement enough if it were not so obviously natural to him—tell the story of his appearance before "Judge Glynne, the Lord Chief Justice of England, a Welshman" without a hint that he sees anything ludicrous in the event and without recognizing, apparently, that

13 *Journal*, pp. 155, 156, 229-30, 350.

he and the judge appear to the reader not as two formidable champions representing God and Satan but as two rather foolish, if sincere, lunatics. The circumstances of the hearing were, undoubtedly, serious enough, but Fox is so solemn in his righteousness and the judge so heated and impotent in his attitudinizing that the story must seem rare farce indeed to most readers.

When first brought into court, Fox is moved, as he invariably was, to make the most impolitic of comments. This time, fortunately, the remark produces its effect immediately and needs not to be repeated as in fact the Lord, testing the loyalty of Fox's spirit, often required that it be: "We stood with our hats on a pretty while, and all was quiet. And I was moved to say: 'Peace be amongst you.'" For the redoubtable Judge Glynne once is enough, and so he to the jailer: "'What be these you have brought here into court?' 'Prisoners, my lord,' said he." For the judge, a social distinction, requiring respect from Fox, is obvious; for Fox, any distinction must be spiritual and must tell in his own favor. The stage is set for their circus of legal sparring and scriptural jockeying. Fox, by contemporary account, possessed a knowledge of the Bible sufficient that, had all copies been lost, he could have written it anew from memory; knowing his own strength, he cunningly leads the contest ever so quickly in that direction, while the judge, having misstepped into Fox's den, gathers his rags and tatters of social dignity, like judicial robes, as best he may about his embarrassingly exposed person.

"Why do you not put off your hats?" said the judge.
And we said nothing.
"Put off your hats," said the judge again.
But we said nothing.
Then again the judge:
"The court commands you to put off your hats."
And then I replied and said, "Where did ever any magistrate,

178

king, or judge from Moses to Daniel command any to put off their hats when they came before them into their courts amongst the Jews the people of God or amongst the heathen, or where did any of the heathen command any such thing in all their courts or their kings or judges? Or show me where it is written or printed in any law of England where any such thing is commanded; show it me and I will put off my hat."

And then the judge grew very angry and said, "I do not carry my law books on my back."

Then said I, "Tell me where it is printed in a statute book that I may read it."

Then said the judge, "Take him away, prevaricator, I'll firk him!"

Then they took us away and put us amongst the thieves; and presently after he calls to the gaoler, "Bring them up again."

"Come," said he, "where had they hats from Moses to Daniel? Come, answer me I have you fast now," said he.

Then I said, "Thou mayest read in the third of Daniel that the three children were cast into the fiery furnace by Nebuchadnezzar with their cloaks, hose, and hats on." And you may see that Nebuchadnezzar was not offended at their hats.

This plain instance stopped him: so that, not having anything else to say to the point, he cried again, "Take them away, jailer."[14]

To take off the shoes is one thing; to take off the hat quite another. Of course, it is true that God commanded in the one case, society in the other. If only Fox could see the comedy— but if he were outwardly conscious enough to see the joke he would not be George Fox. He always appears thus in his own description: sober, solemn, triumphant, righteous—and self-righteous. Finally brought to full trial, and after some by-play about his refusal to swear an oath, Fox concludes his account of the hat trick thus: "Then they let fall that subject [the oath]; and the Judge fell upon us about our hats again,

[14] *Journal*, pp. 243-44. The last paragraph, which is omitted in Nickalls' edition, is taken from the *Autobiography*, ed. Jones, pp. 246-47; cf. Everyman *Journal*, p. 122.

bidding the jailer take them off; which he did, and gave them to us; and we put them on again." The comedy is delicious—and all unconscious.

Another, and currently much more damaging, reason for the disregard into which Fox has fallen is the fact that exercise of the rational faculty is very far from being his strong suit. We are almost all, nowadays, rationalists—or pride ourselves on being so—open to conviction only through verifiable sensory experience in the external world. Intelligent and scientific thinkers, we do not want irrational or superrational experience; we do not want knowledge that we cannot handle and grasp with the rational intellect, that we cannot explain, that we cannot set down in "because," "thus," and "therefore" language and communicate persuasively to others; we refuse any understanding that suggests irresolvable paradox or final mystery, however profound or beautiful. And further, which is why we mistreat George Fox, we not only refuse that experience for ourselves by calling it hard names ("abnormal," "psychopathic") but we would also deny it to others. Our immediate reaction to someone who claims the experience and maintains its value is "lock him up." What we have not known intellectually is not accessible to anyone else in any other way, and to claim such experience is to be well deserving of punishment. "Prevaricators" should be taught a lesson. Tell all George Foxes that it cannot be, it must not be, it will not be. Explain, if necessary, about malfunctioning glands or organs and about manic-depressive states and sublimation and about the effects of geographic, economic, social environment. Or, like Francis Bugg, the disaffected Quaker, write a painstaking, endless, "rational" refutation of the "errors" of Fox. Show the Quakers and the world the eight or the twenty-three or the sixty-five points in which they are perverse and wrong. Reveal, as Bugg did in 682 folio pages, *The Great Mystery of the Little Whore* in which are "Hidden Things brought to

Light, whereby the Fox is Unkennell'd."[15] Reason with them. But if reason fails thus far, then kick them, for they are unreasonable, and when reason is frustrated by something beyond and outside itself, it has every reason to use force to convince unreasonable people. And George Fox is, beyond doubt, unreasonable.

But it does not all really matter. This is the cream of the mystic jest; this it is which so infuriates us as rational, logical, good (until crossed by irrationality), scientific people. We are justly enraged because these people still claim to know, to have the revelatory experience which we are sure we have proved cannot be. We will never forgive George Fox for having been so certain of himself, for having been happy, content, serene, undisturbed by our reasons against his experience. Why could he not at least take off his hat? We will never forgive him for not acknowledging his madness. We would like all to have been psychoanalysts of the time, so that we might reduce him to the sum of his childhood traumas; or at least let him know that we see through his game. Failing that, we are mostly like the judge: "I'll firk you George Fox, if you don't become reasonable and observe social amenities." We use what power we have against him, however, and "not having anything else to say to the point," we echo the judge's cry: "Take them away, jailer." So the rational world goes on, in this way at least like the mystic, that it may be too content in its half-world; goes on firking George Fox and denying the reality of the half of human experience that he represents but that it happens to be incapable of knowing.

[15] Francis Bugg's career is an interesting epiphenomenon in the history of Quakerism. After Bugg left the Quakers (in a dispute over money owed by Bugg), he made an entire career out of attacking Quakers. For forty years he scourged them in folio books of almost endless length: *DNB* lists something over twenty publications; W. C. Braithwaite, the Quaker historian, says there were over sixty books and pamphlets from Bugg's pen, all attacking Quakers and Quakerism.

2. Darwin: "observing and reasoning"

Darwin's *Autobiography*, written at the request of "A German Editor" who had asked for "an account of the development of my mind and character with some sketch of my autobiography," intended originally not for publication but for the interested perusal of immediate family and descendants, is a curious and touching document in the literature of self-description. The flavor of the book is, in interesting and revealing ways, both like and unlike what one finds in Darwin's other, his purposefully and completely scientific, books. There is the point of size, first of all. Describing his observations of barnacles (a project of eight years, published in "two thick volumes"[1]), or coral reefs, the fertilization of orchids, or the action of earthworms, Darwin could hardly contain himself; the books went on and on and on until Darwin, at length, recognized himself as the original for Bulwer-Lytton's portrait of "a Professor Long, who had written two huge volumes on limpets."[2] In the *Autobiography*, however, in the

[1] *Autobiography*, p. 117. The only text of the *Autobiography* available until recently was that of 1887, edited in three volumes by Francis Darwin and including a selection of letters (*Life and Letters of Charles Darwin*; London: John Murray). Francis Darwin omitted a fairly considerable amount from his father's *Autobiography*: an account of stealing fruit as a child, for example, and "two odd stories about bleeding" told to Charles by his father; some of Charles Darwin's discussion of his religious skepticism; and many passages that were critical of friends and acquaintances. In 1958, Charles Darwin's granddaughter, Lady Nora Barlow, re-edited the *Autobiography* and restored all the omitted passages. References are to this edition of the *Autobiography* (London: Collins); when it is a question of letters, references are to the three-volume edition of 1887.

[2] *Auto.*, p. 117. The Bulwer-Lytton novel is *What Will He Do With It?* (1858). An actor named Waife, seeing a bill in a stationer's window advertising a "Lecture on Conchology" by Professor Long, "Author of 'Researches into the Natural History of Limpets,'" stops to talk with the stationer: "'Conchology,' said the Comedian, 'is a subject which requires deep research, and on which a learned man may say much without fear of contradiction. . . . Possibly the lecturer may have found an audience rather select than numerous'" (*What Will He Do With It?* 2 vols. [London:

reversion to private life, Professor Long does an about-face into extreme reticence. The description of Darwin's own life, composed over three months of writing "for nearly an hour on most afternoons," is really no more than an essay in length. Darwin's writings provide us with a public-private Dr. Jekyll and Mr. Hyde: Professor Long, of limpet and barnacle fame, when he turns his gaze from the barnacle to the barnacle-observer, is as if miraculously transformed into the Mr. Short responsible for the *Autobiography*. Professor Long and Mr. Short, the public-scientific and the private-experiential faces of Charles Darwin, thus far seem little related to one another. And yet, if the *Autobiography* is in length quite unlike his scientific work, Darwin expressly intends to be as objective and as detached in the one as in the other. As if he were a coral reef in the South Seas, Darwin deliberately looks at himself from without, studying a creature, presently not living, to whom a series of things happened in the past and over whom a series of changes came in sixty-seven years of life. Darwin is clear and revealing in the expression of his intention: "I have attempted to write the following account of myself, as if I were a dead man in another world looking back at my own life. Nor have I found this difficult, for life is nearly over with me."[3] It is an interesting fact that in his *Autobiography* Darwin says almost more about himself unconsciously, in the

Routledge, Warne, and Routledge, 1864], I, 125-26). The Comedian's remark is ironic since, the year after Bulwer-Lytton's novel, Darwin's *Origin Of Species* found a numerous audience indeed (rather numerous than select perhaps). While Darwin was probably not much read on barnacles, his books on earthworms and orchids had, undoubtedly because of the *Origin of Species*, a circulation that surprised everyone, including their author.

[3] *Auto.*, p. 21. Cf., as a point of curiosity, the first sentence of another autobiographer who, though very different as a man, was also a scientist (and whose "Autobiographical Notes" are about the same length as Darwin's *Autobiography*): "Here I sit in order to write, at the age of 67, something like my own obituary" (*Albert Einstein: Philosopher-Scientist*, ed. Paul Arthur Schilpp, 2 vols. [New York: Harper, 1959], I, 3).

mode of his expression, than he says consciously in deliberate statement. A thinker who supposes himself not at all given to metaphoric expression, Darwin, as here, significantly reveals a great deal about his personality through metaphor and simile ("as if I were a dead man") without, apparently, ever realizing what he is doing.

Perhaps the most immediately remarkable quality in Darwin's tiny book, aside from its distinctive charm and grace but not altogether separable from these two things, is a sense of modest bewilderment. We feel questions, implied and essential, constantly behind Darwin's effort. He seems never assertive enough to say, with Walt Whitman, that endless and untiring, monumentally assertive self-affirmer, "I am the man, I suffer'd, I was there." Instead, there is an unbelieving note of interrogation: "Am I that man? Was I ever that person? Did I suffer?" But one should say again: the questions are always implied and not stated, as if they lay outside the circle of Darwin's conscious awareness and interest. In his *Autobiography* Darwin is, in effect, out of touch with his subject as a living being, and the reader, overcome by Darwin's very real modesty, shares his wonder and bewilderment at what he was, at what he is, at the shattering effect of publication of his theory of evolution. As we read his *Autobiography* we wonder that this recluse, the aging valetudinarian of Down, should be the same person there described: ". . . in many ways a naughty boy . . . much given to inventing deliberate falsehoods"; or the young man who wasted his time at Cambridge and "got into a sporting set, including some dissipated low-minded young men . . . and we sometimes drank too much, with jolly singing and playing at cards afterwards."[4] Indeed,

[4] *Auto.*, pp. 22-23 and 60. An autobiographical fragment, written in 1838 (that is, almost thirty-eight years before the *Autobiography*), recounts much the same sort of memory of his childhood. This fragment is included in *More Letters of Charles Darwin*, ed. Francis Darwin, 2 vols. (London: John Murray, 1903), I, 1-5.

the connection between the two men, the man who "was there" and the man who looks "back at my own life" from the dead, is so tenuous and nearly unbelievable that Darwin's son and editor feels constrained to qualify with a footnote his father's account of those mild Cambridge orgies: "I gather from some of my father's contemporaries that he has exaggerated the Bacchanalian nature of these parties.—F.D." (*Auto.*, p. 6on.). This may be the unkindest cut of all—the careful son who disallows his father's wild oats sowed in younger years. To his father's "We have heard the chimes at midnight," Francis Darwin seems to respond with Falstaff: "Lord, Lord, how subject . . . old men are to this vice of lying." The reason for Francis Darwin's disbelief, however, is probably obvious and goes well beyond the mere desire of a good Victorian son for a proper Victorian father. The reader, like Francis, can discover no living connection between the retired and famous scientist who, throughout his adult life, could not work for more than three or four hours a day without terrible suffering from undiagnosable bad health and the young man in Tahiti who corrupted the good, temperance-society intentions of the natives with "a flask of spirits, which they could not refuse to partake of,"[5] and, in the Galapagos Archipelago, "frequently" clambered on the backs of the giant tortoises for a ride around the countryside.[6]

The question which lies behind Francis Darwin's disbelief and which has puzzled readers of Darwin for a century is more often and perhaps better stated thus: how could Darwin—so gentle, generous, sensitive, and modest as his *Autobiography*, as his writings everywhere, as the testimony of acquaintances reveal him to have been—how could he ever have upset things so much? The question of course occurred to Darwin himself,

[5] *The Voyage of the Beagle*, ed. Leonard Engel (Garden City, N.Y.: Doubleday & Co., 1962), p. 411.

[6] *Beagle*, p. 385. These are the tortoises that Darwin eventually rode right into the *Origin of Species: Beagle*, pp. 394 and 397-98.

manifesting itself in the tone of bewildered modesty that we have noted in the *Autobiography*. With no more noise than he made, or wanted to make, how could Darwin have effectively propounded a theory so vast in its implications, so shattering for traditional philosophies, cosmologies, and world-views? The conclusion of Darwin's *Autobiography* is both astounding and characteristic in its surprise and in its modesty: "With such moderate abilities as I possess, it is truly surprising that thus I should have influenced to a considerable extent the beliefs of scientific men on some important points" (p. 145). Here, as everywhere, the good Englishman, Darwin brings off his colossal understatement in the plainest of manners and the quietest of voices. Even as he points to the obvious truth about the effect of his long-developed, painfully elaborated and argued theory of evolution (a lifework in every sense), Darwin almost completely effaces himself from the accomplishment. Self-effacement: this, in fact, is the quality that one finds everywhere characteristic of Darwin, and that ties together the autobiographer and the scientist.

Consider the nature of Darwin's scientific achievement, for this says much about his autobiographic effort, what it is and why it should be that. Darwin's one great theory, to elaboration of which he devoted his life, we see gradually appearing in *The Voyage of the Beagle*, then coming to full and controversial expression in the *Origin of Species*, and finally drawing itself out in illustrative expansion in a series of later books (*On the Contrivances by which Orchids are Fertilised by Insects; The Variation of Animals and Plants under Domestication; The Descent of Man and Selection in Relation to Sex; The Expression of Emotions in Man and Animals*). The *Origin*, which is the keystone in the exposition, reveals the logic of Darwin's theory; it begins with a chapter on "Variation under Domestication" and proceeds to one on "Variation under Nature," for Darwin is essentially concerned with just this:

186

variation and how it has occurred in the history of life on earth. With a phrase borrowed from Malthus (whom Darwin, in October 1838, "happened to read for amusement"; *Auto.*, p. 120), the argument proceeds to a consideration of how certain species, in a "struggle for existence" with other species, are selected for continued existence. The answer, in the fourth and climactic chapter, is that nature, operating through immutable laws, continually selects those forms of life best fitted to existence under particular environmental conditions, rejecting less qualified forms by allowing them to die off. In the structure of his book one sees Darwin's argument: as we can artificially and experimentally produce species mutations and variations, so similar mutations and variations occur naturally and, as it were, experimentally in the long history of the world. Specific variations, observable in the myriad forms and faces of living nature past and present, result from "natural selection" which is the controlling and directing "will" behind the process of evolution. (This is not, Darwin would say, a Lamarckian will to evolve, residing in the creature, but a will expressing the being of nature.) The complete title of the book tells the same story: *Of the Origin of Species by means of Natural Selection, or the Preservation of Favoured Races in the Struggle for Life.*

It will be apparent that Darwin's theory is first, and almost last, concerned with mutation and variation, with change per se. There is a point in his *Voyage of the Beagle* when Darwin, excited by the extraordinary symbiotic existence of polypi which are closely united yet distinct beings, strikes a note not at all characteristic of his thought or writing: "Well may one be allowed to ask, what is an individual?" (*Beagle*, p. 95). There we have a question that Darwin almost never did ask. He was concerned instead with changes forming an abstractable process divorced from the living organism. He sought and elaborated a rule or law of variation common to all the observable phenomena, quite in disregard of "what is an individual." Peculiarly, Darwin exhibits no more sympathy with his own known life, with the question of "what is [this] individual," than he does with other, essentially unknown, unknowable lives of plants, animals, and men. Darwin seldom or never has to do with what Stephen Dedalus calls the "I, entelechy, form of forms," as he muses on individual change and constancy in *Ulysses*, thinking that though every cell in the human body changes in a few years' time yet there remains something stable and constant, an essential "I." Darwin's subject is the law of moving "forms," not the "form of forms," and in choosing he is only acting the part of the disciplined scientist in search of a general law. He looks always for changes passed around by common rule over living things. He can hardly concern himself with that which makes the being not common but unique, not subject to general law but faithful only to its own law; he can hardly, that is, concern himself as a scientist—and the scientist is soon the man—with the life of the particular, the irreproducible being.

"I have, also," Darwin says in another book, but it is equally true for the *Origin*, "often personified the word Nature; for I have found it difficult to avoid this ambiguity."[7] Indeed, Darwin not only personifies but he regularly deifies nature—"Dame Nature," as he grandly calls her in one place (*Beagle*, p. 199). She may not be what others call the First Cause, but she is the highest order of cause that Darwin conceives or allows. He goes on, however, to say of his goddess: "I mean by nature only the aggregate action and product of many natural laws—and by laws only the ascertained sequence of events." Darwin's knowledge of his divinity is, of necessity, all a posteriori and inductive, never a priori or deductive; and she is a sort of conglomerate goddess, composed of demigods

---

[7] *The Variation of Animals and Plants under Domestication*, 2nd rev. ed., 2 vols. (New York: Appleton & Co., 1894), I, 7.

and goddesses which are the immutable natural laws. In a letter to Asa Gray (June 5, 1861), Darwin refers to "my deity 'Natural Selection'" (*Life & Letters*, II, 373), that being the highest of the demigods in the pantheon and the major channel through which the power of nature operates to regulate the affairs of creation.

Almost any subject whatever furnished grist for Darwin's mill, for his great theory of evolution and the variations that must have come and gone in a million years of adaptive change. Even when it is a question of *The Expression of the Emotions in Man and Animals*, Darwin is much less concerned with the emotion itself, or with its relation to a sufficient expression, than he is with the way in which an expression with no present use might be explained as a variant trace of an archaic and functional expression. Everything is traced down and back— a sneer, for example (recollection of a canine snarl), or tears; for Darwin, these emotional expressions do not have a purpose but only a history. A smile ("The tendency of the zygomatic muscles to contract under pleasurable emotions") is not an incipient laugh but is the nonfunctional, habitual residue of aeons of laughter ("the last trace of a habit, firmly fixed during many generations, of laughing whenever we are joyful").[8] Man, for Darwin, is an object of study over which change is constantly passing, and not something unique experiencing a state of being. In this book, as in nearly everything he wrote, Darwin is in the grip of his particular daimon, his idea, his theory of evolution; in consequence, a more accurately descriptive title would be *The Evolution of Emotional Expressions in Man and Animal*.

According to Darwin's own account of his method of working and of his formulation of a theory, he was simply led on by accumulated facts to the necessary conclusion. He had no

[8] *The Expression of the Emotions in Man and Animals* (New York: Appleton & Co., 1894), pp. 205 and 211.

preformed theory to impose; rather the body of facts, brought all together, imposed the theory upon him, pointed inexorably, unavoidably to the one theoretic end to be recognized. The facts, Darwin might say, spoke, and their voice was the theory of natural selection. The movement is all in one direction: from facts to theory. Darwin, by temperament and conscious, felt need a pure empirical thinker, at the far pole from intuition and feeling, expresses the inductive scientist's disappointment in rereading Grandfather Erasmus Darwin's *Zoonomia*, because "the proportion of speculation [is] so large to the facts given" (*Auto.*, p. 49). For the Darwinian observer and thinker this is the rankest heresy, discovery of a speculative skeleton rattling around in the family closet. And what if it should prove to be a heritable character trait? For Darwin's theory, of course, ascribed a great many things to heredity. Whether we find the horror in grandfather, in ourselves, or in a stranger, we should be capable of diagnosing the case, and, as good scientists, should do our bit to help stamp out speculative, imaginative thinking, for such intuitive procedure takes hold of the scientific stick at the wrong end. In good, moralistic terms, pledging himself to a purer life, Darwin castigates the dirty habit when uncovered in himself: "I must try not to fall into my common error of being too speculative. But a drunkard might as well say he would drink a little and not too much!" (*Life & Letters*, III, 123). If such a thing is possible, then one might say that Darwin as conscious scientist is an upright, moralistic, Sunday Puritan and empirical thinker, but as unconscious, psychic man is a slovenly, drunken speculator and imaginative/intuitive type. Having taken the pledge, however, having suppressed the Satanic unconscious with its alluring phantoms, and sworn himself to pure, scientific living, Darwin could feel himself reclaimed and secure, prospering like any Puritan and redeemed sinner: "I am a complete millionaire in odd and curious little facts, and I have been astounded at my own industry" (*Life & Letters*, III, 27). That Darwin was a "millionaire in . . . facts" in the *Origin of Species* was unquestionably true, as J. D. Hooker in admiration could tell him: "I am perfectly tired of marvelling at the wonderful amount of facts you have brought to bear" (*Life & Letters*, II, 242). It is well that Darwin should have been so prosperous, for by his own testimony in the *Autobiography* he was very deliberate and very conscious in his method if not in either his goal or his intention. "I worked on true Baconian principles," he says, "and without any theory collected facts on a wholesale scale. . . . Nor did I ever intermit collecting facts bearing on the origin of species" (*Auto.*, pp. 119 and 99). And in letters of the time: "I was so struck with the distribution of the Galapagos organisms . . . that I determined to collect blindly every sort of fact, which could bear any way on what are species. . . . Note-book after note-book has been filled with facts which begin to *group themselves* clearly under sub-laws."[9] The voice of the amassed facts, it is true, might not be perfectly audible to the human ear, or might have a slight catch in it (thus the fact of sterile progeny, "the acme of the difficulty," as Darwin calls it in the *Origin*, rather confused his hearing and had to be worked in before the theory confidently asserted itself through the total body of facts: "I fairly struck my colours before the case of neuter insects"; *Life & Letters*, II, 170); but Darwin strained to hear the voice of physical facts expressing themselves in theory as intensely as any neo-Pythagorean to hear the Music of the Spheres. And he heard the voice, too, speaking of nat-

[9] *Life & Letters*, II, 23, and I, 298. Cf. *Origin of Species*, first page of "Introduction": "On my return home [from the *Beagle* voyage], it occurred to me, in 1837, that something might perhaps be made out on this question by patiently accumulating and reflecting on all sorts of facts which could possibly have any bearing on it. After five years' work I *allowed myself to speculate* on the subject, and drew up some short notes" (Everyman ed. [1928], p. 17). Italics, both here and in the text, are mine.

ural selection and adaptation to environment: "I can remember the very spot in the road, whilst in my carriage, when to my joy the solution occurred to me; and this was long after I had come to Down" (*Auto.*, pp. 120-21).

With Darwin the careful, continuous, blind collecting of facts until they should corporately speak, or even if they should never speak, was more profoundly rooted than a mere method of his professional discipline. His beloved but autocratic father might call Darwin good for nothing but "rat-catching" (*Auto.*, p. 28), yet the truth is that his enthusiasm for catching rats, for collecting beetles, for gathering every fact he could lay his hands on in the natural world was Darwin's abiding passion and it was this primarily that made him a great scientist. By temperament Darwin was avid of facts, greedy to collect and classify every detail of the natural world—to the degree that he finally becomes a type character and, like an animal in Aesop, points a moral for the reader: a beetle in the mouth is not worth two in the hands.

> But no pursuit at Cambridge was followed with nearly so much eagerness or gave me so much pleasure as collecting beetles. It was the mere passion for collecting. . . . I will give a proof of my zeal: one day, on tearing off some old bark, I saw two rare beetles, and seized one in each hand; then I saw a third and new kind, which I could not bear to lose, so that I popped the one which I held in my right hand into my mouth. Alas it ejected some intensely acrid fluid, which burnt my tongue so that I was forced to spit the beetle out which was lost, as well as the third one.　　(*Auto.*, p. 62.)

"Dame Nature," enjoining temperance in beetle-collecting as in all things, might be supposed to have given here also a demonstration in the ways of evolution through natural selection. That beetle, most fit to survive because it could escape the enemy by a squirt of acrid fluid, undoubtedly lived another day to pass on its valuable modified talent to numerous progeny. Sadder perhaps, and wiser certainly, but no less passionate, Darwin kept the beetles in their proper place and continued to collect ("The passion for collecting, which leads a man to be a systematic naturalist, a virtuoso or a miser, was very strong in me, and was clearly innate, as none of my sisters or brother ever had this taste"),[10] until he could read the meaning of evolution in the face of nature.

Darwin sees and presents himself in the scientific process as a collector with a blessedly rational mind—that *par excellence* and no more. We find Darwin summed up, by himself, in two recurrent words, "observing and reasoning": these two words, on which all theory is founded, are inseparable companions in the scientific method and very characteristic of Darwin all through his self-description. Observing, for the natural scientist, is the equivalent of collecting: not content with looking, he would take the natural subject with all his senses, would possess it in every way. In Darwin's case, the observer-collector was not only born but also made. The voyage of the *Beagle* brought before Darwin's attentive eyes and into his eager hands collectible facts in "several branches of natural history, and thus my powers of observation were improved, though they were already fairly developed" (*Auto.*, p. 77). The capacity which was not, perhaps, innate in Darwin, the capacity he had to acquire and to couple with the inborn passion for observing-collecting before he could move through facts to theory, the capacity which Darwin rather piqued himself on possessing though others might hint critically at its absence, was "reasoning." "The investigation of the geology

---

[10] *Auto.*, p. 23. Indeed, Erasmus, the brother mentioned, never had Darwin's passion for collecting or his reverence for fact; cf. a letter from Erasmus to Charles Darwin in November, 1859: "In fact, the *a priori* reasoning [of *Origin of Species*] is so entirely satisfactory to me that if the facts won't fit in, why so much the worse for the facts is my feeling" (*Life & Letters*, II, 234). Of course, there is, by Darwin's own account, no *a priori* reasoning there.

AUTOBIOGRAPHY SIMPLEX

of all the places visited" by the *Beagle*, he points out, "was far more important, as reasoning here comes into play. . . . I discovered, though unconsciously and insensibly, that the pleasure of observing and reasoning was a much higher one than that of skill and sport. The primeval instincts of the barbarian slowly yielded to the acquired tastes of the civilized man."[11] In the very modest appraisal of his capacities near the end of his *Autobiography*, Darwin is willing to give away much ("I have no great quickness of apprehension or wit. . . . I am . . . a poor critic. . . . My power to follow a long and purely abstract train of thought is very limited. . . . My memory is . . . hazy"), but he claims the two essentials and is clearly hurt by those who would deny him one of the two. His plea that he be allowed "reasoning" is simple, direct, pained, and pathetic, and it leads him back around to the beginning: only observing and reasoning can legitimately discover a single theory in a billion facts.

> Some of my critics have said, "Oh, he is a good observer, but he has no power of reasoning!" I do not think that this can be true, for the *Origin of Species* is one long argument from the beginning to the end, and it has convinced not a few able men. No one could have written it without having some power of reasoning. . . .
>
> I think that I am superior to the common run of men in noticing things which easily escape attention, and in observing them carefully. My industry has been nearly as great as it could have been in the observation and collection of facts. . . . From my early youth I have had the strongest desire to understand or explain whatever I observed—that is, to group all facts under some general laws.   (*Auto.*, pp. 140-41.)

Observation of many facts and reasoning on them will produce

---

[11] *Auto.*, pp. 77 and 79. "The primeval instincts of the barbarian"—i.e., shooting. Francis Darwin discreetly dropped this sentence from his edition of the *Autobiography*, presumably in order not to offend bird-shooting squires.

194

one rule, the General Law. The method is, apparently, quite scientific, quite objective, quite perfect.

What Darwin desired to be—what, in fact, he felt he was in the very essence of what seems to us a paradoxical selfhood —was a purely and totally impartial observer of and detached reasoner on a phenomenal system altogether apart from and outside himself. This is not to say that Darwin did not embrace humanity in his theory. Of course he did; that was the scandal of it for all Special Creationists. But as he observed and experimented, it never occurred to Darwin that the observer and experimenter stood at the very center of the process and so had to be taken into account with the result. Instead, Darwin would be an analytic observer not involved in the process, a rational theorizer still in no way a part of the experiment itself. Thus—and the metaphor, presented with modesty and puzzlement occasioned by a "curious and lamentable loss of the higher aesthetic tastes,"[12] is Darwin's own—he would be and, in fact, became a sort of machine for observing and reasoning, an efficient, infallible, unliving machine. "My mind seems to have become a kind of machine for grinding general laws out of large collections of facts, but why this should have caused the atrophy of that part of the brain alone, on which the higher tastes [i.e., poetry, pictures, and music] depend, I cannot conceive" (*Auto.*, p. 139). In order that he might become a perfect and mechanical device, and in the interests of science, Darwin murders the organism—and then is surprised to find it dead.

Now the reader is presented with the peculiar notion of a machine writing its autobiography. But the real truth is, *must*

[12] *Auto.*, p. 139. Darwin's rigid and single-minded discipline not only robbed him of the "higher aesthetic tastes" but of the capacity of deep feeling for friends as well: "Of late years, though I still have very friendly feelings towards many persons, I have lost the power of becoming deeply attached to anyone, not even so deeply to my good and dear friends Hooker and Huxley, as I should formerly have been" (*Auto.*, p. 115).

be, and this is doubly, triply true for someone who writes autobiography, that as long as it is a living consciousness, then, by the very fact of observing, the central receptor and perceptor is a part of the shifting experiment, a part of the evolving system. Try as he might to be mechanical or dead (ill-health "is enough to make one wish oneself quiet in a comfortable tomb"; *Life & Letters*, III, 106), Darwin could not do it, any more than anyone else acting as an observer on himself and life. To observe is to live, to join and to connect subject and object, to be a part of the whole and individual process of life. Darwin tried and tried to deny a half and more of the psychic organism, and that whole and outraged organism, it seems reasonable to suppose, took its revenge on this attempt of Darwin's at self-effacement or self-destruction, took its revenge in the form of all the various, plainly psychosomatic illnesses (cf. the "palpitations and pain about the heart" before he boarded the *Beagle*; *Auto.*, p. 79) that he suffered from, and very intensely, his life long. The psychic bewilderment, which at first glance seems strange in a man possessed of such supereminent observational capacities as Darwin, becomes eventually explicable in precisely those same terms. Enormously and minutely conscious of the world of natural phenomena, of the physical world past and present which he so assiduously collected and classified, Darwin was, as if by a compensatory lack, largely unconscious of the nature and place of the collector and classifier in this careful process. Always conscious of the significance of external phenomena, Darwin was almost equally and oppositely un*self*-conscious; for the self does not present collectible and classifiable facts. Hence the brevity of the *Autobiography*. The scientific genius who could bring to synthetic expression a theory of the origin of species—a theory which had evolved over a period of generations with incremental advances here, qualifications and modifications there, and reversals elsewhere, eventually to come to completion in Darwin's experiments and thoughts at Down—this same man is the very definition of naïveté when he comes to look within instead of without; then he seems quite incapable of conceiving that the essential self, out of which the embracing theory is produced, has in any sense a part to play in the shape and quality of that theory. By the time he wrote his *Autobiography* Darwin had become, on the one hand, "a kind of machine for grinding [out] general laws" and, on the other hand, a melancholy recluse who questioned little and understood less of his own place in the "dubious experiment" of life.

One has only to compare Darwin as autobiographer with Montaigne and Jung and the point is made. These two scientists of autobiography included, as an essential component in their experiments or their essays in truth, the recording consciousness itself, at least so far as this is ever humanly possible. To do this is to make the closed system of the experiment more inclusive; it is to reach toward a consciousness transcending and comprehending all the forces and terms involved in a life. There may, after all, be forces in a life that are not entirely external, not altogether observable and reasonable, and that, unless considered and understood, will surely bias the experiment. If we look out upon the billion phenomena of the world from the center of the phenomenal existence into which we are born—notice that we do not exist at one end or the other or outside that swarm—then it will be most intelligent for us to consider that the observant eye is itself one of the phenomena and a vital part of our living experiment. Darwin sought to give order, in a formulated law, to the pre-existent and continuing-to-exist phenomena that surrounded him, but without acknowledging that he was inescapably at the center and that he, like all of us in the aggregate, *was* the very process that he wished simultaneously to order externally and to efface internally.

Darwin, if we think of him in comparison with Jung and Montaigne—or Newman or Mill or Eliot, for that matter—was unsophisticated. He had little or nothing in the way of perspective awareness on himself and his situation that would permit him to include his self in his observations. This lack of philosophical sophistication or perspective is the reason for the modest bewilderment in Darwin's *Autobiography*; it explains also the melancholia which affected Darwin for so much of his adult life; and it suggests why Darwin did not really understand—but rather retreated like a snail whose antennae have been touched, leaving Huxley (qualified and proud to be "Darwin's Bulldog") to perform in the market-place—when a considerable part of an age poured contumely on his head for his theory. His bewilderment is consequent finally upon his particular and scientific temperament: upon his restricting the area of his experiment, as he believed necessary, to externally observable evidence and phenomena.

Observation and reasoning versus intuition and speculation: Darwinian science draws the line very sharply, and it is a line that Darwin himself will not overstep no matter what the subject may be. On this basis he could effectively put down an opponent who did not agree that the earthworm is largely responsible for the entire surface of the earth ("But M. D'Archiac must have thus argued from inner consciousness and not from observation"[13]); on this basis also he found himself disapproving of Herbert Spencer ("His deductive manner of treating every subject is wholly opposed to my frame of mind"; *Auto.*, p. 109); and on this basis, finally, Darwin had to consider himself, though it gave great pain to some members of his family, as, at most, an agnostic in religious matters. One of the ironies of his personal history is that Darwin,

[13] *The Formation of Vegetable Mould, Through the Action of Worms, with Observations on Their Habits* (New York: Appleton & Co., 1895), p. 4.

on the suggestion of his father, who was himself a skeptic or worse, should have taken a degree at Cambridge with the intention of becoming a clergyman. But Darwin says that early in life he believed as much as any clergyman would be expected to do, and that, as a young man, he dreamed of some evidence—preferably in writing and incontrovertible—that might be suddenly discovered ("in Pompeii or elsewhere") to confirm the literal and factual truth of the Gospels. Then his belief might have remained. As years passed and the discovery was not made, Darwin was still "very unwilling" to give up his religious belief, but eventually "disbelief crept over me at a very slow rate," and he found it more and more difficult "to invent evidence which would suffice to convince me" (*Auto.*, pp. 86-87). The kind of evidence Darwin sought was hard and masculine, the same kind as he sought—and found—in geology and botany. He rejected with good-humored contempt the soft, feminine, and intuitive sort of evidence with which a Mrs. Barlow tried to convert Robert Darwin: "Doctor," she told Darwin's father, "I know that sugar is sweet in my mouth, and I know that my Redeemer liveth" (*Auto.*, p. 96). For himself, Darwin says in another passage, "The clearest evidence would be requisite to make any sane man believe in the miracles by which Christianity is supported" (*Auto.*, p. 86), and he does not appear to have found the sugar in Mrs. Barlow's mouth answerable to his criteria.

In his mature years, the furthest concession that Darwin would make to those who wrote piously requesting information on his "religious views" was to say that he simply did not know and thought no man could know; that it was beyond the reach of the human mind to have any understanding of a First Cause. The religious answer to this state of mind would presumably be faith which, like its object the First Cause, transcends mere intellect. But Darwin, for his own part, rejected faith outright (in a passage cautiously deleted from the *Auto-*

biography by Francis Darwin): "It never struck me [in the days when he was a "believer"] how illogical it was to say that I believed in what I could not understand and what is in fact unintelligible. I might have said with entire truth that I had no wish to dispute any dogma; but I never was such a fool as to feel and say 'credo quia incredibile' " (*Auto.*, p. 57). The strong words and the tone of outrage reflect nicely the force of the insult felt by the intellect in Tertullian's Rule of Faith. "Science," Darwin told a German student-correspondent, "has nothing to do with Christ, except in so far as the habit of scientific research makes a man cautious in admitting evidence. For myself, I do not believe that there ever has been any revelation" (*Life & Letters*, I, 307). Even if there were a God, it seems he would be powerless to abrogate the laws of nature: "Everything in nature is the result of fixed laws" and "the more we know of fixed laws of nature the more incredible do miracles become" (*Auto.*, pp. 87 and 86). Anyhow, the "law of natural selection" came to seem to Darwin a more than adequate replacement for a personal God—and for his law he had evidence in excess, as he did not for God.

"Science," Darwin says, "consists in grouping facts so that general laws or conclusions may be drawn from them" (*Auto.*, p. 70). It has been often enough remarked that Darwin's great scientific book is not really what the abbreviated title seems to suggest. He does not intend to trace an actual origin of species, but to formulate a general law that will account for the way changes in species have occurred. Nor, of course, does he ever propose any end for the evolutionary process, whether the evolution be of the individual or of the race. This is of crucial significance when we are talking not about the scientific formulation but about the scientist's life. How do we account for a life that developed in just this way? Where is the life going, and why? There is no theory for it, and no accounting for it, because no general law can be made to apply to the individual, the singular and the unique. Scientifically, Darwin could formulate a general law without apparently recognizing that that general law was autobiographically involved with an individual law. Had he been challenged, as Newman was, to say, "What, then, does Charles Darwin mean?" Darwin would, in logic, have had to deny that he "means" anything. For in his discipline, the observable changes and abstractable laws were everything, the man nothing. And even facts do not "mean"; only a person can do that.

Darwin concludes his *Origin of Species* with a sort of breathless awe before the huge field opened up to study by his theory of natural selection. When we accept that "species are only strongly marked and permanent varieties, and that each species first existed as a variety," then, he says, "how far more interesting—I speak from experience—does the study of natural history become!" In particular, "A grand and almost untrodden field of inquiry will be opened, on the causes and laws of variation" (*Origin*, pp. 446 and 460). Variations are accessible to sensory observation; principle of being, or essential unitary life, is not. Darwin, the sensationist, was a scientist of variation who, when he agreed to consider the question at all, posited some vague "nerve force" (*Expression of the Emotions*) or prototypical life-force flowing through all creation; but he notably never attempts a study of that life-force, which would mean, at least in part, going intuitively and speculatively inward rather than observationally and analytically outward. It would mean, in effect, living with George Fox for a while. It is difficult, in a sense, to think of Fox and Darwin as of the same species, let alone of the same nation. If one tries to imagine a meeting of the two—it cannot be done; it is simply unimaginable. There would be nowhere that either could or would start a dialogue with the other. They represent two incompatible extremes of human nature and suggest between them the great variety possible in human nature, though neither, of course, contained anything like full variety in himself. It is relevant to remark that Darwin and Fox are both very much the type of individualistic eccentric for whom Mill makes an impassioned plea in his essay "On Liberty," but at the same time neither one is at all like the complete individual, full and rich within his own character, that Mill there maintains as the ideal.

The reader of Darwin is left with the great single achievement in science to which its author in a very real sense gave over his whole life. Beyond that, he can only speculate on the interesting advice given to Darwin by the fourth Earl of Stanhope, father of the historian who was a contemporary of Darwin. The old Lord, Darwin says, "was a strange man, but what I saw of him, I liked much. He was frank, genial, and pleasant . . . and his clothes, when I saw him, were all brown. He seemed to believe in everything which was to others utterly incredible." Though he was a Fellow of the Royal Society and one-time president of the Medico-Botanical Society, Lord Stanhope may yet have been rather eccentric in his scientific interests. At least it would seem reasonable to guess that, as a scientist, he was almost certainly quite un-Darwinian. "Why don't you give up your fiddle-faddle of geology and zoology," he once asked Darwin, "and turn to the occult sciences?" (*Auto.*, p. 112). Darwin, a man of infinite patience and considerable tolerance, but a scientist possessed by the passion to observe everything and intuit nothing, was merely amused at the notion.

3. Newman: "He asks what I *mean*"

"Genius eludes definitions," Henry Tristram says in his edition of Newman's scattered autobiographical papers. "Let it be granted," he continues of Newman, "that he was not a

202

theologian, nor a philosopher, nor a historian, nor a preacher, nor a poet, at least not in the front rank."[1] Nor, though he was sometimes these things also, can he be adequately described as religious administrator or educator or novelist or psychologist. It is not at all easy to know where to place Newman or how, most rewardingly, to approach him; even such a loose grouping as "man of letters," or "scholar," though in a sense he was both, does not satisfy Newman's interests or his achievement. Yet, in spite of the protean variety of his writings, there is undoubtedly something that draws all the separate volumes together into one coherent body, that makes of them a distinct *œuvre*, and that stamps each of them as unmistakably Newman's. Maybe a new designation, not very neat but perhaps more likely therefore to be valid, would serve a useful purpose: "autobiographical artist." In this somewhat amorphous category Newman might at least join St. Chrysostom and the other early saints who, he says with deepest admiration, "have written autobiography on a large scale; they have given us their own histories, their thoughts, words, and actions, in a number of goodly folios, productions which are in themselves some of their meritorious works."[2] Like these early saints, Newman paradoxically makes available to the whole world as the real subject of all his writings, whether in philosophy, psychology, history, theology, or education, what he calls "secretum meum mihi." Every volume Newman gave to the world has reference to and is a reflection of, takes its source in and derives its strength from, his own most private, secret, religious experience. "Bien que, en effet," Henri Bremond says, describing Newman's practice, "le *je* et le *moi* soient relativement assez rare dans les livres de Newman, prédicateur,

[1] *The Autobiographical Writings of John Henry Newman*, ed. Henry Tristram (London: Sheed and Ward, 1956), pp. 17-18.
[2] *Historical Sketches*, 3 vols. (London: Basil Montagu Pickering, 1872-73), III, 218.

romancier, controversiste, philosophe, poète, il s'expose, il se raconte toujours."[3] Drawing on the personal present and the remembered, equally personal, past for his true subject, Newman elaborates a complex autobiographic portrait throughout the forty or so volumes of his collected works. "By their fruits ye shall know them": If a man is justified not by faith alone but by his works as well, then, as he implies of Chrysostom and his fellow saints, Newman himself should be greatly merited in his works, those fruitful productions and artistic reflections of a profoundly spiritual lifetime.

When one turns to the *Apologia pro vitâ suâ*,[4] it is a very near thing whether one should consider Newman, along with such unwonted bedfellows as Fox, Darwin, and Mill, as an autobiographer simplex, or whether he should not instead be taken in the round, like Montaigne and Jung, as an autobiographer duplex. Of them all, excepting probably Montaigne, Newman is the supreme artist, which very fact alone tends to remove him from a grouping with Fox, Darwin, and Mill. Moreover, Newman understands entirely the sources and the terms of autobiography, and to him must be ascribed in the highest degree the consciousness and self-consciousness that is the double mark of the theoretical autobiographer. Nor is it at all easy to say of Newman which was his primary mode of response to the world, whether feeling or thinking, intuition or sensation. Here again he is more like Montaigne or Jung than he is like Fox, Darwin, or Mill. Newman had, for example, according to contemporary testimony, extremely acute senses[5] and, as one can see in his work, a brilliantly logical in-

---

[3] *Newman: Essai de biographie psychologique* (Paris: Librairie Bloud, 1906), p. ix.

[4] All quotations from the *Apologia* are from the critical text edited by Martin J. Svaglic for Oxford Univ. Press in 1967.

[5] James Anthony Froude says that Newman's "senses, even the commonest, were exceptionally delicate. I was told that, though he rarely drank wine, he was trusted to choose the vintages for the college cellar"

tellect; he was moved by complex and refined feelings, un-
erring in their judgment of value, and by an intuitive grasp of
spiritual reality the equal of any that can be named.

These are the marks of the complete man and writer, at
once artist and philosopher. And yet it is more practical to
consider Newman as an autobiographer uncompounded because these capacities and tendencies, the exposition of theory
and its elaboration in practice, are spread out, as it were par-
celed out, over his collected works and not, as with Montaigne
and Jung, combined and concentrated again and again in each
book or essay and particularly fully in the autobiography. It
was perhaps the artist in Newman, faithful ever to the singleness and unity of the idea lying behind and threaded through
each work, that enjoined this separation of theory from practice. The portrait painter, after all, executes his single plan,
realizes the particular vision; he does not attach a philosophical
treatise as a part of the work in explanation of how the portrait, in general theory and in particular fact, comes to make
its appeal and demand on us. No more does Newman mix
logical theory with imaginative self-portraiture. He insistently
maintains the integrity of the work of imagination even at the
sacrifice of much that would seem interesting and probably
relevant in the view of a casual observer. But this is very far
from saying that Newman had no theory, no explanation of
the philosophy and the psychology of autobiography that he
might have produced with the *Apologia* had he so chosen.
What Newman does instead is to argue a rational theory of
epistemology and psychology (which is implicitly a theory of

(*Short Studies on Great Subjects*, 4th series [New York: Charles Scribner's
Sons, 1886], p. 183). Sensation with Newman was a very different thing,
of course, from what it was, for example, with Darwin: Newman always
referred sensory data to the subjective center of feeling for proper valuation; Darwin held such data at objective arm's length, never corrupting it
with feeling.

autobiography), of how we know and why we assent, in his *Grammar of Assent*, and a rational theory of history and philosophy, of the origins and ends of religious evolution, personal and communal, in his *Development of Christian Doctrine* (and elsewhere); and the terms of these theories he makes real, vivid, and particular in his *Apologia*, the epistemological, psychological, historical, and philosophical portrait of one man, *this* man, growing through experience to religious knowledge, doctrinal belief, and dogmatic assent. In our analysis, we shall look at both theory and practice, taking them, as Newman does, more or less separately, and consider how the *Apologia* is structured and why it should be so.

An Essay in Aid of a Grammar of Assent[6] presents a typically subtle, careful, and complex argument about human nature and religious belief, about the psychology of human assent to propositions in general and of human belief in religious dogma in particular. The book analyzes and hypothesizes about the psychology of what William James called the "will to believe." What is that will? How and by what is it moved? What do belief and assent humanly mean, and what do they involve? These are Newman's questions, this is his subject. His work is a construct in personal philosophy, a coherent world-view, fundamental and elaborate, based on a comprehensive and exact concept of the psychological na-

---

[6] In chronological fact, the *Grammar* (1870) was written six years after the *Apologia* (1864), twenty-five years after the *Development of Christian Doctrine* (1845). The idea for it, however, had long been in Newman's mind—indeed, on his conscience ("Rightly or wrongly I had ever thought it a duty, as if it was committed to me to do it"; *Auto. Writings*, p. 273). Since Newman's theories and personality were steady and consistent in development, it does no injustice to take the books out of order and to say that the earlier *Apologia* is a complete manifestation of the theory that had yet to be elaborated in the *Grammar of Assent*. Newman considered his *Grammar*, like almost everything he wrote, a "first essay" toward statement of the subject: hence the title. Page references in the text are to the Longmans, Green, & Co. (London) ed. of 1909, vol. VIII in *The Works of John Henry Newman*.

ture of man. By a very slight shift of terms one could say that the *Grammar* concerns itself with the process of self, seeing that process, in a general, and Newman would say, scientific way, as an actualizing, under human conditions of time and space, of innate and spiritual, peculiarly human, possibilities; or, again, seeing that process as a progressive expansion through experience into comprehension of the nature of self-existence and the nature of an existent and related Other.

Human knowledge Newman separates into two kinds, according as it comes to us through experience or through the rational intellect. We know something to be, either because we have experienced it or because, logically and rationally, we deduce that it should be or must be. We apprehend a truth by experience of it or by a syllogism which leads our reason, the premises being valid, necessarily to the truth as conclusion. The first kind of knowledge and truth, and the first kind of proposition and assent following upon this knowledge, must be, like the experience from which it springs, singular, unique, particular, concrete, a-logical, *sui generis*, not at all subject to the generality of law but only to the fact of its being. The second kind of knowledge and truth, proposition and assent, being not apparently self-existent but a characteristic creation of the human mind, is common, shared, general, abstract, logical, typical. "All things in the exterior world are unit and individual, and are nothing else; but the mind not only contemplates those unit realities, as they exist, but has the gift, by an act of creation, of bringing before it abstractions and generalizations, which have no existence, no counterpart, out of it" (*Grammar*, p. 9).

Thus Newman distinguishes, in his psychological scheme of belief, two kinds of apprehensions, two of propositions, two of assents. These he denominates real and notional apprehensions, real and notional propositions, real and notional assents. Experience presents us with realities, logic with notions. The total man, with passion, intellect, and will—all that he is and means—engages himself as a living being in real assent; only the rational faculty, saying "Yes, that is logical," is involved in notional assent. Experience, according to Newman, touches us differently a million times with its many singulars; out of these many contacts, the mind, in its characteristic working, raises the abstraction of a general rule. "Each use of propositions has its own excellence and serviceableness, and each its own imperfection. To apprehend notionally is to have breadth of mind, but to be shallow; to apprehend really is to be deep, but to be narrow-minded. . . . However, real apprehension has the precedence, as being the scope and end and the test of notional."[7] Thus Newman in effect throws his lot in with real apprehension, claiming the primacy of that immediate, irrefutable, inexpressibly private experience (biographically, for example, Newman's conversion at fifteen) by which the individual judges and values all that the senses thereafter touch and the mind subsequently creates and beholds. Though the mind, Newman continues, operates over experience to abstract its own generalities, the rules and laws thus lifted from out of the many do not apply back on the particular and unique, the real and living; they have validity only in their own realm of the general and common, the theoretical and abstract. Newman was famously a believer in miracles—and how could he fail to be, given his terms? There is no general rule for particular life. In a search for causes and a first cause we must finally and blankly stop before the fact of life itself. What law is it that causes life to be? Life itself, and not that it *should* be but that it *is*, is the great miracle. Like all real knowledge

[7] *Grammar of Assent*, p. 34. One might here make brief reference, by way of illustration, to Darwin, a notional apprehender after broad and general laws which would ask for notional, abstract assent, and to Fox, a deep, narrow-minded and real apprehender, balanced treacherously and unconditionally on the razor-edge of his momentary and entirely concrete, even if intuitive, experience.

and assent this comes to us, *must* come to us, in experience. With human reason, the probability or necessity of life and consciousness could never be deduced. One might paraphrase Newman's own words on the doctrine of transubstantiation ("It is difficult, impossible, to imagine, I grant; but how is it difficult to believe?"; *Apologia*, p. 215) on this first and quintessential miracle: "Life is difficult, impossible, to deduce, I grant; but how is it difficult to experience?" It is the paradox of living awareness that to it, the center of consciousness, life should be rationally impossible but experimentally actual. Beyond those terms—the blank wall that faces the inquirer into the mystery of life—there is no going.

Life, as Newman says in so many ways, is always and only in the particular, scientific or philosophic knowledge of that life always in the general. Development and growth of the self consists in the continuous interchange and transformation between the two, in the constant individual growth to fit the general terms of human nature. The individual human being is what he peculiarly is, this individual, by the fact of his real assents, but is a human being by reason of his notional assents. These latter, whereby each man succeeds to the estate of man, "rising from particulars to generals, that is from images to notions" (*Grammar*, p. 31), bind men together in the same condition, "a common measure between mind and mind" (*Grammar*, p. 83). One might say, then, that notional apprehensions and assents contain the forms of life *in posse*, real apprehensions and assents life *in esse*. Notional assents suggest the continuous, as yet unreal, possibilities of human shape available for actualization in the detailed, moment-to-moment life of the one man, and this actualization, as it comes to the sum of concrete experiences here and now, time after time, is unique and, after the fact (but not before), irrevocably determined. Real assents, in Newman's definition, "are of a personal character, each individual having his own, and being known by them"

209

(*Grammar*, p. 83). So the self is defined from minute to minute through a thousand and hundred thousand of meetings between evolved and evolving spirit, on the one hand, and formative experiences actualizing the possible on the other. And like life itself, the all-decisive real assent "is proper to the individual. . . . It cannot be reckoned on, anticipated, accounted for, inasmuch as it is the accident of this man or that" (*Grammar*, pp. 83-84). All the progressive moments of selfhood, those points at which the individual really assents with the whole being and thus becomes a new whole being out of the old—all the past real assents brought to and contained effectively in the present one—all these moments of completion "depend on personal experience; and the experience of one man is not the experience of another" (*Grammar*, p. 83).

Only real apprehensions, calling responses from all the individual has been and is, move the will and affect the living being. Advances of self come unceasingly (even as we falsify by our reason in trying to break down process into successive points) with real apprehensions and concurrent responses of the will: "Acts of Notional Assent and of Inference do not affect our conduct, and acts of Belief, that is, of Real Assent, do (not necessarily, but do) affect it" (*Grammar*, p. 90). The self is not changed by notions but, when it is changed, by realities, among which realities must be importantly included the very self in change. "After all," Newman says in a well-known passage in the *Grammar of Assent*, which he quotes from his own earlier "Tamworth Reading Room," "After all, man is *not* a reasoning animal; he is a seeing, feeling, contemplating, acting animal" (*Grammar*, p. 94). He is all this, Newman suggests, and more, an existent fact whose true being is inaccessible to language. He is an ineffable, organic complex in motion, conscious of himself but without the ability to describe or communicate what he is conscious of. That complex moves and changes as it lives into and so realizes the terms of generally human propositions; that is, the individual evolves as he comes to be capable of giving real assent—because he has acquired experience—to propositions to which, before, he could only give notional assent. Thus, while Newman declares that "individual conviction"—the beliefs and meanings that compose our being—"is *sui generis* and varying with the individual," he also maintains the twofold nature of spiritual assent: "the *motivum credibilitatis* is personal to each individual as well as formal, public, and what may be called objective, after the manner of a science."[8] Consider an instance of this growth (a process not altogether unlike "individuation" in Jung's psychology) from merely notional to intensely real assent. Poetry, being the reflection not of a part but of the whole of embodied, individual experience, the product and metaphor of a complete and unified, unique self, calling for us not to do but to see and to be made anew, demands real assent to its terms. It appeals to the whole experience of the reader who is, however, not at first or always capable of such assent as poetry requires.

> Passages, which to a boy are but rhetorical commonplaces, neither better nor worse than a hundred others which any clever writer might supply, which he gets by heart and thinks very fine, and imitates, as he thinks, successfully, in his own flowing versification, at length come home to him, when long years have passed, and he has had experience of life, and pierce him, as if he had never before known them, with their sad earnestness and vivid exactness. Then he comes to understand how it is that lines, the birth of some chance morning or evening at an Ionian festival, or among the Sabine hills, have lasted generation after generation, for thousands of years, with a power over the mind, and a charm, which the current literature of his own day, with all its obvious advantages, is utterly unable to rival. Perhaps this is the reason of the medieval opin-

[8] From a paper dated Jan. 5, 1860, published in Adrian J. Boekraad and Henry Tristram, *The Argument from Conscience to the Existence of God* (Louvain: Editions Nauwelaerts, 1961), p. 169.

ion about Virgil, as if a prophet or magician; his single words and phrases, his pathetic half lines, giving utterance, as the voice of Nature herself, to that pain and weariness, yet hope of better things, which is the experience of her children in every time. (*Grammar*, pp. 78-79.)

The truths, for apprehension and assent, remain always the same, holding ever the freshness and the vivid emotional and intellectual precision by which the poet was informed and with which he informed his rhythms and images. In our memorized, notional response we recognize the rightness for verse of the rhythms, the diction and syntax, the images—but not the truth of the metaphors. These have not yet represented and created our experience. We have not really apprehended the terms of the proposition, for we have not lived these terms. As Keats says (and, recognizing the rightness of his idea, he repeated it in letters written several months apart), "Axioms in philosophy are not axioms until they are proved upon our pulses: We read fine things but never feel them to the full until we have gone the same steps as the Author. . . . Nothing ever becomes real till it is experienced—Even a Proverb is no proverb to you till your Life has illustrated it."[9] When the terms of the proposition have been transformed into what we know—or turn it around, rather: when we have grown into the terms—then our assent is real; we are serenely certain and unified in response because we know. "From the nature of the human mind," Newman says, "time is necessary for the full comprehension and perfection of great ideas";[10] and so also of great religious truths or of experience richly rendered in poetry: they are none of them really available to the young,

[9] Letters to John Hamilton Reynolds (May 3, 1818) and to George and Georgianna Keats (Feb. 19, 1819): *The Letters of John Keats*, ed. Maurice Buxton Forman, 4th ed. (London: Oxford Univ. Press, 1952), pp. 141 and 316.
[10] *Essay on the Development of Christian Doctrine* (London: Longmans, Green, & Co., 1909), p. 29.

212

the innocent, and the inexperienced. The truth really does not change, "for there is but one truth," but we, its apprehenders, who enact and embody the truth, do. We see that which we saw not, because our sight, grown old in experience, is finally fresh enough to respond to the poet's freshness. The many moments of our experience have come together until they click, and they click with the poet's experiential, metaphorized sum. For our life, as we know it in this epitomizing moment, the poem is suddenly, briefly, a sufficient and necessary metaphor.

Like poetry, religious belief is a matter of real assent and total response, which distinguishes the one from rote memory, the other from theology. "Theology, as such, always is notional, as being scientific: religion, as being personal, should be real" (*Grammar*, p. 55). The form that religious propositions take we call dogma, which, in its proper signification, "when long years have passed" weighting its terms with meaning, is capable of evoking the realest of assents: "From the age of fifteen," Newman tells us in the *Apologia*, "dogma has been the fundamental principle of my religion" (p. 54). To such a dogmatic proposition as "The Son is God," which is, according to Newman, a proposition shaped by the experience of generations of believers, and which is, again, the form that their experiential knowledge has gradually acquired, the individual, himself at first unshaped, unformed, inexperienced, can only give a notional assent; but this notional assent will not at all move the will, or change a man or his conduct. For such sure and deep response we must live and learn, waiting until the terms are filled by our growth and, in the filling, apprehended. That is to say, we must become capable of comprehension; we must hold an image, out of present and past lived experience, of (1) sonship, (2) Godship. Take the second term first. We have, according to Newman, an innate knowledge of God, an "image" of him, determined by and

213

given evidence through individual conscience. The conscience, for Newman (lest it be said that everyone does not have a conscience, or that there is no such thing), is quite simply the voice of "what I am." Kingsley's question, "What, then, does Dr. Newman mean?"—the question which set the *Apologia* in motion—would be the same in other words as, "What, then, is Dr. Newman's conscience?" Everyone, Newman argues, is, after all, "one"; everyone is something, more or less coherent. In this sense, then, everyone does have a conscience which impels him to act thus rather than otherwise, makes him be himself, chaotic or partial as that self may seem, rather than someone else. "Conscience is a personal guide, and I use it because I must use myself; I am as little able to think by any mind but my own as to breathe with another's lungs" (*Grammar*, pp. 389-90). But conscience, Newman claims, is also the "voice of God" (*Grammar*, p. 122), so that to our apprehension the self and God speak with one voice, and "conscience is a connecting principle between the creature and his Creator" (*Grammar*, p. 117). Conscience, consciousness of the self, and awareness of God are, in effect, all coequal, "prior," Newman asserts, "to all questions of trust or assent" (*Grammar*, p. 61). We give, then—we cannot but give—real assent to the proposition "God is," and we give it because "I am."

This leaves us with an apprehension of one of the terms: God. The second term is not apprehended by us innately nor by the fact of what we are. We do not, that is, know the complex relation of "sonship" as a principle concomitant upon conscious existence, but only as knowledge of experience. It remains, before we can give a real assent to "The Son is God," to fill our second term with the evolution of a life. There is, conveniently, a description extant of Newman living, as it were, exactly these terms, the terms of the dogmatic principle that "The Son is God," and bringing his hearers to a similar living response. James Anthony Froude recalls the effect of a passage from Newman's sermon on "The Incarnate Son, a Sufferer and Sacrifice":

> Again, I am not sure whether it was on the same occasion, but it was in following the same line of thought, Newman described closely some of the incidents of our Lord's passion; he then paused. For a few moments there was a breathless silence. Then, in a low, clear voice, of which the faintest vibration was audible in the farthest corner of St. Mary's, he said, "Now I bid you recollect that He to whom these things were done was Almighty God." It was as if an electric shock had gone through the church, as if every person present understood for the first time the meaning of what he had all his life been saying. I suppose it was an epoch in the mental history of more than one of my Oxford contemporaries.[11]

Newman has frequently been charged or credited, depending upon the point of view, with the spiritual changes in a great many young men at Oxford, both during the time he was there and later. It must often, more than a century later, be difficult to imagine just how real and deep his influence was, and while a passage like this gives some hint, we still miss the voice, the appearance, the whole man speaking and moving both himself and his hearers. "I am touched by my five senses," Newman says, and this holds for his readers as well, "by what my eyes behold and my ears hear. . . . I gain more from the life of our Lord in the Gospels than from a treatise *de Deo*."[12] J. A. Froude and others could observe the living man; we must depend upon the portrait in the *Apologia*.

Just as life is a process occurring in time, so real assent can only come with the accretion of personality realized in past

[11] *Short Studies on Great Subjects*, p. 188. The sermon is number six in vol. VI of the *Parochial Sermons* (London: Rivington & Parker, 1842), esp. pp. 80-81. Froude, when he recalled this sermon, was no particular friend of Newman's ideas or position. He was Kingsley's brother-in-law, and it was his book that Kingsley was reviewing when he tossed off the slander on Newman.

[12] *Historical Sketches*, III, 217.

and passing time. We move; we can see and show that we have moved; but we can seldom or never say when, for the process is unbroken, accretive, and evolutionary. We might produce a rational record or a diagram of process, but we will never thereby convey the subtle fact and feel of process itself which ever slips away, will never stay. The attempt is like breaking a straight stick into pieces and putting the pieces over a curved line. One can break the stick into as many pieces as one wants; it will never quite form the real curve. A logical record of process must always be more or less untrue, more or less angular, broken, abrupt, unfaithful to the gradual curve of self, being but a rational fitting to a more than rational process. The self or consciousness is, like a curve, rationally but not really a succession of theoretical points. How shall one take it or break it at any point, then, and hope to hold it? "For myself," Newman says in the *Apologia*, referring to his religious progress, "it was not logic that carried me on; as well might one say that the quicksilver in the barometer changes the weather. It is the concrete being that reasons; pass a number of years, and I find my mind in a new place; how? the whole man moves; paper logic is but the record of it" (p. 155). There is the man and the movement; or the man *is* the movement. Speaking of the act or acts by which we exist and are conscious of existing, "Sentio," Newman says, "ergo sum."[13] It is, one may suppose, something more than "solitary, naked, external, logical"[14] mind, but including that, of course, which speaks and moves, means and senses and experiences and today finds itself in a different place from yesterday. "I have done various bold things in my life," Newman declares, as he attempts to communicate to his readers some sense of the unity of his evolving being: "this is the boldest" (*Apologia*, p. 91).

[13] From a paper on conscience published in Boekraad and Tristram, *The Argument from Conscience*, p. 105.
[14] Quoted by Meriol Trevor, *Newman: The Pillar of the Cloud* (London: Macmillan, 1962), p. 307.

This excursion into the theory behind Newman's *Apologia* is no doubt a long way around to get to the beginning, but it does, I think, finally bring us back to the man Newman, his personality and his autobiographic art. Implicit in the dramatic structure of the *Apologia*, but never drawn out in the thin light of abstract statement, is all the autobiographical-psychological theory of the *Grammar*. The *Apologia* is the artistically conscientious portrait of Newman's personal and religious, his real, assent: the picture, that is, of his own growth into the ages-old terms of Roman Catholic dogma. The *Grammar*, one might say, corresponds to the "treatis *de Deo*," the *Apologia* to the life in the Gospels. Newman frequently expressed his dislike of the standard biography, which, done as it is from outside, leaves the essence of being untouched and the personality of the subject reordered or misordered according to the intention of the biographer; he as frequently expressed himself in favor of a different kind of biography—a compilation of letters strung together with as little explanatory narrative as possible. "Letters I don't mind," he explained to Ambrose St. John, "for they are facts, and belong, for good or bad, to the personality of the writer of them" (*Auto. Writings*, p. 23). Because letters are the expression, at a particular moment and in a particular context, of the whole personality of their writer, a "Life" might be built up, and would be more or less valid, from these moment-to-moment coherent images. And Newman characteristically wanted to continue responsible for himself, for what he was or what he meant, even after his death. For every letter he wrote he accepted responsibility, and for his life as a whole he both accepted and demanded responsibility. This insistence that the man who lived and the man who wrote the life should have identical responsibilities Newman carried a step further: he arranged with Anne Mozley to be his first biographer,[15] and sent her, to

15 Only of the Anglican years: *Letters and Correspondence of John Henry*

assist in the composition, the letters that he wished included and, in the third person, an "Autobiographical Memoir" to accompany the letters. As the editor of the *Autobiographical Writings* implies, the adoption of an anonymous, objective, third-person persona—Newman's attempt to be himself and not himself, or to pretend to be someone else describing the experience of himself—is often precarious, a tour de force maintained only very tenuously and with great difficulty. It is no doubt true that time causes a certain disjunction of personality; still, however, the total separation implied in adopting and maintaining the third person is clearly exaggerated, and the reader experiences some considerable difficulty, because Newman did also, in holding simultaneously in mind the identicalness and the separateness of writer and subject in the "Memoir." There is, for example, a time when Newman, either daringly or forgetfully, introduces the first person close on the heels of "Mr Newman": "indeed at a later date Mr Newman availed himself, when accused of Catholicity, of the distinctions which Dr Lloyd in an article in a Review had introduced into the controversy with Rome, and others, who came within his influence, I believe Mr Oakeley, have testified to that influence in their case having acted in a Catholic direction" (*Auto. Writings*, p. 70). Who is that "I"? Anne Mozley? Mr Newman? Anon? In any case, Newman did not willingly let go from his hands at any time the authority for speaking out the person of John Henry Newman.

"A Saint's writings are to me his real 'Life,' "[16] Newman declares, and thereby gives the clue to his own practice and incidentally to his distrust and fear of biography. Newman's "Life" was written in his letters, in his notes and memoranda, in his books that all contained and reflected, each doing its

---

Newman during his Life in the English Church, 2 vols. (London: Longmans, Green, & Co., 1891).

[16] *Historical Sketches*, III, 227.

part, the movements that led imperceptibly into one another so as to become not single and separate movements but a whole growth and evolution, never starting (unless with his conversion at fifteen), never stopping (unless in death, the final completion, culmination, logical transfiguration). "Perhaps I shall be asked," Newman continues, "what I mean by 'Life.' I mean a narrative which impresses the reader with the idea of moral unity, identity, growth, continuity, personality. When a Saint converses with me, I am conscious of the presence of one active principle of thought, one individual character, flowing on and into the various matters which he discusses, and the different transactions in which he mixes. It is what no memorials can reach." A "Life," one comes to see, is a metaphor, ordered, single, coherent, meaningful, for life, which is all too often disordered, multiple, chaotic, meaningless; it is, like his letters and collected writings, a revelation or manifestation of the individual man in his integrated personality, his "moral unity." When Newman undertook the publication of his collected works in a uniform edition, he chose to put the *Apologia* first, then to go on to Sermons, Essays, Treatises, etc., thus making the "Life" the thread or key to his writings and the *Apologia* the focus through which to approach all else in his work and thought.

Some ten years after the publication of his *Apologia*, Newman recorded in his journal his shock and dismay upon the realization of how little he had produced by way of public works in recent time—only two books in fifteen years, "the Apologia and the Essay on Assent—of which the former was almost extempore." Casting about for explanations of this unproductiveness, he hit upon one that is very much to the point of his performance in the *Apologia*: this is what he describes as "my habit, or even nature, of not writing & publishing without a *call*. What I have written has been for the most part what may be called official, works done in some office I held

219

or engagement I had made . . . or has been from some especial call, or invitation, or necessity, or emergency, as my Arians, Anglican difficulties, Apologia or Tales. The Essay on Assent is nearly the only exception. And I *cannot* write without such a stimulus. I feel to myself going out of the way, or impertinent—and I write neither with spirit nor with point" (*Auto. Writings*, pp. 272-73). Newman took a considerable pride, altogether justified by his great and effective skill, in being a controversialist and an occasional writer—and the *Apologia* was preeminently written to an occasion: Charles Kingsley's seemingly casual but in fact (as Kingsley later testified) deliberate remark, "wantonly" thrown out in the course of a review article on the history of Elizabethan England: "Truth, for its own sake, had never been a virtue with the Roman clergy. Father Newman informs us that it need not, and on the whole ought not to be" (*Apologia*, p. 341). That, as Newman says in the correspondence following upon the original article and preceding the *Apologia*, is a charge "direct, distinct, public"; Kingsley, challenged for evidence in support of his proposition, should have been "bound to prove it as directly, as distinctly, as publicly; or to own you can't." Instead of which, however, Kingsley, coming on like the Blatant Beast itself—or, perhaps more significantly, like the last courageous defender of British womanhood—returned to the controversy not with book and chapter but with a shotgun blast of new charges and innuendos and slanders in his truly remarkable pamphlet, *What, Then, Does Dr. Newman Mean?*

The first of Kingsley's original sentences, though not very exact in its statement, contains what Newman would call a merely notional proposition ("in which one or both of the terms are common nouns, as standing for what is abstract, general, and non-existing"), and asks only for notional apprehension and assent. Newman, naturally, would scorn the proposition that Roman Catholic priests have not a very high regard for truth, but he would not have written a book, and that book an autobiography, to refute it. What would be the point and purpose or the occasion, where the possibility of any refutation except a notional, and therefore unmoving, one? The second sentence, however, touching as it does the quick of immediate and individual self—Father Newman: *this* priest—is a real proposition ("composed of singular nouns . . . the terms stand[ing] for things . . . unit and individual. . . ."),[17] looking for real assent. It asks us to realize the terms and to give a willed response in answer. Father Newman—so goes Newman's sharpened restatement of the proposition— is a "liar and counsellor of lying." The implication is that the reader knows and has a real apprehension of the particular, unified moral being signified by that proper name. The anguish of Newman's response, brought with all the authority of close and central self-consciousness ("Proximus sum egomet mihi"; *Grammar*, p. 61), is as real and distinct as the animosity of Kingsley's attack.

But if "Father Newman is a liar" is a proposition requiring real dissent, that can be effectively achieved only in a positive way: that is, Newman must bring the reader not simply to reject a misapprehension (which would leave him with a blank: what, then, is he, if "Father Newman is not a liar"? Perhaps the fool that Kingsley later suggested?), but must persuade him to reapprehend and to give real assent to another, a contradictory proposition, statable as, "Father Newman is conscientious." ("Conscientious" is not a word that one recalls from the *Apologia*; yet this is basically the proposition, positive in direction and real in meaning, which is to be filled, like a vessel of two halves connected by a conduit of active predication, with the realized metaphor of a life, with, that is, "The 'Life' of John Henry Newman.") The truth or falsity of

---

17 Quotations on notional and real assent are from pp. 9-10 of *Grammar of Assent.*

Kingsley's second sentence, unlike the proposition of his first sentence, is, according to Newman, the kind a man will live or die for: "No one, I say, will die for his own calculations: he dies for realities" (*Grammar*, p. 93). To defend that process of what has been and is himself, however, Newman need not die; in defense, he proposes instead his life, and that life, a real thing, the end of a myriad unit experiences, allows no refutation. "Intellectual ideas," Newman says in his *Grammar*, "cannot compete in effectiveness with the experience of concrete facts" (p. 12). With this, the artist's justification, Newman sets about recreating the concrete facts drawn from the well of his own life; unwilling to leave his life in the hands of another, he becomes the apologist *pro vitâ suâ*, and lives again, dramatic and convincing in the portrait of what he has been, vivid and imaginative in the metaphor of what he is. When, fifteen years later, he was made a cardinal, Newman significantly, being the artist he was, chose as his motto, "cor ad cor loquitur." And how does heart speak to heart? "The heart is commonly reached, not through the reason, but through the imagination, by means of direct impressions, by the testimony of facts and events, by history, by description. Persons influence us, voices melt us, looks subdue us, deeds inflame us" (*Grammar*, pp. 92-93). This tells us why the *Apologia* is what it is: a creative construct from personal history, an imaginative work of art. An argument would be nothing to the purpose; only the ordered recreation of persons moving and voices speaking, of looks revealing and deeds inciting will "vanquish, not my Accuser, but my judges" (*Apologia*, p. 12).

Since Kingsley's pamphlet, in its title, inquires after the conscience of a man, asking what it is that makes him this man and not another, questioning the experience and the creative spirit, unique and individual and essentially unknown outside itself, that is existent under the name of John Henry Newman, the "True Mode of Meeting Mr. Kingsley" is to replace

222

a perverted portrait and biography (deliberately perverted by a biographer dabbling in a life not his own) with a faithful one. "Yes," Newman says, "his very question is about my *meaning*. . . . He asks what I *mean*; not about my words, not about my arguments, not about my actions, as his ultimate point, but about that living intelligence, by which I write, and argue, and act. He asks about my Mind and its Beliefs and its sentiments; and he shall be answered; not for his own sake, but for mine" (*Apologia*, p. 12). In his book Newman promises to substitute a true history and description for a false, and if that, being made of language and not life, can never carry the feel of the very experience itself, it can at least convey, by the ways of art, the sense of a "Life" unified by a real and living principle. "I must, I said, give the true key to my whole life; I must show what I am, that it may be seen what I am not, and that the phantom may be extinguished which gibbers instead of me. I wish to be known as a living man, and not as a scarecrow which is dressed up in my clothes" (*Apologia*, p. 12). If he succeeds in this portrait-cum-apology, if he effectively portrays in metaphor the vital being and draws a faithful likeness of how it has been and is with him, then, Newman asserts confidently, truth and triumph will follow. Newman's is the mode of the artist, showing fidelity only to what is, and this—paradoxically, since Newman is here as almost always the controversial and occasional writer—leaves out and behind Kingsley and controversy. Kingsley and his charge are no longer Newman's subject: that subject has been transformed to become life in a particular vessel, life informed by one conscience, life located in a specific time and place. His subject is a particular embodiment of truth, and his technique faithful portrayal of existent being, which carries with it, as a corollary, the truth which shall vanquish his readers, now become— as they always will be when a work of art is in question— his judges.

What Newman convincingly establishes in his *Apologia* (that it *is* convincing is tested on every reader who feels outrage still one hundred years later at the vicious meanness of Kingsley's slander) is his own integrity—that is, the coherence and unity of the self which acts: the moral integrity of the man is assured for us by the artistic integrity, the unity and coherence, of the portrait. "A man's moral being," says a priest in *Loss and Gain* who might as well be the Newman of the *Apologia*, "is concentrated in each moment of his life; it lives in the tips of his fingers, and the spring of his insteps."[18] That a man's life is thus unified and coherent does not, of course, mean that there is in it no change or development; and the reader of the *Apologia* is left with no doubt that Newman's was such an integrated, directed, destined life, though the direction and destiny became apparent only after the fact, only when all the various, earlier movements were perfected in the conversion to Rome. "Gentle pressure," the Soul of Gerontius thinks, in "The Dream of Gerontius," as it separates itself in death from the body, "gentle pressure tells me I am not / Self-moving, but borne forward on my way." This gentle pressure of Gerontius' personal guardian Angel, representing both the will of God and intuition of inner being, is not altogether unlike that conscience, the source and meaning of Newman's movement, called into controversy by Kingsley's question. "In a higher world it is otherwise," Newman says in *The Development of Christian Doctrine* (like all his books a record of movement, this one written at the crucial moment when he was moving from the English to the Roman Catholic Church), "but here below to live is to change, and to be perfect is to have changed often" (p. 40). Exemplifying, in this book on doctrinal and ideological development, the concept that he is also explaining, Newman displays the change

---

[18] *Loss and Gain: The Story of a Convert* (London: Burns & Oates, 1962), p. 215.

224

occurring in himself by copious quotations from his own earlier, specifically Anglican and controversial, writings. The extensive self-quotations lie in this text that bridges Newman as Anglican and Newman as Roman Catholic like seeds in ripened fruit—seeds that look back to an earlier stage of the fruit and that also promise new life, more growth, development, and perfection in the future. Depending on the perspective, one can see in these earlier writings the promise of the later, as in the young Newman we see the essential spirit of the mature priest; or, in the writings of the Roman Catholic (e.g., the *Grammar*), we see the completion and perfection of a work began and hesitantly expounded, with occasional error and corrigible heresy, in the Anglican papers.

In this matter of evolution, there is a clear analogy to be drawn between scriptural revelation, which is the objective, historical, and public seed of all church doctrine, and Newman's conversion at fifteen, the subjective, momentary, and private seed of personality, thereafter to be exfoliated in years of experience. Through a "unitive power" that Newman describes as "an eclectic, conservative, assimilating, healing, moulding process" (*Christian Doctrine*, p. 186), Christian doctrine and the self, motivated respectively by revelation and conversion, develop naturally to perfection, presided over in the one case by the infallible voice of the Church, in the other by the integral conscience. Echoing the words of Montaigne, Newman describes evolution, doctrinal or personal, as "the legitimate growth and complement, that is the natural and necessary development" (*Christian Doctrine*, p. 169) of the first motive to spiritual life. "Wonderful it is to see," Newman exclaims in a sermon of 1843 on "The Theory of Developments in Religious Doctrine," "with what effort, hesitation, suspense, interruption—with how many swayings to the right and to the left—with how many reverses, yet with what certainty of advance, with what precision in its march, and with what ultimate completeness, it has evolved; till the whole truth 'self-balanced on its centre hung,' part answering to part, one, absolute, integral, indissoluble, while the world lasts!"[19] As with belief and doctrine so also with the self and personality, development is gradual and imperceptible, made up of an infinite number of continuous movements, "so that it were as easy to follow the growth of the fruit of the earth," Newman says four pages on in the same sermon, " 'first the blade, then the ear of corn, after that the full corn in the ear,' as to chronicle changes which involved no abrupt revolution, or reaction, or fickleness of mind, but have been the birth of an idea, the development, in explicit form, of what was already latent within." It was such a chronicle that Newman bravely undertook to produce in his answer to Kingsley's pamphlet.

It is notable that in his "History of my Religious Opinions" —the body, that is, of the *Apologia*—Newman does not begin, as one might have supposed he would, with 1801, the year of his birth, or anywhere near it. Of his attitude toward religious "liberalism," Newman says, "What I held in 1816, I held in 1833, and I hold in 1864" (*Apologia*, p. 54). The last is the year of the *Apologia*, 1833 the year of the beginning of the Oxford Movement, 1816 the year of Newman's conversion ("of which I still am more certain than that I have hands and feet"; *Apologia*, p. 17); and it is with this year, the date of his complete transformation and spiritual birth—not a development but an entire change of identity and total reordering of personality—that Newman begins. "Of course I cannot myself be the judge of myself," Newman wrote to Anne Mozley, apropos of this determinative conversion; "but, speaking with this reserve, I should say that it is difficult to realise or imagine the identity of the boy before and after August 1816 . . . I can look back at the end of seventy years as if on an-

[19] *Fifteen Sermons Preached before the University of Oxford* (London: Rivingtons, 1880), p. 317.

other person."[20] The change of identity (he was one boy then another) was simultaneous with Newman's first real assent. This may have been the single time in Newman's life when a move exteriorly caused, he felt, interiorly effected, could be more or less dated. From this point on his life was a single, coherent, integrated development, and there was thereafter a "History of Religious Opinions" to chronicle, in the course of which changes could be discerned but never dated. According to his biographers, Newman was constantly going over his papers—letters, journals, memoranda, notes, documents published and unpublished—shuffling and reshuffling his records of development, ordering and reordering those successive stages and extensions of personality evolving. Thus one of the papers, the "Autobiography in Miniature" (see Chapter I), shows him circumscribing at each further step on the way the early selves as, while moving, they had been recorded: within the Cardinal was the Priest and Father of the Oratory, within whom was the converted Catholic, within whom was the Vicar of St. Mary's and Fellow of Oriel, within whom was the Scholar of Trinity, within whom was the converted schoolboy, within whom must have been, though forever unimaginable to the mature man, the child unconverted; this last one could not be touched by the Vicar, the Priest, or the Cardinal, because it was another life, or another state prior to life.

Looking back with the aged Cardinal on his long career, we see that it could not have been otherwise than it was; yet how incredible it would have been to Newman to have had, like Adam at the end of *Paradise Lost*, his whole history projected before him in 1821 or 1833 or 1841. The growth, the development, the moves were all "natural and therefore necessary and just," and, once enacted (again in Montaigne's phrase), "they are in the great stream of the universe and in the chain of Stoical causes," but in the early years they were no more than

20 *Letters and Correspondence*, I, 22.

phantoms, possibilities that the young Newman could surely never have believed possible. "It is over," Newman recorded on June 13, 1824, the day of his ordination as an Anglican priest. "I am thine, O Lord; I seem quite dizzy, and cannot altogether believe and understand it. At first, after the hands were laid on me, my heart shuddered within me; the words 'for ever' are so terrible." On the next day he noted similar feelings: " 'For ever,' words never to be recalled. . . . What a blessed day was yesterday. I was not sensible of it at the time —it will never come again." And yet one more record to the same purpose on June 15: "What blessed days are these! how, in after life, shall I look back with a mournful pleasure on the time of my espousals! O God grant it may not be with grief" (*Auto. Writings*, pp. 200-201). What would have been Newman's emotion if, instead of looking back from the future, he had been able in 1824 to look ahead and to see that the same Pope (Leo XIII) who would make him in 1879 a cardinal would in 1896 declare invalid for all men these very orders of the English Church under which he was even now trembling? Those would have been complex emotions indeed. But Newman had far to go and much to realize before he would have fulfilled the end for which he was made.[21] Only from an afterview, however, can we see that, like Charles Reding, the hero of *Loss and Gain*, no matter how much he resisted the fate, no matter how many hard names he called the Pope and the Roman Mariolaters, no matter how attractively he defined the *via media* of the Anglican Church, Newman "could not ultimately escape his destiny of becoming a Catholic" (*Loss and Gain*, p. 117). Newman went the way and realized his destiny, and the *Apologia* is his metaphor for the experience.

[21] From notes on a spiritual exercise done at Maryvale in 1846: "I thought also of the horror, at the judgment, of Xt's saying to me, 'Here is the end he was made for—look at it—this was the end and this has been his life— he was made for this end & he has not fulfilled it' " (*Auto. Writings*, p. 237).

Newman's metaphor, arranged to a particular rhetorical end, is a highly selective one: his is a religious, a personal/ spiritual portrait. Looking into that portrait and holding it against the other works, one sees that the careful argument of the *Grammar of Assent*, for example, or *The Development of Christian Doctrine*, is really dependent, for first motive and final formulation, upon the private experience narrated in the *Apologia*. What Newman hypothesized publicly, he already knew and was privately, and in that private world of interior consciousness, of intuition and feeling, he had discovered (*pace* John Stuart Mill) real and sure religious evidence. From childhood, or from first converted awareness of being, he was guided, so Newman tells us, by a belief "isolating me from the objects which surrounded me . . . confirming me in my mistrust of the reality of material phenomena, and making me rest in the thought of two and two only absolute and luminously self-evident beings, myself and my Creator" (*Apologia*, p. 18). Behind the creative power of Newman's portrait, shaping it at every turn, is "what I am," the enacted drama of the two beings "face to face, 'solus cum solo,' "[22] the conscience of the being John Henry Newman, a conscience from within and beyond, defining him and giving evidence of God: "and if I am asked why I believe in a God, I answer that it is because I believe in myself, for I feel it impossible to believe in my own existence (and of that fact I am quite sure) without believing also in the existence of Him, who lives as a Personal, All-seeing, All-judging Being in my conscience" (*Apologia*, p. 180). Grant Newman but this much, the ground of his becoming—and there is no way to refuse it, since Newman is not arguing, he is doing a portrait of argument and of process: we can only grant the artist his subject—and the complete

[22] The phrase "what I am" occurs in both the *Apologia* and the *Grammar* with the same significance: *Apologia*, p. 12, and *Grammar*, p. 347; "solus cum solo" is from *Apologia*, p. 177.

metaphor ("the concatenation of argument by which the mind ascends from its first to its final religious idea"; *Apologia*, p. 179) spins itself out without a flaw.

> Starting then with the being of a God (which, as I have said, is as certain to me as the certainty of my own existence . . .), I look out of myself into the world of men, and there I see a sight which fills me with unspeakable distress. The world seems simply to give the lie to that great truth, of which my whole being is so full; and the effect upon me is, in consequence, as a matter of necessity, as confusing as if it denied that I am in existence myself. . . .
>
> What shall be said to this heart-piercing, reason-bewildering fact? I can only answer, that either there is no Creator, or this living society of men is in a true sense discarded from His presence. . . . And so I argue about the world; *if* there be a God, *since* there is a God, the human race is implicated in some terrible aboriginal calamity. (*Apologia*, pp. 216-18.)

Thus the concatenation of argument, leading like a "Kindly Light" toward assent in "unam sanctam catholicam et apostolicam Ecclesiam," evolves from the seed of consciousness; and the Roman Church, the end of Newman's spiritual journey, is already luminous in the distance even here at the beginning of the way.

In his *Autobiography*—which is very different from Newman's *Apologia*, the two men being of essentially opposite psychologies—John Stuart Mill, giving the principle justifying each element of his education but never realizing the scene in dramatic recall, leaves the reader floating in a high and sparse air of reason that is nearly incapable of sustaining imaginative life. His education, for example, remains something stated, his relation with James Mill and Harriet Taylor emotional experience forever unrecreated. Mill sacrifices every anecdotal particular to statement of the general and logical. Newman, by contrast, understanding the superior power of the real to the notional when it is a question of moving men's wills, and of the felt to the thought when a work of art is in hand, sacrifices nothing on that altar. There is always an awed wonder in Newman at the thought of time past and passing, hurrying the one individual through his many moments and places, through the manifold forms of his being. "What a dream is life," Newman says; "the days are come and they are gone; but, so it is, time is nothing except as the seed of eternity" (*Auto. Writings*, p. 138). Near the end of *Loss and Gain*, Charles Reding, another of Newman's metaphors for his experience in evolution, comes in sight of Oxford, perhaps for the last time, "and the spires and towers of the University came on his view, hallowed by how many tender associations . . . wood, water, stone, all so calm, so bright, they might have been his, but they were not. . . . He could not have another Oxford, he could not have the friends of his boyhood and youth in the choice of his manhood." And, on the next page, with him as with Newman, "All had passed as a dream, and he was a stranger where he had hoped to have a home" (p. 201). The reader of the *Apologia* will always remember the drama of Newman's life by the time and place of incident.

I left Oxford for good on Monday, February 23, 1846. On the Saturday and Sunday before, I was in my house at Littlemore simply by myself, as I had been for the first day or two when I had originally taken possession of it. I slept on Sunday night at my dear friend's, Mr. Johnson's, at the Observatory [in Oxford]. . . . I called on Dr. Ogle, one of my very oldest friends, for he was my private Tutor, when I was an Undergraduate. In him I took leave of my first College, Trinity, which was so dear to me, and which held on its foundation so many who had been kind to me both when I was a boy, and all through my Oxford life. Trinity had never been unkind to me. There used to be much snap-dragon growing on the walls opposite my freshman's rooms there, and I had for years taken it as the emblem of my own perpetual residence even unto death in my University.

231

On the morning of the 23rd I left the Observatory. I have never seen Oxford since, excepting its spires, as they are seen from the railway. (P. 213.)

Here, in the record of his movement from the Church of England to the Roman Catholic Church, Newman's artistry, calling out a complex of emotional response, is definitive and convincing. The whole integral, developmental process is made real for the reader—that "seeing, feeling, contemplating, acting animal" who is also judge of this work and this man—in the snapdragons that remain in memory but now stripped of their former significance, in the spires that, like the village on Keats's urn, will be forever desolate and unvisited because transformed into the part of a work of art. The "towery city and branchy between towers" is for Newman now the past, seen only from the railway—but at what time does the present ever become the past? The spires, metaphors for old religious opinions, belong to yesterday, and when seen vaguely on the distant horizon are difficult to connect with the self living in the present. But they serve well the great purpose of the autobiographical artist: to recreate the miracle of his own life.

4. Mill: "an advantage of a quarter of a century"

> "The child is father to the man."
> How can he be? The words are wild.
> Suck any sense from that who can:
> "The child is father to the man."
> No; what the poet did write ran,
> "The man is father to the child."
> "The child is father to the man!"
> How *can* he be? The words are wild.

Hopkins' nonsensical little poem, taking off Wordsworth, provides a convenient point of departure for discussion of John Stuart Mill, in whose education we discover not only that "the

232

man is father to the child" (James Mill being dominantly that to John Stuart), but also that "the child is father to the man" (the adult John Stuart Mill having been born of the child shaped by the father). What every reader remembers about Mill's life, of course, is the education—that education, in his own characteristic understatement, "unusual and remarkable,"[1] which was conducted at times by two very different masters, at other times by himself, and which he describes with extraordinary but typical detachment in his *Autobiography*. The education shows us the man in the making, the child reaching one hand back to the father, the other hand forward to the man he is to be—the man who, shaped by the process, will sit down years later to try to describe and recapture it. The formation of character, as Mill came later to affirm, is thus circular and continuous. It was only when he was able to break free from an educational theory of linear progress to perfection, however, that Mill's individual education was complete. There is, Mill discovered, no such progress, no such simple perfection; human experience, to avail ourselves of Yeats's visionary figure, is more a matter of spiraling and interlocking, interchanging cones than it is of a straight line to a goal of happiness. Mill never ceased to be the product of his father's programmatic formation, but he was not completed as a man until, under the tutelage of Harriet Taylor, he discovered that there was another half to the circle, and that the circle ideally signified full and various individuality.

Mill originally intended to divide his *Autobiography* into two halves: Part I, Before Harriet Taylor; Part II, After Har-

---

[1] *Autobiography of John Stuart Mill* (New York: Columbia Univ. Press, 1960), p. 1. References are generally to this Columbia edition of the *Autobiography*. For this final version, Mill deleted and rewrote extensively from an earlier version that has been published as *The Early Draft of John Stuart Mill's "Autobiography,"* ed. Jack Stillinger (Urbana, Ill.: Univ. of Illinois Press, 1961). Some of the material deleted is relevant in the present study, so occasional reference is made also to this *Early Draft*.

riet Taylor. This structural division remains in the final version, but there the two parts, instead of lying directly together, are separated and balanced against one another by a central chapter, a sort of pivot in the development of J. S. Mill: "A Crisis in My Mental History. A Stage Onward." The logic of this structure suggests that the experience of Part I (the first four chapters) led inevitably to the mental crisis; and that this crisis found resolution and cure in the experience of Part II (Chapters VI and VII). We see, in effect, John Stuart Mill as he was and as he is, the half and the half, or, more truly, the half and the whole, communicating through the focus of self at the point of crucial and, as it happened, painful transformation. Oddly enough, but also characteristically enough, Mill, in his self-presentation, claims almost no part in his own eventual achievement: that intellectual accomplishment, as he describes it, was almost entirely a matter of influence from others, an influence that was paternal for some quarter of a century and uxorial thereafter. Mill's portrait shows the boy coming from the rigorous and unaffectionate hand of the father, into and eventually through the critical shadow of nervous depression or melancholia, to reach manhood under the benevolent warmth and loving cultivation of Harriet Taylor (whether anyone else saw Mrs. Taylor thus scarcely matters: Mill did). If Mill's prose manner were less cool and detached, his *Autobiography* might seem almost a Victorian melodrama with Mind as the hero-heroine. But, for good or bad, the prose of the *Autobiography*, pointing up the relation obtaining between the writer and his material, has the same judicious and rational texture as the prose of Mill's *System of Logic* or his *Examination of Sir William Hamilton's Philosophy*. If the material of his self-portrait suggests a melodrama of the mind, the stylistic medium (so that the ghost of James Mill might rest quietly in the grave) cools emergent feelings very rapidly.

In the first part of his education, as Mill presents it, he was the theoretically lifeless object of an experiment. Like the children in the opening scene of Dickens' *Hard Times*, he was seen as an inanimate vessel to be filled to the top with no-nonsense knowledge by his intensely serious father, a man totally committed to a particular psychological and philosophical theory of education.

> A man who, in his own practice, so vigorously acted up to the principle of wasting no time, was likely to adhere to the same rule in the instruction of his pupil. I have no remembrance of the time when I began to learn Greek. I have been told that it was when I was three years old. . . . I learnt no Latin until my eighth year. . . . My father, in all his teaching, demanded of me not only the utmost that I could do, but much that I could by no possibility have done. . . . Of children's books, any more than of playthings, I had scarcely any. . . . I was continually incurring his displeasure by my inability to solve difficult problems for which he did not see that I had not the necessary previous knowledge.[2]

Mill's record is filled with "My father said. . . ." and "My father thought. . . ." as he depicts that educational scientist in the full heat of experiment, touching the impressionable mind of the boy to the fullest degree of trained response. And the boy—we have only to read any of his writings—did respond.

The center of Mill's studies, a paradigm for his whole education, he locates in logic. Newman's schoolboy, too young yet to understand, is put to memorize lines of Virgil, rhythms and images heavy with the weight and meaning of human

---

[2] *Auto.*, pp. 3, 4, 6, and 8. It seems that even James Mill, devoted as he was to principle and theory, could fail in practice—or so one must judge from a peculiar passage in the *Autobiography* (p. 2): ". . . in his position, with no resource but the precarious one of writing in periodicals, he married and had a large family; conduct than which nothing could be more opposed, both as a matter of good sense and of duty, to the opinions which, at least at a later period of life, he strenuously upheld."

experience immemorial. Mill, on the other hand, similarly too inexperienced at the age of twelve to possess the human substance that would make for meaningful contemplation, was set by his father to study not poems alive with the emotions of humanity but instead the rigid outlines and rules of thought itself. The heart of Mill's education was syllogistic logic, which, as he says in his book on the subject, is not an accurate picture of thought processes but is instead a kind of abstract shorthand by which we can check the validity of thought: "not a correct analysis of that process of reasoning or inference . . . but . . . an indispensable collateral security for the correctness of the generalization itself."[3] That this subject, so very abstract, formal, and impersonal, should have been the virtual culmination of Mill's mental education (he says his paternal education was complete at age fourteen); that syllogistic logic should be the focus of his autobiographical portrait of mind, out from which lines of character radiate to inform the man—this is altogether significant. In pursuit of a theory, the mind of the master impresses itself on the mind of the pupil through the purest forms of logic.

> From about the age of twelve, I entered into another and more advanced stage in my course of instruction; in which the main object was no longer the aids and appliances of thought, but the thoughts themselves. This commenced with Logic, in which I began at once with the Organon, and read it to the Analytics inclusive, but profited little by the Posterior Analytics, which belong to a branch of speculation I was not yet ripe for. . . .
> My own consciousness and experience ultimately led me to appreciate quite as highly as he [James Mill] did, the value of an early practical familiarity with the school logic. I know nothing, in my education, to which I think myself more in-

[3] *A System of Logic, Ratiocinative and Inductive: Being a Connected View of the Principles of Evidence and the Methods of Scientific Investigation*, 8th ed. (New York: Harper & Brothers, 1893), p. 148.

debted for whatever capacity of thinking I have attained. . . .
I am persuaded that nothing, in modern education, tends so
much, when properly used, to form exact thinkers. . . . It is
also a study peculiarly adapted to an early stage in the education of philosophical students, since it does not presuppose the
slow process of acquiring, by experience and reflection, valuable thoughts of their own.   (*Auto.*, pp. 12 and 13-14.)

The impersonal forms of thought on the one hand, something
—it did not much matter what—to fill those forms on the
other: almost any substance whatever could provide grist for
the mill of the mind, and that marvelous device, fed infinitely
with raw material, might, according to the theory of James
Mill, be infinitely perfected. "So complete," Mill explains,
"was my father's reliance on the influence of reason over the
minds of mankind" that for the son as for any human subject
all that was needful was the well-made thinking apparatus
and regular stimulus to set it in operation; then, since "his
fundamental doctrine was the formation of all human character by circumstances, through the universal Principles of Association," there naturally existed "the consequent unlimited
possibility of improving the moral and intellectual condition
of mankind through education" (*Auto.*, pp. 74 and 75). If
nothing else in nature is capable of it, yet the mind might thus
be the long-sought perpetual motion machine; or, since the
mind requires continued stimulus for movement, it suggests
perhaps a windmill grinding and grinding, turned by the variety of sensational experience that supplies it constantly with
stimulus in daily existence.[4] It was just such a mind, capable

[4] Carlyle's half-veiled reference to Mill and his father in *Sartor Resartus*
(written before Carlyle conceived the pleasant possibilities of Mill as a
disciple) is apposite: "Shall your Science proceed in the small chink-
lighted, or even oil-lighted, underground workshop of Logic alone; and
man's mind become an Arithmetical Mill, whereof Memory is the Hopper,
and mere tables of Sines and Tangents Codification, and Treatises of what
you call Political Economy, are the Meal?" (*Sartor Resartus*, chap. X; cf.
Michael St. John Packe, *The Life of John Stuart Mill* [London: Secker &
Warburg, 1954], p. 168).

237

of grinding exceeding fine, that James Mill set about producing. And John Stuart was undoubtedly, up to a point, the perfect product and the exemplary proof for his father's theories.

> In the course of instruction which I have partially retraced, the point most superficially apparent is the great effort to give, during the years of childhood, an amount of knowledge in what are considered the higher branches of education, which is seldom acquired (if acquired at all) until the age of manhood. The result of the experiment shows the ease with which this may be done. . . . If I had been by nature extremely quick of apprehension, or had possessed a very accurate and retentive memory, or were of a remarkably active and energetic character, the trial would not be conclusive; but in all these natural gifts I am rather below than above par; what I could do, could assuredly be done by any boy or girl of average capacity and healthy physical constitution: and if I have accomplished anything, I owe it, among other fortunate circumstances, to the fact that through the early training bestowed on me by my father, I started, I may fairly say, with an advantage of a quarter of a century over my contemporaries.   (*Auto.*, p. 7.)

Mill's characteristically dry praise for the results of the experiment in education sounds to the reader curiously like a lament for lost youth, or not perhaps lost, but simply unknown.

"Childhood and Early Education" (Mill's first-chapter title) was, then, altogether a manner of sensation/thinking, and Mill, as his father's experiment intended, came out an almost perfect "empirical/thinking" type. He was provided by his education with a finely rational intellect which, as with Darwin, could accurately (i.e., logically) judge the evidence and turn out of the inductive machine a law or theory embracing and explaining all received facts, flowing in from phenomenal experience. Darwin, a collector and natural scientist, observed and reasoned on natural facts; Mill, since he moved out into the moral and social sciences, merely translated observation and reasoning into experiencing and thinking. It is a cardinal principle of the adult J. S. Mill's sensationist, associational psychology, or of what he called his "philosophy of experience," that all human knowledge, all marks on what was originally a *tabula rasa*, must be experiential. "Of nature, or anything whatever external to ourselves," he maintains, "we know . . . nothing, except the facts which present themselves to our senses, and such other facts as may, by analogy, be inferred from these. There is no knowledge *a priori*; no truths cognizable by the mind's inward light, and grounded on intuitive evidence."[5] Mill's entire *System of Logic* was directed, according to the *Autobiography*, against "the ontological and 'innate principles' school," against the "German, or *a priori* view of human knowledge, and of the knowing faculties" (*Auto.*, p. 157). Even deductive reasoning, Mill argues, is merely inductive reasoning once removed: analyze any general principle informing the deductive method and you will always discover, whether this is immediately apparent or not, a pyramid of inductive logic building up to it; analysis will inevitably reveal a source in sensory experience. So, to his contemporary Newman, who found evidence for God in innate, individual conscience—who, indeed, founded everything he was on the certainty that conscience is a priori and inborn—to him Mill would respond, as he does generally in the *Logic*, that what is called conscience is not at all innate: that it is instead based on repeated experiences (actions and punishments) from which, by the inductive process, we have inferred a principle (certain actions lead to punishment), given it a name (conscience), then forgotten where it came from and supposed its source to be superhuman. While Newman was sure that conscience was the voice of a Heavenly Father, Mill was equally sure that it was the voice of his own, dangerously irascible,

[5] "Coleridge," *Dissertations and Discussions: Political, Philosophical, and Historical*, 4 vols. (London: Parker & Son, 1859), I, 404.

earthly father: "Another evil I shared with many of the sons of energetic fathers. To have been, through childhood, under the constant rule of a strong will, certainly is not favourable to strength of will. I was so much accustomed to expect to be told what to do, either in the form of direct command or of rebuke for not doing it, that I acquired a habit of leaving my responsibility as a moral agent to rest on my father, my conscience never speaking to me except by his voice" (*Early Draft*, pp. 184-85). Newman was born with a conscience, Mill inferred from the empirical facts of his education a moral system whose standard was happiness, and across the wheel of psychological types there was little likelihood of communication between the two. Mill, for his part, was very firm and very clear: "The notion that truths external to the mind may be known by intuition or consciousness, independently of observation and experience, is, I am persuaded, in these times, the great intellectual support of false doctrines and bad institutions" (*Auto.*, p. 158). Mill *père et fils*, in league against "the opposite school," perhaps best (or worst) represented by Newman's Church with its infallible voice, would show intuition and feeling the door before they might gain any serious foothold.

Mill's system of psychology, of course, treated only the conscious mind—and hence seems today only a partial psychology—but the irony of his case was that it was not conscious mind that temporarily undid him and stopped cold his mental progress. It was something older and more unmanageable, something deeper and more elusive, more insidious and more dangerous than conscious mind that whispered to John Mill during his "mental crisis" that there would surely come a time when there would be no original musical composition any more because all the possibilities would have been exhausted. To such horrid forebodings, the conscious, rational mind could offer little consolation and no answer because the

240

anxiety was neither conscious in origin nor rational in content. One psychic function, it would seem, is always developed at the expense of its opposite—thinking, for example, at the expense of feeling;[6] and while a main function determines our conscious attitude (according to Jungian psychology), an inferior function balances and opposes this main function by its dominance in the unconscious, whence, uncontrolled unless at least acknowledged by the conscious mind, it may erupt dangerously and inexplicably to engender neuroses—or, shall we say, mental crises. If, in looking back over his experience, John Stuart Mill rejects intuition as a valid ground of knowledge, James Mill had long since, in provision for his son, thoroughly scouted feeling from educational theory and practice. Mill says his father was possessed of strong feelings, and that may be; whatever the personal case with James Mill, however, in his conscious plan of education for his son—than which there has never been a plan *more* conscious—he coolly and completely repressed feelings in himself and scorned them as unworthy of notice in the development of another.

> The element which was chiefly deficient in his moral relation to his children was that of tenderness. . . . He resembled most Englishmen in being ashamed of the signs of feeling, and by the absence of demonstration, starving the feelings themselves. . . .
>
> My father's teachings tended to the under-valuing of feeling. It was not that he was himself cold-hearted or insensible; I believe it was rather from the contrary quality; he thought

[6] Cf. Einstein: "If an individual enjoys well-ordered thoughts, it is quite possible that this side of his nature may grow more pronounced at the cost of other sides and thus may determine his mentality in increasing degree" (*Einstein: Philosopher-Scientist*, 1, 5). Which, one might ask, comes first—well-ordered thoughts and then an education to suit that "side of his nature," or an education in syllogistic logic, then a resultant character? In either case, as Einstein suggests, as Mill's history proves, there is a "cost." Or, as Mill himself says, "No youth of the age I then was, can be expected to be more than one thing, and this [a pure reasoner] was the thing I happened to be" (*Auto.*, p. 76).

that feeling could take care of itself; that there was sure to be enough of it if actions were properly cared about.

(*Auto.*, p. 77.)

Or, as Mill put it in a passage that he later felt it more circumspect to delete: "It was one of the most unfavourable of the moral agencies which acted on me in my boyhood, that mine was not an education of love but of fear" (*Early Draft*, p. 66). Consciously, then, it is out with intuition and down with feeling, forward with sensation and up with thinking. For John Stuart Mill, because of his father's experiment with his life, the circle of types was more like a fixed roulette wheel, heavily loaded in advance: he could not but fall into the predetermined hole.

In theory, it is obvious, Mill should have been an empirical thinker; in fact, he was; and in style, that being a mirror of the made man, we can trace and demonstrate his typical configuration. For, although Mill suffered a mental crisis, although he changed and grew, although he underwent a further education and development, although the child was not exactly and identically the man, yet James Mill got him first. The father really did shape the child's mind, as in theory he hoped he could. All sorts of things might change after that, but the twig had been well bent, and the branch could only live out the bent pattern. Whatever did change, Mill's style, one to one with his education, continued cerebral to the end. "It would often *tell* better on the reader," Mill once hesitantly advised Carlyle, "if what were said in an abrupt, exclamatory, and interjectional manner were said in the ordinary grammatical mode of nominative and verb."[7] Carlyle was not likely to change his style on the advice of Mill (or any other man), and he, naturally, had his own opinion of Mill's mind and manner—an opinion that was, appropriately, about equal and

[7] Packe, *Life*, p. 184.

242

opposite to Mill's judgment on him. Recommending his new acquaintance to Jane, Carlyle described him as "a fine clear enthusiast, who will one day come to something; yet to nothing poetical, I think: his fancy is not rich; furthermore, he cannot *laugh* with any compass."[8] Laughter Carlyle had in abundance, of course, though there might be those that would think it unbalanced, hysterical, or insane laughter. John Mill, lucid, abstract, as coolly sane in expression as in thought, never gave himself to Carlyle's laughter; or, indeed, to any noticeable amount of laughter at all. For all his massive and synthesizing intelligence, it would be fair to say of Mill that he lacks somewhat in humor as well as stylistic verve. In this, as in so many ways, Mill is a truly dispassionate writer "in the ordinary grammatical mode of nominative and verb"—interjectional on infrequent occasions, abrupt and exclamatory never. In its rational clarity, in its high and dry thinness, Mill's prose is quite emptied of affective feeling; in its emotional poverty, it offers no hook, no variation of texture, for the reader's sensory imagination. The mind might be fed on sensation, as Mill claimed, but somehow, in its typical functioning, the mind must retain all sensory detail, for none of it turns up on the page in Mill's writing. The reader of Mill must be content with the ratiocinative product since Mill offers him so little of the felt, raw material of thought. It is certainly true that his reader very seldom dares to disagree with Mill, but he equally seldom gives a total, Newmanesque assent, or feels his will moved by the argument, for the fact is that Mill very infrequently makes a total—i.e., more than intellectual—appeal. As reluctant with fictions as Swift is said to have been with metaphors in *Gulliver's Travels*, "the rogue never hazards an anecdote."

Even, or perhaps especially, when he writes of Harriet Taylor's influence on his thought, practice, and writing, Mill re-

8 Packe, *Life*, pp. 169-70.

mains always general and abstract and rational. Stylistically, Mill seems unwilling to share emotional experience as his mind goes about cutting the facts, drying them, gathering them into generalities, and laying them out for the reader's circumspect consideration. Particularized scenes and anecdotes, drawing the reader to participation in Mill's self-portrait and -progress, are almost deafening by their absence (contrast the autobiography of an artist like Yeats—a string of revealing and more or less factual anecdotes from beginning to end—or Montaigne). Some few abstractions serve to suggest the mental quality of the people who shaped and formed Mill, but there is scarcely a hint of any stories which, by their dramatic precision, relevance, effectiveness, might, like poetry, carry the subject alive by passion into the heart. Mill never, that is, captures total character and personality in significant gesture that would carry and embody the same sort of truth, recaptured from personal history, as a meaningful fiction might. In the end, we have not a sense of Harriet Taylor, the living woman, but a disembodied paean of praise to her influence on Mill's thought. Mill can tempt the reader's interest with such a promising start as, "The steps in my mental growth for which I was indebted to her were far from being those which a person wholly uninformed on the subject would probably suspect." "Oh?" the reader may think, "perhaps we're getting into something now; perhaps a speck of drama will find its way from the life to the page." Nothing of the kind: Mill has no intention of satisfying the reader's curious imagination, or of pandering to his itching desire for what both Mill and Harriet would have considered revoltingly "sensual" detail. Mill offers instead these dusty abstractions that choke the reader's imaginative response at its source:

It might be supposed, for instance, that my strong convictions on the complete equality in all legal, political, social and domestic relations, which ought to exist between men and women, may have been adopted or learnt from her. This was so far from being the fact, that those convictions were among the earliest results of the application of my mind to political subjects. . . . But that perception of the vast practical bearings of women's disabilities which found expression in the book on the "Subjection of Women" was acquired mainly through her teaching. But for her rare knowledge of human nature and comprehension of moral and social influences, though I should doubtless have held my present opinions, I should have had a very insufficient perception of the mode in which the consequences of the inferior position. . . . etc. (*Auto.*, p. 173.)

So much for the reader's impassioned, "sensual" curiosity—and let that be a lesson to him.

Stylistically, Mill did not change. He does claim, however, that during the period of his crisis there occurred an "important transformation in my opinions and character" (*Auto.*, p. 93). The other half of Mill's education was yet to come, but that could only be after he had passed through the shadow, only after the inferior function of feeling, willfully suppressed and consciously denied, had exploded into a mental crisis that manifested itself significantly as an inexplicable depression in feeling ("tormented by the thought of the exhaustibility of musical combinations").[9] Mill says that during his depression he was able to continue with his conscious activity as well as ever: "During this time I was not incapable of my usual occupations. I went on with them mechanically, by the mere force of habit. I had been so drilled in a certain sort of mental exercise, that I could still carry it on when all the spirit had gone out of it" (*Auto.*, p. 98). This time of crisis and trans-

[9] *Auto.*, p. 102. We see Mill's susceptibility to this fantastic kind of despair or melancholy or accidie again, at a later date (December 1854), in a letter to Harriet: "If I let myself dwell on the idea I could get into the state of being unable to bear the impossibility of flying to the moon —it is a part of human nature I never saw described but have long known by experience—" (F. A. Hayek, *John Stuart Mill and Harriet Taylor: Their Correspondence and Subsequent Marriage* [London: Routledge & Kegan Paul, 1951], p. 213).

formation is like an interim period, or a "centre of indifference," in Mill's history: suspended between a father past and a wife to come, between an education of acquisition and a cultivation of feeling, between his need for human love and his theoretical indifference to it, Mill was through with the old world but as yet incapable of the new. There was some four years between Mill's crisis and his meeting with Harriet Taylor. The exhaustion of what he so desperately needed from life without being able to specify what it might be (the depletion of musical combinations being merely a symbol for the emotional poverty of life: what was there to live for?) stands, a terrible and ironic frustration, in the way of Mill's further individual development. What he had not been taught by his tutor to name and know, he could hardly expect, alone and unaided, to spell out. The associational circle of cause and effect closed on Mill, to be broken only by a new, intervenient perception or presence from without. And yet not entirely or really from without either, since the energy necessary to effect such an internal change in the self, and to give it a meaning or a reason for being, comes only from within the self. The strength of transformation was to be personal and suprapersonal for Mill, granted and yet achieved.

His youthful industry as a Utilitarian propagandist, Mill says, was "little else . . . than zeal for speculative opinions. It had not its root in genuine benevolence, or sympathy with mankind; though these qualities held their due place in my ethical standard" (*Auto.*, p. 77). Even this slight motive to corporate life, insufficient and inappropriate as it seems for individual human existence, disappeared during Mill's depression: "I became persuaded, that my love of mankind, and of excellence for its own sake, had worn itself out" (*Auto.*, p. 95). How long, after all, is it possible to love an abstraction? Abstractions, perhaps, may have continuing relations with abstractions, but can an individual human being continue

246

the lover of mankind? Mill found not. "I sought no comfort by speaking to others of what I felt. If I had loved any one sufficiently to make confiding my griefs a necessity, I should not have been in the condition I was" (*Auto.*, p. 93). "Mankind" is an unreality in the face of "any *one*," but for Mill, as yet, "any one" hardly existed, neither another "one," nor, consequently, his own "one." "But there was no one," he continues, "on whom I could build the faintest hope." Naturally, Mill considered whether he might not turn to his father, his acknowledged maker up to this time: "My education . . . was wholly his work." And there, for the son, is the cruel irony. The theory had worked perfectly—only too perfectly; there was no way the conceiving mind could be expected to see the experiment from without and to be dissatisfied with its result: any disabilities in the theory were the disabilities of James Mill's mind. The son, broken on the wheel of that very circumstantial experience which alone, according to the doctrine of his own and his father's associational psychology, is the basis of character and knowledge, could hardly appeal his inadequacy back through the chain of experiences to the theoretician, for that man could only and truthfully say: "Yes; such is what I intended." James Mill was clearly not the "one"; the new day had to begin elsewhere. The mental crisis stands, in Mill's life and in his portrait, as the focal point of breaking and rebuilding: out in either direction, and drawing the two halves together, the whole individual begins to find his own shape.

James Mill made an efficient thinking machine; it remained for Harriet Taylor to help the machine see how it might be a man. Like Darwin hesitant and modest, though not, like Darwin, bewildered, since by the time he wrote the *Autobiography* he had succeeded in coming through to self-understanding, Mill introduces the mechanical metaphor himself: "I conceive that the description so often given of a Benthamite, as a mere reasoning machine . . . was during two or three years of my life not altogether untrue of me" (*Auto.*, p. 76). The progress of Mill's education from father to wife may be conveniently traced in a developing metaphoric thread that runs through the account in the *Autobiography* of the making of a mind and the cultivation of an individual. The essence and product of James Mill's exclusively intellectual educational program finds expression most often in a machine metaphor: Mill was shaped and formed by another's hand, a functioning, stamped, thinking, manufactured machine, "acquiring" an "amount of knowledge" external and transferable (this is partly Mill's notion, partly the idea of others about Mill before he read Wordsworth and began to cultivate the feelings). But the other, the heretofore neglected half of education for life, is always expressed by a submerged organic metaphor (as if Mill were completing himself by borrowing their favorite metaphor from the opposite school, from the Coleridgeans). After the crisis it is not a question of shaping or forming, of acquiring something external or finished, but of "cultivating," of "nourishing" with an emotional "fount" that had been "sealed up" in youth; now the "sacred fount" is forced by unconscious pressure to crisis and to flow before the organic whole will be realized. "It is impossible," the son says of James Mill,

> not to feel true pity for a father who did, and strove to do, so much for his children, who would have so valued their affection, yet who must have been constantly feeling that fear of him was drying it up at its source. . . . When [fear] . . . predominates so much as to preclude love and confidence on the part of the child to those who should be the unreservedly trusted advisers of after years, and perhaps to seal up the fountains of frank and spontaneous communicativeness in the child's nature, it is an evil for which a large abatement must be made from the benefits, moral and intellectual, which may flow from any other part of the education. (*Auto.*, pp. 36-37.)

Harriet Taylor, in Mill's all too brief and abstract characterization of her, is everything that James Mill was not and could not be; happily, therefore, "My Most Valuable Friendship" can follow immediately in the plan of the *Autobiography* upon "A Crisis in My Mental History."

> In the deserts of the heart
> Let the healing fountains start,
> In the prison of his days
> Teach the free man how to praise.

W. H. Auden's metaphor for the curative power of Yeats's poetry expresses what Mill found in Wordsworth's poetry and Harriet Taylor's person: "a woman of deep and strong feeling, of penetrating and intuitive intelligence, and of an eminently meditative and poetic nature," informed by "noble and elevated feeling" which "co-existed with a highly reverential nature." Her "sensitive as well as her mental faculties would, with her gifts of feeling and imagination, have fitted her to be a consummate artist," and she was possessed of a "lovingness ever ready to pour itself forth upon any or all human beings who were capable of giving the smallest feeling in return" (*Auto.*, pp. 130 and 131). With this metaphor of healing and fertility in mind, it may not seem altogether insignificant that the first hopeful sign of rebirth for Mill (some years before he knew Harriet) comes with the flow of tears induced by reading of sad and brave events in an autobiography: "A vivid conception of the scene and its feelings came over me, and I was moved to tears. From this moment my burthen grew lighter. The oppression of the thought that all feeling was dead within me, was gone. I was no longer hopeless: I was not a stock or a stone" (*Auto.*, p. 99). The healing waters having broken through, Mill, no longer a "mere reasoning machine" from his father's workshop, cultivates the seeds of self and nourishes them to full individual growth from the founts of feeling.

249

The other important change which my opinions at this time underwent, was that I, for the first time, gave its proper place, among the prime necessities of human well-being, to the internal culture of the individual. . . .

I had now learnt by experience that the passive susceptibilities needed to be cultivated as well as the active capacities, and required to be nourished and enriched as well as guided. . . . The maintenance of a due balance among the faculties, now seemed to me of primary importance. The cultivation of the feelings became one of the cardinal points in my ethical and philosophical creed.[10]

It was Harriet who, years before she could become his wife, provided Mill personally with a "cultivation of the feelings."

Whether his "dear one," his "inspiration," his "prize in the lottery of life" was exactly what Mill said she was or not, is, of course, an interesting and vexed question. The extraordinary development of his character is often the reverse of what would be expected in a young man: when we read of Mill's intellectual and literary achievements at three or twelve or nineteen, we have continually to remind ourselves of his extreme youth; when, on the other hand, we come upon his expressions of feeling in letters to Harriet written at the age of twenty-eight or thirty-two or forty-seven, it is with amazement and some embarrassment for Mill that we recall that they were not written by a schoolboy of fourteen. Or again, when Mill expresses himself to Harriet in hyperbole (or is it hyperbole? It might be truer to say that what we take as hyperbole, Mill intended literally), it is a matter of squirming discomfort for the reader: "Every possible good that the

---

[10] *Auto.*, pp. 100-101. Cf. the metaphor in Jung: "Just as the great personality acts upon society to liberate, to redeem, to transform, and to heal, so the birth of personality in oneself has a therapeutic effect. It is as if a river that had run to waste in sluggish side-streams and marshes suddenly found its way back to its proper bed, or as if a stone lying on a germinating seed were lifted away so that the shoot could begin its natural growth" ("The Development of Personality," *CW*, xvii, par. 317).

new year can possibly bring to the only person living who is worthy to live, and may she have the happiest & maniest new years that the inexorable powers allow to any of us poor living creatures."[11] It has been suggested that Mill's extravagant eulogies of Harriet, his frequent confessions of complete emotional, intellectual, and moral dependence upon her, were a result of her cleverness in giving Mill's ideas back to him for his wondering admiration; that she served as a sort of intellectual mirror in which he could narcissistically love his own reflected ideas.

It is true that in his exaggerated devotion to Harriet (which, after her death, he transferred with suspicious ease to her daughter Helen) Mill specifically ascribes to her great intellectual powers. Even so, Mill is not precisely admiring himself or his own mind in Harriet, but rather investing her with those ideal properties lacking in his own conscious make-up, but present, by compensation, in his own unknown, unconscious, undeveloped self. She was the embodiment for Mill of all the feeling and intuitive side of his character that had been systematically repressed throughout his education, and he became a whole man by realizing his unconscious potentialities in Harriet, or by projecting them onto her person. She had a quickness of mind and intuition that allowed her to understand the questions her husband was working with and to come to an answer very like his eventual answer, but by a different route and different means, and this, I think, is the reason for Mill's adoration. His answers were attained by a careful process of logic and reasoning, hers by an intuitive perception. This is the sort of person that Mill was constituted—even, paradoxically, by his education—to admire, to love, to be infatuated with. If he was made foolish by his display of feeling, as many people thought (and continue to

[11] Dated January 1, 1855: Hayek, *Mill and Harriet Taylor*, p. 214.

think) he was, then that is the risk taken in a one-sided education such as his had been. The needs of the man whose feelings had been "starved" in childhood were supplied by the woman who described herself in these words:

> It seems to me that personal feeling has more of infinity in it than any other part of character—no ones *mind* is *ever* satisfied, nor their imagination nor their ambition—nor anything else of that class—but feeling *satisfies*—All the qualities on earth never give happiness without personal feeling—personal feeling always gives happiness with or without any other character. The desire to give & to receive feeling is almost the whole of my character.[12]

Abrupt interjection and exclamation never entered Mill's own style, but he does not seem to have minded it in Harriet. Her pre-eminence in their relation reminds one rather of the picture Virginia Woolf gives in *To the Lighthouse* of Mrs. Ramsay, who sits serenely in full, intuitive possession of the fruits of contemplation, never having struggled to get there, while her husband toils two-thirds of the way there in painful ratiocination but can get no further. While Mr. Ramsay frustratedly wonders how his wife got to the end, however, Mill only praises and praises his wife for being there. The way Mill described her in an early version of the *Autobiography*— a passage that Harriet marked and that he later rejected—is more than sufficient confirmation for this reading of their relationship:

> But at a very early period of my knowledge of her she became to me a living type of the most admirable kind of human being. I had always wished for a friend whom I could admire wholly, without reservation & restriction, & I had now found one. To render this possible, it was necessary that the object of my admiration should be of a type very different from my own; should be a character pre-eminently of feeling, combined how-

[12] Letter to Mill, undated, about 1835 or 1836: Hayek, *Mill and Harriet Taylor*, p. 98.

ever as I had not in any other instance known it to be, with a vigorous & bold speculative intellect. . . . The best thing I . . . could do for the world, would be to serve as a sort of prose interpreter of her poetry, giving a logical exposition to those who have more understanding than feeling, of the reasonableness of that which she either knew by the experience or divined by the intuition of one of the richest & strongest of natures.   (*Early Draft*, pp. 198-99.)

Onto Harriet, to put the matter perhaps oversimply, Mill projected his *anima*. And in her, it might be noticed, he no longer scorned intuition as a basis of knowledge, nor feeling as the proper judge of it.

Mill's contemporaries smiled at Mill's praises, or laughed outright, and generations of readers have been sure that Harriet was quite different from Mill's (almost always vague) descriptions. She was "a clever and remarkable woman," George Mill, one of John's younger brothers, said, "but," he discreetly added, "nothing like what John took her to be."[13] For an understanding of Mill's character and his *Autobiography*, however, the important point is that he *saw* her thus— he endowed her, out of his own needs and in his own estimation, with those characteristics that he had been denied, that he denied himself, and that he required in a partner. If others were skeptical, she fortunately believed what he said of her, and so could be the partner Mill needed. Certainly, it is hard to believe that she was all that her husband claimed: it is hard to believe that anyone could be that; and the picture of her that emerges from, for example, the recent studies by Hayek and Packe and Pappe is much less impressive and very much less pleasant than Mill could ever have wished. *Tant pis*— in Mill's mind and eye, not to say in his heart, she was what he said, and when it is a question of how he became what he eventually was, that is surely all that counts.

[13] Quoted by Guy Linton Diffenbaugh, "Mrs. Taylor Seen Through Other Eyes than John Stuart Mill's," *Sewanee Review*, XXXI (April 1923), 201.

With the advent of Harriet and the full resolution of his mental crisis, with much now to live for, Mill discovers—or rediscovers: he gives real assent to something long known and often forgotten—that internal culture of the individual is a way of resolving the oppressive question, forced on him "like an incubus" by the doctrine of associational psychology, of free will and necessity. In the tension created between inner will and outer circumstance, the fortunate individual finds that self which he must be and chooses to be. Until now, however, Mill has seen only the external and necessary, has seen only that circumstances, absolute and necessary, shape character. "The state of the whole universe at any instant," Mill says, thus providing in his *Logic* a basis for inductive premises, is "the consequence of its state at the previous instant; insomuch that one who knew all the agents which exist at the present moment . . . could predict the whole subsequent history of the universe" (*Logic*, p. 250). And, because he would establish the validity of the moral sciences, Mill must and does claim that it is not otherwise with human character and action. They are as exactly linked to circumstances by cause and consequence as any other phenomena in the universe. Clear recognition of this might well, as in the *Autobiography*, issue in despair: how could Mill hope ever to reverse the circumstances that had plunged him into depression? "I felt as if I was scientifically proved to be the helpless slave of antecedent circumstances; as if my character and that of all others had been formed for us by agencies beyond our control, and was wholly out of our power" (*Auto.*, pp. 118-19). Turning the coin over, however, it becomes apparent that the flow of cause and effect is not in one direction only: if circumstances shape character, so too does character transform circumstances. So long as we look in the direction of circumstances→character and cause→effect, without observing that they compose but half a circle, we shall, with Mill, fall into depression and mental crisis; when we see the half-circle, however, which is antecedent to circumstances and consequent upon the will or desire of character, we may, again with Mill, recover joy and realize the simultaneous necessity and beauty of full individual development. Mill resolves "the doctrine of what is called Philosophical Necessity" by "discarding altogether the misleading word Necessity" (*Auto.*, pp. 118 and 119), by disavowing Fatalism (which has, as he says in his *Examination of Sir William Hamilton's Philosophy*, "a paralyzing effect on conduct"),[14] and by discovering his own Determination in a distinction between Predestination and Fatalism. His Determinism turns out to be very similar to, perhaps no other than, what one would call "realization of the self": a process which reaches out to the predestining will of the divine on the one hand, is touched by necessity on the other, and freely wills that which is thereby determined. In his essay "On Liberty," Mill argues that if God creates man and is a good being, then he must delight in "every nearer approach made by his creatures to the ideal conception embodied in them."[15] This is truly a hopeful predestiny: fructification of seeds deposited, carried, realized. The channels of becoming are to be discovered in the forms of creation. Thus, in a world split between good and evil (Mill's three essays on religion, "Nature," "Utility of Religion," "Theism," are consistently Manichaean), the individual may contribute his small portion to the struggle by becoming that self which was predestined and preordained by its creator: "We may be cooperating with the unseen Being to whom we owe all that is enjoyable in life. . . . requiting the good he has given by a voluntary co-operation which he, not being omnipotent, really

[14] *An Examination of Sir William Hamilton's Philosophy* (London: Longmans, Green, & Co., 1889), p. 606.

[15] "On Liberty," *Utilitarianism, Liberty, and Representative Government* (New York: Dutton, 1951), p. 161.

needs."[16] The entire universe, except for the evil force, is joyous with the cultivation of self. "For if God acts according to general laws," Mill says, in distinguishing Predestination from Fatalism, "then, whatever he may have preordained, he has preordained that it shall take place through the causes on which experience shows it to be consequent: and if he has predestined that I shall attain my ends, he has predestined that I shall do so by studying and putting in practice the means which lead to their attainment" (*Sir William Hamilton's Philosophy*, p. 606). Whether this constitutes an argument for or against free will, it is, and was for Mill, a liberating doctrine.

In at least this way a Utilitarian to the end of his life, Mill never, as he says in the *Autobiography*, "wavered in the conviction that happiness is the test of all rules of conduct, and the end of life" (p. 100). But if he did not waver in this conviction, he did come to believe that happiness might be less easily calculable than he had supposed, and that the pursuit of happiness should be both indirect and redirected. Mill concludes *A System of Logic* with his most carefully considered statement of this principle: "I . . . declare my conviction, that the general principle to which all rules of practice ought to conform, and the test by which they should be tried, is that of conduciveness to the happiness of mankind, or rather, of all sentient beings; in other words, that the promotion of happiness is the ultimate principle of Teleology" (*Logic*, p. 658). On the other hand, from the *Autobiography*, "I now thought that this end was only to be attained by not making it the direct end" (p. 100). It sounds very much like a first or a

[16] *Three Essays on Religion* (London: Longmans, Green, Reader, & Dyer, 1874), p. 256. Given the forces contending within him, it is perhaps significant that Mill was attracted to Manichaeism. "No religious system," according to Peter Brown, "had ever treated the visible world so drastically, and with such liberalism, as an externalization of an inner, spiritual conflict" (*Augustine of Hippo* [London: Faber & Faber, 1967], p. 56).

priori principle, the very existence of which Mill denied, but the position he eventually takes is something like this: happiness is the proper standard of all human conduct, but it is not something you can salt on the tail and take directly; instead, happiness is to be found indirectly in cultivation of individuality, plenary and various. There, on a principle otherwise unexplained (the creator so intended it?), is the source of happiness.

> The character itself should be, to the individual, a paramount end, simply because the existence of this ideal nobleness of character, or of a near approach to it, in any abundance, would go farther than all things else toward making human life happy, both in the comparatively humble sense of pleasure and freedom from pain, and in the higher meaning, rendering life, not what it now is almost universally, puerile and insignificant, but such as human beings with highly developed faculties can care to have. (*Logic*, pp. 658-59.)

Finally, shaped by his father, cultivated by Mrs. Taylor, new-born but with the authority of experience in every line, the whole Mill stands forth in what, excepting his *Autobiography*, is his finest work, "a kind of philosophic text-book of a single truth" and that truth the truth of individuality. The epigraph to the essay "On Liberty," again sounding like an original principle, insists on its single truth: "The grand, leading principle, towards which every argument in these pages directly converges, is the absolute and essential importance of human development in its richest variety." The style of this essay, mirroring the man, takes on new color and life under the impetus of the subject and out of the inspiration provided by Mill's intellectual and marital daimon. One is inclined, that is, to agree with Mill in his valuation of the book—and for the reason he suggests: "The 'Liberty' was more directly and literally our joint production than anything else which bears my name. . . . It is in consequence of this that, although it never underwent her final revision, it far surpasses, as a mere specimen of composition, anything which has proceeded from me either before or since" (*Auto.*, p. 176). And Harriet, after all, represented only the freeing or the realization of something potential within Mill himself. Cooperating in full with the "lovingness" of Mrs. Taylor—she humanizing, cultivating, nourishing the theretofore incomplete man—Mill demonstrates that love makes the machine turn and even, such are its wonders, brings the machine to life and creative individuality.

Though Mill asked her often for advice in writing the *Autobiography*, there is little evidence, either internal or external, that Harriet contributed much to that composition. And it would probably be fair to say that Mill's *Autobiography* strikes the perceptive reader as a curious anomaly: a self-portrait that is yet a nonfigurative painting, a sketch of the personal and particular in impersonal and general terms. Surely, a more abstract portraitist than Mill scarcely exists. Who has ever, for example, merely from reading the *Autobiography*, succeeded in *seeing* James Mill? But, it might be objected, Mill intended to describe the education given by his father and not his father's person. Then what about Harriet Taylor? Mill certainly tries to give some sense of what she was and what she seemed to him; yet a a century of readers have confessed themselves unable to see or to understand or to believe in the reality of Mill's Harriet Taylor. And the notion that most people hold of Mill himself—as cold and high and thin and dry as the air of the mountains he loved to climb—is unquestionably due for the most part to the fleshless picture that he gives us in the *Autobiography* of the making of pure mind. Mill's character, with the arrival of Harriet, may have taken on some of the warmth and emotionality that she claimed and he proclaimed; but the form of the *Autobiography*, both in overall structure and in local expression, bears the clear stamp of the school logic so carefully impressed on Mill's mind by his father some fifty years before he came to write it down. It is all very like a syllogism on private human experience—but no less interesting or significant for that.

five : *Four Quartets*

the pattern more complicated

1. "significant emotion"

Though the limitations are not of course the same in every case, there are, nevertheless, very clear limits to the universality of the metaphors created by Darwin and Fox, by Mill and Newman. Darwin's general law of evolution and Newman's personal history in evolution, Mill's educational syllogism and Fox's private voice, closely tailored as they are to their creators' specific needs, and partly because of that close tailoring, do not fit the experientially determined necessities of all men. Darwin, Fox, and Mill projected their appropriate and single metaphors for the most part unconsciously, and even when they were aware of what they were doing they seldom considered why; Newman, although he created his metaphors consciously, did it largely for polemical, and thus for circumstantially confined and autobiographically impure, purposes. In the autobiographical writings of Montaigne and Jung, however, and indeed in the entire lifeworks of these two men, one discovers metaphor-making that is purer in intention, wider in application, and more entirely aware of itself, of its source and its object, than is the case with the four simple autobiographers. Montaigne and Jung were both, as I have suggested, artists of moral experience, and for such writers no demarcating line exists to indicate where life, whether taken as their own life or as the stuff of moral artistry, leaves off and where the disciplines of psychology and philosophy begin; nor, of course, does such a limiting line, which would restrict the sufficiency of his metaphor, exist for the artist in a more traditional sense—the poet, for example. Poetry, like psychology and philosophy, is about life, not about part of it but potentially about all of it. The truth that poetry embodies, large or small as it may be, is a whole truth, and ideally it engages thought equally with feeling, intuition equally with observation; it engages, that is to say, the whole man and his entire consciousness, all his experience, and his vision, recollected in tranquillity, of that experience. If it is legitimate to say that there is art of a sort behind the autobiographies of Jung and Montaigne, or that these two writers avail themselves of some of the same means and seek much the same ends as the artist, then one can also observe that there is, in a reciprocal sense, considerable autobiography, both individual and universal, behind the art of a poem like *Four Quartets*, though I think Hugh Kenner was quite right to call his book on Eliot *The Invisible Poet*, for the personal and historic Eliot tends to disappear in his poem into patterns of universalized experience. What Eliot does, in a general way, in *Four Quartets*, as Jung does in his *Memories* and Montaigne in his *Essays*, is to weave together personal allusions in such a way as to create a generalized significance, so that the work becomes, in effect, an autobiography of and for Everyman as a philosophic and spiritual being. The artist who, like Eliot, treats his own experience as representative and symbolic, resolves and merges those dualities of consciousness and the unconscious, of the individual and the race, that have long attracted and teased the minds of psychologist and philosopher. The individual self—a self belonging indistinguishably to poet, reader, and poem—that is realized by the process of a work like *Four Quartets* stands for the whole integrated psyche of mankind; it becomes, for the moment, an epitome representation of the human effort toward consciousness.

That the unity of autobiography is, as Montaigne might say, consubstantial with the unity of the autobiographing personality seems to me a fact we cannot escape in discussing the con-

261

ditions and the possibilities of autobiography as art, or art as autobiography. "Mais les thèmes essentiels," Georges Gusdorf quite rightly maintains, "les schémas de structure qui s'imposent au matériel composite des faits extérieurs sont les éléments constituants de la personnalité."[1] How could it be otherwise with autobiography, that narrative of recall and discovery that Gusdorf describes, in an elegant formulation, as "le symbole, en quelque sorte, ou la parabole, d'une conscience en quête de sa propre vérité" (*ibid.*, p. 119). But one would not be misunderstood here: this is true also for the drama or the novel, for the Einsteinian formula and the Socratic theory; and it is the very rock on which an understanding of the mode of *Four Quartets* should be founded. Yet, because one would not be guilty of confusing art with life, as one might be accused of doing by those who insist on the rules proper to the "genre," and because one did not, in any case, know the T. S. Eliot of Monday and Tuesday existence, it is necessary to hold to and emphasize a distinction between the merely personal personality of T. S. Eliot and the artistically transformed personality of the poem. Recall and recapitulation, I would suggest, are the twin techniques by which Eliot effects this transformation of personality in the poem, and I would suggest further that recall and recapitulation are of the very essence of great autobiography: they provide the substance and the method of Montaigne's *Essays*, with his double and triple perspective on his own past, and they are the matter and the manner of Jung's *Memories*, with his ontogenetic-phylogenetic presentation of human experience; recall and recapitulation, to put the matter otherwise, signify the use of memory for artistic and universalizing ends. "In literature," Stephen Spen-

---

[1] "Conditions et limites de l'autobiographie," in *Formen der Selbstdarstellung: Analekten zu einer Geschichte des literarischen Selbstportraits* (Festgabe für Fritz Neubert), ed. Günther Reichenkron and Erich Haase (Berlin: Duncker & Humblot, 1956), p. 113.

der says in his essay on "Confessions and Autobiography," "the autobiographical is transformed. It is no longer the writer's own experience: it becomes everyone's. He is no longer writing about himself: he is writing about life. He creates it, not as an object which is already familiar and observed, as he is observed by others, but as a new and revealing object, growing out of and beyond observation."[2] It is through the operation of memory, which draws all the significant past up into the focus of the present, that the autobiographer and the poet succeed in universalizing their experience and their meaning. Each of them discovers, in fact, by looking through the glass of memory, a meaning in his experience which was not there before and which exists now only as a present creation.

"Memory," André Maurois once said, directing his amused irony against the autobiographer and against one of the major psychological tools of the autobiographer's art, "Memory is a great artist. For every man and for every woman it makes the recollection of his or her life a work of art and an unfaithful record."[3] Being a great biographer, Maurois naturally states the case for his own, perhaps more objective and certainly more external, art as strongly as possible, and he shows little concern whether autobiography shall survive the comparison or not; what he says, moreover, has an unquestioned bit of truth in it. However, mere falsification of the past with the intention of justifying the present, which is apparently what Maurois has in mind, will hardly produce a work of art from the materials of the lived, recalled, and recapitulated past in the sense that one would intend when one says that *Four Quartets*, which puts memory to use as both a technique and a theme, is a great work of art; nor, turning the matter over, will such "artistic" falsifying result in a great work of auto-

---

[2] "Confessions and Autobiography," *The Making of a Poem* (New York: Norton Library, 1962), pp. 65-66.
[3] *Aspects of Biography* (New York: D. Appleton & Co., 1929), pp. 157-58.

biography, and *Four Quartets*, representing and recreating the philosophic quest, comes in the end to be both the meditative autobiography of the poet and a spiritual autobiography for his readers. The record that memory reconstructs is no doubt, as Maurois says, "unfaithful" to the past, but this infidelity seems at most a very minor sin if one considers memory not as an orderly summoning up of something dead—a sort of Final Judgment on past events—but as a creative figuration of the living present and a summary reconstruction of how the present came to be that which it is and that which it represents itself as being. Memory, even ideally, is not something that begins in the far-distant past and that then follows a course to the present. The past is past; we do not exist in the past any longer and so cannot exercise memory or any other function from within it. But why should this essential fact about memory bother us? Why should we not take memory for what it richly is—a function of present consciousness—rather than worrying about what it is not, and cannot be? Of course memory will never give us objective truth about the past. And are we sure that we ever knew the objective truth about the past anyway ("so that it appears," as Camara Laye says in *Dark Child*, the autobiography of his African childhood, "as if we are ceasing to be what we were, and that truly we are no longer what we were, and that we were not exactly ourselves even at the time when these miracles took place before our eyes"[4])? Though it is powerless in the past, however, memory can and will create a subjective and vastly important truth about the present. Memory issues in and validates present being because it is simultaneously a tracing that leads to present consciousness and a product of that same present consciousness; it integrates all the old, half-remembered, or perhaps misremembered, selves, which were ade-

[4] *The Dark Child*, trans. James Kirkup and Ernest Jones (New York: Farrar, Straus & Giroux, 1954), p. 75.

quate to their own proper moments, into the pattern of the new self, which is born in the moment now out of this very exercise of consciousness and memory. "Autrement dit, l'auto-biographie est une seconde lecture de l'expérience et plus vraie que la première, puisqu'elle en est la prise de conscience." *Four Quartets* constitutes a recapture of experience, "une seconde lecture de l'expérience," in Gusdorf's phrase (p. 114), "et plus vraie que la première"; a recapture and a renewal of Eli-ot's experience and the reader's experience and Everyman's; a series of recollections and a revitalization of selfhood and, in the recapitulative technique that operates within the work, a constant recall and compression of these metaphorized recol-lections from earlier passages of the poem. But this is all rather complicated, and how it is, in a more specific analysis, that the poet is able to refigure past experience as present con-sciousness, and how it is, as a corollary to this refiguring proc-ess, that he succeeds in expanding the circumference of his metaphor to make it available as expression and creation for any man, requires and will bear considerable investigation.

Let us, like Socrates, try to subdue the confusion of poetic theory by proceeding on an hypothesis: that the poem com-municates an experience. What does it mean to say that it is possible to communicate an experience? We clearly, from the subjective nature of individual experience, have no objective assurance that it can be communicated. I feel something, you feel something; how shall we ever meet to communicate? How shall we ever, even, know that we feel the same or similar things, have known the same or similar experiences? Emotions begin at home, and so does poetry, which is concerned with "how it feels": how it feels to have experienced this or that; what the total experience of myself at this moment feels like. And that is so profoundly subjective that it would seem to lie quite beyond the reach of communication, at least and cer-tainly beyond rational communication. Hopkins, in one of his Ignatian meditations, records the question which, he says, fascinated him as a child: "What must it be to be someone else?" He of course never knew; nor do any of us. Yet the poet and the reader, insofar as they take poetry seriously, demonstrate their faith that the poem is there as the meeting point of two quite differently formed men. They accept the poem, that is, as the conjunctive point for two conscious beings, each shaped by his own unique complex of experiences, and each with a reservoir of unconscious being of unknown extent lying beneath that consciousness.

Susanne Langer, pursuing her argument that the human animal is possessed of a distinctive (also, she maintains, instinctive) capacity for symbol formation, speaks of "an unexplored possibility of genuine semantic beyond the limits of discursive language."[5] "Unexplored," one must assume, would refer specifically to the work of logicians, linguists, and aesthetic philosophers. The "possibility" has unquestionably been explored by poets, and not only of this century. Eliot looks toward the same realm of "semantic" when, in "The Music of Poetry," he suggests that "the poet is occupied with frontiers of consciousness beyond which words fail, though meanings still exist."[6] This area of real meaning, lying beyond the capacities of discursive intellect and rational language, is to be explored, in literature, through rhythm, image, and metaphor, or through what I shall call, in attempting to draw these three and more together under one term, "motif." Each of these motifs is designed to capture, as it were, and to re-evoke in present, memoried consciousness, an emotional experience of the past, the feeling of an old self or a partial self. One cannot, as I have suggested earlier, hope to capture with a straight-on

---

[5] *Philosophy in a New Key* (Cambridge, Mass.: Harvard Univ. Press, 1942), p. 86.

[6] *On Poetry and Poets* (New York: Farrar, Straus & Cudahy, 1957), pp. 22-23.

266

look, or expect to transmit directly to another, one's own sense of the self; at most one may be able to discover a similitude, a metaphor, for the feeling of selfhood—such metaphors as the body's sudden blazing, for example, or the soaring and gliding of a windhover, or the laughter of children hidden in leaves. A motif is thus adapted, on the side of the poet, to emotional life, and it calls forth, from the reader, a response; it does not present, by itself and with a one-to-one correspondence, a statable meaning.

Now the hypothesis again: the poem communicates an experience. It does this, however, not directly but by transforming the experience (itself incommunicable) into a motif available to *more or less* free association, simultaneously limiting the freedom of possible associations by the contextual circumstances under which the motif occurs. Each of us brings to the poem his own experiences, which need not be—indeed, cannot be—the same as the poet's, and there finds these private experiences more or less, depending on the effective power of the motif, conformed to the motif and so expressed in it. Notice that this responsive reading of the poem is a new and creative experience in itself: as much an experience that creates and re-creates the self as any transcendent moment in a rose-garden or idyllic day on a frozen stream.

After reading the poem, the reader is two full removes from the poet's experience (the poet being already at one remove when he wrote the poem). But the poem, not the poet, has indisputably communicated to him an experience. It has, besides, made the reader's own experience significant, transforming personal emotion into something suprapersonal. "There are many people," Eliot says, "who appreciate the expression of sincere emotion in verse, and there is a smaller number of people who can appreciate technical excellence. But very few know when there is an expression of *significant* emotion, emotion which has its life in the poem and not in the history of the poet [one might add: 'or in the history of the reader']. The emotion of art is impersonal."[7] The poet who seeks a meaning in experience and who attempts a meaningful communication about experience can never be content with a merely rational argument or with a representation of events and actions. He must rather shape his metaphor to his subjective experience, to what we may call his vision of himself, and make external events fit that significant pattern.

"What every poet starts from," Eliot maintains, "is his own emotions,"[8] and though this must be so, what he moves toward in the poem is expression not of those emotions but of "significant emotion"; and these are two quite different things. It is worth remarking that the movement, in the words Eliot chooses, is from multiple emotions of life to the single emotion of an art work, from the disorganized multiplicity of experience to the intensely organized unity of the artifact. The reader, too, in his responsive act, moves from emotions private to himself to the impersonal and significant emotion of the poem. In simple schematic form, the total process of the poem might be rendered something like this:

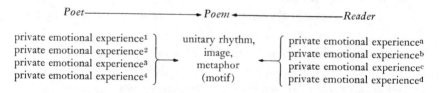

Poet————————→*Poem*◄————————————*Reader*

private emotional experience[1]		unitary rhythm,		private emotional experience[a]
private emotional experience[2]		image,		private emotional experience[b]
private emotional experience[3]	→	metaphor	◄	private emotional experience[c]
private emotional experience[4]		(motif)		private emotional experience[d]

We rest atop the unitary metaphor of the art work, our consciousness joined therein with the poet's, and hold in ordered composition the emotions which lie below it. No longer caught within the experience of the emotions, we hold them and not they us.

[7] "Tradition and the Individual Talent," *Selected Essays*, 3d ed. (London: Faber & Faber, 1951), p. 22.

[8] "Shakespeare and the Stoicism of Seneca," *Selected Essays*, p. 137.

Whatever poetry succeeds in doing must be done with words or with language. Words, however, in their conceptual capacity—thus far created by reason to convey rational ideas and more or less fixed within their own definitions—are not adequate to the subtle and hidden complexities of emotional experience. The poet who explores the "frontiers of consciousness" will find conceptual language alone largely insufficient. Without, of course, neglecting the conceptual, he must be equally and continuously alive to the rhythmic and visual properties of language. Words, for the poet, have the power of sound and picture as well as of abstract ideas. His language is not only conceptual but also sensuous, not only rational but also rhythmic.

The expressive powers of language as used in poetry might be put into a scale of increasing flexibility thus:

1. words as words (least flexible because somewhat fixed in conceptual use; symbolic forms hardened, more or less, into dictionary definitions);
2. words as images and images as metaphors (to be defined not from a dictionary but by contextual placing);
3. words as rhythms (sound and stress patterns coming before and lasting after the words themselves and the images; suggesting a meaning inaccessible to "definition");
4. words as images, metaphors, and rhythms (i.e., motifs), themselves rhythmically organized, a particularly prominent technique in *Four Quartets*.

In this ascent from words to rhythms, from relatively closed to relatively open forms, one moves from the prosaic to the musical. Poetry, like music, is rhythmically oriented and so has the openness of association to be found in music; but it also shares with prose the specifying moral significance of language. On the basis of how things are, it can hint at how things should be. This kind of poetry, that exploits the sensuous and rhythmic properties of language equally with its conceptual and rational capacities, can avail itself of the emotional-expressive freedom of (say) Mozart's Clarinet Quintet at one end and of the moral specificity of *Nostromo* at the other.

Our assumption is that experience per se, at least so far as humans are concerned, until given formal ordering and completion in the art work, until given the satisfaction of a new life in structural design, is void of meaning; and that design or pattern is the thing which, relating part to part and part to whole and implying an end in the beginning and middle, demonstrates significance in otherwise meaningless experience. But pattern is not discovered by us—mere details and parts, after all, of the whole design of life—within experience. Instead we, insofar as we are artists, create the pattern and impose it on experience. Art formalizes experience; form implies an end and an intention, and so a meaning. Thus goes one of the major themes of *Four Quartets*: "we had the experience but missed the meaning." Necessarily we missed the meaning, for we, the composite of our acts and intentions, *were* the meaning. How could we, at that moment fully engaged in living the meaning, be sufficiently removed to grasp the whole design subsuming our detail? Emotion, experience, life—whatever name we give it—is merely a subjective fact for us at loose ends, a formless and chaotic and painful mass, until we are far enough removed to see the total pattern, from beginning to necessary end and, if it be a circle, as so many poets and mystics would have it, to new beginning. Then, in the recapture of the experience as a formal, patterned whole, we realize at last the meaning, and perception of meaning is the greatest satisfaction, the richest reward. This, the art experience, is what Beethoven describes as "an incorporeal entrance into the higher world of knowledge which comprehends mankind, but which mankind cannot comprehend." Yeats means the same when he says, in his last letter, "Man can embody truth but he cannot know it." The poem does more for its creator and its reader: it embodies *and* it comprehends; in its forms is the "higher world of knowledge." Any significance that experience may bear becomes apparent only when the total pattern is achieved and the painful moment takes its place, as something "behovely," in the rich design, the completed form. Just as art has no substance without life, so life is meaningless without art, both poetic and autobiographic; and in lyric poetry subjective emotion finds its momentary objective expression, valid, however, only in the reader's subjective response.

If poetry begins in personal emotions, and if it intends to be an expression of emotion but at a new, transmuted, universal level; if, further, the art process is a formalizing process which contains meaning through channeling experience into regularly recurrent forms—then perhaps we can agree on an inclusive term which comprehends as many as possible of the "rhythmic," formalizing elements of poetry. I have suggested the term "motif," defined as "an essential component element of any sort in the design of a work of art (poem) which recurs with some frequency and which eventually helps to establish the design or pattern and consequently the overall meaning of which it is a part"; or, more simply, "a figure which recurs in and eventually contributes to the overall design of a poem." More or less regular recurrence within a pattern, for there can be no pattern without recurrence, is the indispensable element in this definition. Here it is that motif has obvious connections with rhythm, taken in a large sense, which one sees as the definitive characteristic of both poetry and music, and an essential element, perhaps, in all art. Further along in this chapter I shall maintain that "motif" is essentially the same as "rhythm," or is an instance of "rhythm." But before one can do that, it is necessary to develop a definition of rhythm that will accommodate the present definition of motif. For now the matter will be clearer if we distinguish motif

271

from rhythm and let "rhythm" apply to one motif element: viz., the patterned recurrence of *sounds*. For the apprehension of this sound motif one will require what Eliot calls the "auditory imagination," but for other kinds of motifs one will require a variety of other faculties or imaginations as well: at the very least, visual, tactile, kinetic, and relational imaginations. Motif, explicitly and by definition, includes the "rhythmic" use of words, images, phrases, sounds, metaphors, symbols, and even themes: for our purposes, motif is the more or less regular recurrence of any of these.

The motif technique followed in *Four Quartets* consists in introducing a motif, varying it, exploring the possibilities of its significance under the contextual circumstances of its introduction, then dropping it; reintroducing it under new circumstances, again examining and varying it, again dropping it; and so on until the single motif, which has been dipped alive into bucket after bucket of complex, swarming, and active elements and which lives in meaning dependent upon its multifarious neighbors, comes out dripping with meanings which have gradually stuck themselves to it from the various contextual placings it has been subject to. Finally, the richest, weightiest of all these motifs, having become gradually meaningful, gradually charged with significant emotion in the process of the poems, are brought into relationship and climactic ordering, into action and interaction, in the summary conclusion of each of the four poems and ultimately in the magnificent sweep of the grand symphonic close to the whole *Four Quartets*. But by this time the emotions expressed through given motifs are no longer loose, free, personal, or disordered. They give no pain now. They, like the motifs, have acquired a formal and relational significance, taking their place, as "something rich and strange,"[9] in the whole grand design. In-

[9] The phrase occurs in "Shakespeare and the Stoicism of Seneca," p. 137. Eliot apparently borrowed it from Ariel's song in *The Tempest*.

deed, taken all together, they compose that design which is their meaning in the serenity of the finished work of art. The motif and attendant emotion, alive in their relational pattern, become significant by the accretions of contextual "definitions." This congeries of emotionally charged motifs, if we can hold the entire poem as a single, complex unit, is seen to stand as metaphor for the whole self, reborn artistically complete, which informs the poem at every point with its own achieved integrity.

"If we can hold the entire poem as a single, complex unit . . . ." *Caveat lector*: one should not assume that this is something easily achieved. In the case of the *Four Quartets* it is very difficult—it may, indeed, be impossible. The poem is too long, too complex, and too varied for us to maintain a sense of secure possession throughout. This might be undesirable anyway: what poem of any complexity at all yields itself to us as a single effect (Poe's requirement) whenever we pick it up and read it through? But what Eliot's poem does do, again and again and supremely at the very end, is to recapitulate meanings and draw them together through the very motifs we have been describing. Georges Gusdorf, describing the relation between an entire life and the focal compression of that life which is an autobiography, introduces into the discussion an exact and suggestive analogy that comes very conveniently to hand in an analysis of Eliot's technique: "L'autobiographie est un moment de la vie qu'elle raconte; elle s'efforce de dégager le sens de cette vie, seulement elle est elle-même un sens dans cette vie. Une partie de l'ensemble prétend refléter l'ensemble, mais elle ajoute quelque chose à cet ensemble dont elle constitue un moment. Certaines peintures d'intérieur, flamandes ou hollandaises, montrent au mur un petit miroir où le tableau lui-même se répète une seconde fois; l'image au miroir ne redouble pas seulement la scène, elle lui ajoute comme une dimension nouvelle, une perspective de fuite" (*op. cit.,*

273

p. 118). Throughout the *Quartets*, Eliot draws his meanings up behind him into a narrowing mirror that contains and reflects earlier mirrors until the self in the end seems entirely realized and fully revealed. The recall of experience through metaphors and the constant recapitulation of metaphorized selves that is the twofold technique of *Four Quartets* gives the poem its Montaignesque sense of being at once both a re-evocation of experience and an adumbration of meaning achieved through a longer perspective and a fuller perception of pattern; and it gives the poem its Jungian sense of being a summary repetition in the individual of the evolution of consciousness in humanity to the present epitomizing moment.

Eliot's dual technique is also a way, among other things, of preventing a disjunction between present consciousness and the past, a way of bringing the past to be an important component of the present. For Darwin or Mill, the past, as looked upon in an *Autobiography*, was over and finished, simply dead; for Montaigne, on the other hand, in the dialogue between selves —the dialogue engaging *a*, *b*, and *c* Montaignes—no part of the past that was previously recorded and is now recalled can ever be dead, for it is a partner in the creation of present reality. Eliot's redeployment and recapitulation of motifs has the same effect of renewal as this communication of Montaigne with his earlier selves that occurs within the sentence and across the years. Included among the subjects of *Four Quartets* are poetry itself and memory, or the relation of the poet to his experience and of the autobiographer to his life. Thus, like Montaigne, like Jung, like the Dutch painters, Eliot incorporates into his poem a perspective contemplation of the methods, processes, techniques of his art, and he provides a sort of double perspective —at first the whole scene as delivered up by memory and then a mirror-image of that scene that comports a meaning for it— on the life-study of himself-in-becoming. In the end of the

274

poem, Eliot does not so much summarize meaning as renew it, so that what we have felt and understood when spread before us over many lines and pages we now can recall (conjoined with other feelings and perceptions, and thus made new) in a moment. In consequence, when we concentrate on the final twenty lines of the poem, what we should experience there is a richly renewed, while intensely compressed, metaphor of the self.

2. "move in measure, like a dancer"

With this cursory view of lyric poetry as introduction, and with these comments on the "motif technique" of *Four Quartets* as basis, let us examine in some detail the conclusion of Eliot's poem. Below are the final lines of the poem. After each line is a series of references, indicating where motifs in that line have occurred earlier in the *Quartets*. (On notation: Eliot divides the four separate poems which compose the *Quartets*—"Burnt Norton," "East Coker," "Dry Salvages," "Little Gidding"—into five sections each; thus, Roman numerals I through v. Unfortunately, lines are not numbered in any standard edition. For exact reference it is necessary to go through each section and number the lines. "BN, I, 19," for example, refers to line nineteen in the first section of "Burnt Norton." For this schematic presentation I would argue neither completeness nor absolute consistency of references included. I hope, however, that it will serve at least as an effective demonstration of the comprehensive, summary richness of the final lines of the poem.)

With the drawing of this Love and the voice of this Calling
LG, v, 25

BN, I, 19; BN, I, 26; BN, I, 40 & 42-43; BN, v, 17 & 20; BN, v, 27; EC, III, 24-25; EC, III, 26; EC, v, 29; DS, I, 24-25; DS, I, 27; DS, I, 32; DS, II, 28; DS, III, 24; DS, v, 21; LG, I, 48; LG, II, 45; LG, II, 66; LG, III, 10; LG, III, 15; LG, III, 35; LG, IV, 8-9.

We shall not cease from exploration   26

    EC, v, 18; EC, v, 31; DS, v, 45-46; LG, II, 68.

And the end of all our exploring   27

    BN, I, 10; BN, I, 46; BN, v, 10-12; BN, v, 28; EC, I, 1; EC, I, 14;
    EC, II, 48; EC, v, 38; DS, I, 45; DS, II, 1-36; LG, I, 25; LG, I, 34
    & 36; LG, II, 4; LG, II, 26-27; LG, v, 1-3; LG, v, 11.

Will be to arrive where we started   28

    BN, I, 21; EC, I, 50; EC, II, 22; EC, III, 35-43; EC, v, 4; EC, v, 19;
    DS, III, 6; DS, III, 9; DS, III, 17; LG, I, 40; LG, v, 3; LG, v, 14.

And know the place for the first time*.   29

    BN, I, 21 & 22; BN, II, 29-30; BN, III, 1; EC *passim*; EC, I, 3; EC,
    II, 29 & 33-34; EC, III, 38 & 44; LG, I, 22; LG, III, 15; LG, III, 20.
    *time BN, I, 1-5; BN, I, 44; BN, II, 23; BN, II, 36-43; BN, III, 2;
    BN, III, 11; BN, III, 16 & 18; BN, III, 37; BN, IV, 1; BN, v, 2; BN,
    v, 29-30; BN, v, 38; EC, I, 9-11; EC, I, 39-44; EC, v, 26-27; DS,
    I, 36-45; DS, II, 21; DS, II, 60; DS, II, 67; DS, III, 8; DS, III, 25;
    DS, III, 30; DS, III, 35 & 36; DS, v, 19; DS, v, 24; LG, I, 3; LG,
    I, 11; LG, I, 13 & 14; LG, I, 23; LG, I, 38; LG, II, 52; LG, v, 21.

Through the unknown, remembered gate   30

    BN, I, 13; BN, I, 20; DS, I, 12; LG, II, 40; LG, II, 47; LG, II, 57.

When the last of earth left to discover   31

    BN, II, 29; EC, I, 6; EC, I, 37-38; EC, IV, 11; EC, v, 12; DS, I, 16;
    DS, I, 37; DS, II, 56; DS, v, 47; LG, I, 12; LG, II, 16.

Is that which was the beginning;   32

    BN, v, 10-12; EC, I, 1; EC, I, 14; EC, I, 50; EC, v, 8; EC, v, 38; DS,
    I, 46; LG, v, 1-2; LG, v, 11.

At the source of the longest river   33

    EC, III, 29; DS, I, 1; DS, I, 15; DS, II, 68.

The voice of the hidden waterfall   34

    BN, I, 27; BN, I, 35; BN, I, 41; BN, v, 35; EC, III, 29; DS, v, 27.

And the children in the apple-tree   35

    BN, I, 24; BN, I, 40; BN, II, 2; BN, II, 9-10; BN, v, 35-36; EC, III, 16;
    EC, III, 31; DS, I, 26; DS, II, 69; DS, v, 49; LG, v, 19.

Not known, because not looked for 36

BN, I, 23; BN, I, 27-29; BN, I, 33; EC, III, 30; DS, II, 45; DS, V, 26; LG, I, 27.

But heard, half-heard, in the stillness* 37

BN, I, 27; EC, I, 25; DS, I, 28; DS, V, 27-28; DS, V, 29-30; DS, V, 32.

*stillness BN, I, 36; BN, II, 16-19; BN, II, 20; BN, II, 27; BN, II, 28; BN, III, 4; BN, III, 35; BN, IV, 9-10; BN, V, 4; BN, V, 6 & 7; BN, V, 8; BN, V, 17; BN, V, 27; EC, I, 13; EC, I, 22; EC, I, 48; EC, II, 20; EC, III, 12; EC, III, 19; EC, III, 23 & 28; EC, V, 33; DS, I, 34; DS, II, 2, 3, & 33; DS, II, 17; LG, II, 46 & 48; LG, III, 30; LG, III, 41.

Between two waves of the sea. 38

BN, V, 32; EC, I, 48; EC, II, 49; EC, III, 18; EC, V, 2; EC, V, 37; DS, I, 15-25; DS, I, 26-33; DS, II, 34; DS, II, 71; DS, III, 29; DS, III, 39-41; DS, IV, 12 & 14; DS, V, 2; LG, I, 11; LG, I, 36; LG, II, 32; LG, II, 69; LG, III, 4 & 6; LG, V, 13.

Quick now, here, now, always— 39

BN, I, 19; BN, III, 1; BN, III, 23-24; BN, V, 11; BN, V, 13; BN, V, 33; BN, V, 37; EC, I, 14; EC, I, 49-50; EC, V, 1; EC, V, 30 & 32; DS, II, 44; DS, II, 56; DS, II, 75; DS, III, 4; DS, III, 8; DS, III, 29; DS, V, 18-19; DS, V, 33 & 35; DS, V, 44; DS, V, 50; LG, I, 16; LG, I, 38-39; LG, I, 42, 43, & 45; LG, I, 51; LG, I, 52-53; LG, II, 45-46; LG, II, 52-53; LG, II, 67; LG, III, 14; LG, V, 22-24.

A condition of complete simplicity 40

EC, V, 16; DS, V, 20; LG, III, 1-16.

(Costing not less than everything) 41

DS, V, 21-22; DS, V, 31-32.

And all shall be well and 42

All manner of thing shall be well 43

BN, V, 13; EC, I, 44; EC, IV, 13; DS, II, 42; DS, III, 44; DS, IV, 15; DS, V, 33-38; DS, V, 47-50; LG, III, 18-19; LG, III, 47-48; LG, V, 17.

When the tongues of flame are in-folded 44

BN, II, 19; BN, II, 28; BN, IV, 7; EC, I, 34; EC, IV, 20; LG, I, 5; LG, I, 51; LG, II, 28; LG, III, 42; LG, IV, 2; LG, IV, 3; LG, IV, 11.

Into the crowned knot of fire   45

    LG, II, 77.

And the fire* and the rose* are one.   46

    EC, V, 35; DS, II, 36; DS, V, 34; LG, I, 50; LG, II, 41; LG, III, 25;
    LG, V, 40-41; LG, V, 42 & 43; LG, V, 44; LG, V, 45—and this line
    is LG, V, 46.

    *fire EC, I, 5 & 6; EC, I, 27; EC, I, 33; EC, II, 16; EC, IV, 19; EC,
      V, 23; LG, I, 4; LG, I, 9 & 10; LG, I, 51; LG, II, 2; LG, II, 17,
      19, 21, & 24; LG, II, 28; LG, II, 92; LG, IV, 6-7; LG, IV, 14; LG,
      V, 13; LG, V, 45.

    *rose BN, I, 14; BN, I, 16; BN, I, 28; BN, I, 36; BN, II, 39; EC, II,
      7; EC, IV, 20; DS, I, 25; DS, III, 3; LG, II, 2; LG, III, 35; LG,
      V, 19.

Choosing illustrations from these heavily charged lines, a
motif, as I have defined it, can be a word (e.g., "stillness"),
a sound and a rhythm ("And all shall be well and"), a
phrase ("Quick now, here"), an image ("gate"), a metaphor
("tongues of flame"), a theme ("And the end of all our exploring / Will be to arrive where we started"), a symbol
("the fire," "the rose"). These motifs, constituted as such
by their working in the poem, are placed in rhythmic organization (recurrence with variation), finally to reach climax here
at the end. I am aware, of course, that the discussion of motifs
that follows (in the order given above: from the single word
to the rhythmically organized symbol) is more a meditation on
the techniques of *Four Quartets* and more an attempt, as it
were, to live into a part of the poem than it is a strict analysis
of the *Quartets*; but I would suggest (see below, section 3) that
this is a proper way, and perhaps the only proper way, to
"read" the *Quartets*: the right way to read them, that is to say,
is to live them.

stillness (including synonymous phrases and variant forms)

    still: *adj., n., adv., conj., v.*
      adj.   1. Motionless; being at rest.
           2. Not disturbed by agitation or noise; quiet; calm.

3. Uttering no sound; silent.

n.　　　Absence of noise; silence.

adv.　1. Silently; quietly.

2. In continuation by successive or repeated acts; always; ever; constantly; continually.

3a. Until and during the present; at present; yet.

　b. In the future as now and before.

conj. Nevertheless; after all.

v.　1. To stop, as physical motion or agitation; to cause to become quiet; to check the agitation of.

2. To appease; calm; quiet; allay.

3. To stop, as noise; to silence.[10]

Notice how very quickly this simplest of motif elements—a constant word, with several possible dictionary senses and operating in varied contexts—proliferates into a thematic element. The idea of a "still point" at the center of our turning world is pondered in section II of "Burnt Norton," where it is figured in "a white light" that we see as paradoxically "still and moving"; but it is in sections IV and V of that poem that meaning begins to exfoliate in punning uses of the word:

> After the kingfisher's wing
> Has answered light to light, and is silent, the light is still
> At the still point of the turning world.　　(BN, IV, 8-10)

> Only by the form, the pattern,
> Can words or music reach
> The stillness, as a Chinese jar still
> Moves perpetually in its stillness.　　(BN, V, 4-7)

In the "still" that concludes two of these lines one finds nearly all senses of the word present and important: "motionless," "quiet," "silent," "silently," "quietly," "always," "yet," "continually," even "nevertheless." Poised at the line-end, the word draws us back and carries us over by its own echo: we pause in recall of "silent" and "stillness"; we are drawn on by "still

[10] Extract, slightly modified, from Webster's International Dictionary, 2nd ed.

point" and "stillness." And it is not sound alone, or mere dictionary definition, but meaning also that poises in the word: "still," in its crucial position and with its several senses, holds in balance temporal agitation and eternal quiet; it enacts, as the line stops and runs over, both perpetual movement ("yet," "continually") and perfected stasis ("motionless," "quiet," "calm"). This multiple meaning receives a further elucidation in EC, v, 33-35:

> We must be still and still moving
> Into another intensity
> For a further union, a deeper communion. . . .

This suggests that as spiritual man one is committed to un-moving movement, to a movement not in time and space but in intensity and significance. This, however, is a new significance in a new context and it does not cancel or exclude the mean-ing achieved earlier; rather it takes its place with the other meanings of the motif, "the complete consort dancing to-gether," in the final occurrence of "stillness" in "Little Gid-ding."

Elsewhere in the *Quartets*, the motif approaches meaning through other definitions of "stillness." Consider, for example, adverbial use 3b: "In the future as now and before." Thus in a single word we have a compressed recall of the meditation that opens the *Quartets*:

> Time present and time past
> Are both perhaps present in time future. . . .
>
> (BN, I, I-2)

In this sense of the word, the motif also hints at the "stillness," the continuity and integrity, of human personality which evolves into the one thing that it is out of the myriad separate experiences of a lifetime. Each of us is still, with experience incorporated into character, what he was *in potentia* at birth, which is what each of us will still be, only then fully realized, in the moment of death "(And the time of death is every moment)" (DS, III, 36). Thus each of us, in being a one, in being a coherent, integral self, realizes a "stillness" unique to him, which is yet a reflection, like the light from the king-fisher's wing, of the light that "is still / At the still point of the turning world." Life is the process, as indeed is this po-em, of realizing our own "stillness." We hear and half-hear that still, small voice of our potential selves (imagined in "Little Gidding" as "children in the apple-tree" and in "Burnt Norton" as children in the leaves "Hidden excitedly, contain-ing laughter," both still potential before experience), the voice that speaks to us, "Between two waves of the sea," of ourselves. From moment to moment, in the trough between waves, the self speaks and so finds its transient completion—a condition of stillness and complete simplicity, a moment of eternity when, no longer whirled far out on the wheel of hu-man experience, we center in on ourselves to the "still point of the turning world." Eternity is then as Yeats describes it (quoting, he says, Villiers de L'Isle-Adam quoting St. Thomas Aquinas): "Eternity is the possession of one's self, as in a single moment."[11] Being still what we have always been, the last dis-covery we shall come to in death will be nothing other than the being which was us and in us at birth. "In my end is my be-ginning" and vice versa, because there is a "stillness" which is with me and is me.

Contemplating, in "Little Gidding," this last stillness that comes upon individual life, one thinks, perhaps, "of a king at nightfall" (Charles I, beheaded in 1649) and simultaneously "of one who died blind and quiet" (presumably Milton, the chief apologist for regicide). Both these men, moved cease-lessly in time by the spirit of opposition, died "quiet": com-posed, appeased, complete, still, serene, at least from an after-view, in the significance of death. Like the boarhound and the

[11] *Explorations* (London: Macmillan, 1962), p. 37.

boar, they find their antagonistic relation stilled into an eternal and necessary pattern, "the pattern more complicated" of poetry, "the pattern more complicated / Of dead and living" (EC, v, 20-21):

> These men, and those who opposed them
> And those whom they opposed
> Accept the constitution of silence
> And are folded in a single party.   (LG, III, 39-42)

Their significance is not changed, only now fully realized, and they require one another in order that they might

> Pursue their pattern as before
> But reconciled among the stars.   (BN, II, 14-15)

About them now there is an ultimate and, as it seems, an inevitable "stillness"—in every dictionary sense of the word.

The Chinese jar that "still / Moves perpetually in its stillness" demonstrates that art is one of those profoundly paradoxical moments in which the eternal becomes real through the temporal object (which is why "eternity," as Blake says, "is in love with the productions of time"[12]). The jar represents movement held and contained within an unmoving design, desire with all its power yet freed of ineffectual desiring.

> Desire itself is movement
> Not in itself desirable;   (BN, v, 25-26)

but that which draws and motivates creation, whether divine or artistic, is what we call love, and

> Love is itself unmoving,
> Only the cause and end of movement,
> Timeless, and undesiring
> Except in the aspect of time
> Caught in the form of limitation
> Between un-being and being.   (BN, v, 27-32)

[12] "The Marriage of Heaven and Hell," *Poetry and Prose of William Blake*, ed. Geoffrey Keynes (London: Nonesuch Library, 1961), p. 183.

282

When love, however, manifests itself in this world, a world of time and space, it must do so in changing bodies and in the corruptible forms of mortality. Then it is "Caught in the form of limitation / Between un-being and being." Or when, as the creative impulse, love realizes itself in the musical composition or the poem, it takes on itself highly imperfect conditions, and agrees to the limitations of the dying form whether words or notes. It will never perfectly "be," as it may be conceived to have "been" perfectly before limited realization; it will rather exist imperfectly "in the aspect of time . . . / Between un-being and being."

One other way, the Christian way: if Christ is "Love," then *as Love*, as God, he is unmoving. "Timeless and undesiring," he is the "cause and end of movement," but he does not share in that agitation. When, however, he takes on human form— "in the aspect of time / Caught in the form of limitation"— he will be agitated into movement like other men. And this is the point: that the Incarnation (realization of the timeless under conditions of time; embodiment of spirit in a world of time and space, a world of movement) is merely, or profoundly, symbolic of all incarnations. That is, Christ is a perfected symbol for the spiritual experience of humanity. He is spirit embodied; so are we all. As pure and disembodied spirit he was unmoved, desireless; so would we be all under those transcendent conditions. His spirit was symbolically purer and more perfect; his body was symbolically more ideal; the two were symbolically more completely one. But Christ was God as Man—and so, more or less, are we all. And suddenly, in the distraction, the endless movement and purposeless agitation, we have an intuition, a vision of what our spirit purified really is, where its true home is. We hold the spirit in all its "stillness," seeing it *sub specie aeternitatis* (the reverse of incarnation, which is spirit moving *sub specie temporis*), and we

283

know it as spirit; and thereby we have a hint of the unmoving point:

> Quick now, here, now, always—
> Ridiculous the waste sad time
> Stretching before and after. (BN, v, 37-39)

Only at the center—"here, now, always"—can the still point be.

All these meanings, all these hints and suggestions and perceptions, are there by the end of the *Quartets*, to be renewed by the motif-word "stillness"—which is vastly rich in itself but more complex yet in coming, as it does, in the context of "the children in the apple-tree" and figuring in a pattern "between two waves of the sea."

And all shall be well and

The illustrative motif in this line is not simply a question of individual vowel and consonant sounds, though it is that too, but equally of an abstract sound, an abstract form, lying under the line as a whole unit. Robert Frost provides a convenient definition and analogy for this coherent and single sound unit (he happens to be speaking specifically of the sentence, but his remark holds good for the line too):

> I give you a new definition of a sentence:
> A sentence is a sound in itself on which other sounds called words may be strung.
> You may string words together without a sentence-sound to string them on just as you may tie clothes together by the sleeves and stretch them without a clothes line between two trees, but—it is bad for the clothes.[13]

Besides this sort of pure sound (whether individual or drawn into a pattern-unit, a line or a sentence), rhythm includes also syllabic emphasis, i.e., accentual pattern. The rhythmic motif,

[13] *Selected Letters of Robert Frost*, ed. Lawrance Thompson (New York: Holt, Rinehart, & Winston, 1964), pp. 110-11.

then, comprehends individual sounds, a pattern of sounds, and a stress pattern.

As individual sounds in Eliot's line we have the repetition of the "l" sound in "all," "shall," and "well." The short vowel sounds in the line, moveover, provide a neat little paradigm of the rhythmic motif in its simplest form—recurrence with variation—in the pattern they establish:

$$\text{And} \quad \text{all} \quad \text{shall} \quad \text{be} \quad \text{well} \quad \text{and}$$
$$[\text{æ}] \quad [\text{ɔ}] \quad [\text{æ}] \quad \quad [\text{ɛ}] \quad [\text{æ}]$$

That Eliot borrowed this line and did not invent it in no way, of course, changes the effect. (As Frost goes on to say of his "sentence-sounds": "They are apprehended by the ear. . . . Many of them are already familiar to us in books. I think no writer invents them.")

Accentually, also, the line is a nicely enclosed sound unit. Unaccented syllables at beginning and end embrace paired accented syllables which in turn enclose the pair of unaccented syllables at the center of the line—thus:

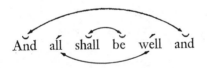

Or, more precisely, one might give a slightly greater emphasis to "shall" and "be" than to the two "and"s, which would produce this accentual scheme:

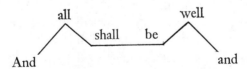

A demonstration of similarity between lines at this level of rhythmic apprehension or "auditory imagination" lies beyond the powers of conscious analysis and proof, but the reader may

285

be convinced that Eliot organizes rhythms rhythmically if I merely cite some lines from elsewhere in the *Quartets* which suggest, to my ear and imagination, something of the same movement as this line. (One should look again at the last five lines of the poem so that the rhythm—essentially a mixture of iambs and anapests, not end-stopped—may re-establish itself in the mind's ear.)

> Or say that the end precedes the beginning,
> And the end and the beginning were always there
> Before the beginning and after the end.
> And all is always now.   (BN, v, 10-13)

> The time of the coupling of man and woman. . . .
>   (EC, i, 44)

> Perpetual angelus.   (DS, iv, 15)

> Here the impossible union
> Of spheres of existence is actual,
> Here the past and future
> Are conquered, and reconciled,
> Where action were otherwise movement
> Of that which is only moved. . . .   (DS, v, 33-38)

> We, content at the last
> If our temporal reversion nourish
> (Not too far from the yew-tree)
> The life of significant soil.   (DS, v, 47-60)

> We die with the dying. . . .   (LG, v, 17)

All these passages where the ultimate rhythm asserts itself (and it is significant that four out of six should be from fifth sections) have to do, appropriately, in one way or another, with the mystical union of human and more-than-human, as if this rhythmic motif were the "right one" for conveying that ineffable, rhythmically oriented experience.

Quick now, here

Three words, any of which might stand alone as an example of a motif-word, compose the exemplary motif-phrase:

286

"quick," "now," and "here." Consider some of the meanings that accrue to these words individually before they are brought into juxtaposition and interplay at the end of "Little Gidding."

"Quick" might signify either "living, life" or "swift, sudden"—but, of course, signifies both equally whenever it occurs. Our "quick" moments, we discover in the exploratory process of the poem, constitute the "real" life, when that life becomes not an extension in time and space but a penetration in sudden awareness. Following the voice of the bird—"Quick, said the bird, find them, find them" (BN, I, 19)—we seek our past selves, both personal and suprapersonal, both potential and actual, to incorporate these selves into our present consciousness of self and so transcend either and transcend the limitations of past and present. Revelation comes—imperfectly, perhaps, "as through a glass darkly," but revelation nevertheless—in "sudden" moments that lie outside time as we know it: in

> The moments of happiness—not the sense of well-being,
> Fruition, fulfilment, security or affection,
> Or even a very good dinner, but the sudden illumination—
> $\qquad$ (DS, II, 42-44)

which reveal the meaning of past experience; or in "the sombre season / Or the sudden fury" (DS, II, 74-75), when we understand the necessary agony caused by the "ragged rock in the restless waters" (cf. "tu es Petrus. . . ."); or in the metaphysical springtime when

> $\qquad$ . . . the hedgerow
> Is blanched for an hour with transitory blossom
> Of snow, a bloom more sudden
> Than that of summer, neither budding nor fading,
> Not in the scheme of generation.
> $\qquad$ (LG, I, 14-18)

These are the moments "in and out of time" (DS, v, 25), moments that are both "sudden" and "living," moments that are in all ways "quick":

> Sudden in a shaft of sunlight
> Even while the dust moves
> There rises the hidden laughter
> Of children in the foliage
> Quick now, here, now, always—
> Ridiculous the waste sad time
> Stretching before and after.
>
> (BN, v, 33-39)

By the end of the *Quartets*, it is "here" and "now" that the spirit is made "quick." Earlier, however, "here" is seen as a place of insignificant vanity and vexation of spirit because, or so long as, we conceive of it as an isolate point, unconnected with "there" and "elsewhere." "Here," the poet says in "Burnt Norton," "Here is a place of disaffection" (III, 1) where the spirit can find neither rest nor silence:

> Not here
> Not here the darkness, in this twittering world.
>
> (BN, III, 23-24)

But, in Forster's phrase, "only connect": only connect here with there, present with past, now with always. The first section of "East Coker" elaborates this theme dramatically around the setting of East Coker and verbally around the motifs of "here," "now," "there," and "elsewhere." This opening section of the second poem is divided into four parts. Part one, echoing Ecclesiastes, presents a generalization on the circular pattern of the elements and of history and civilization. Part two makes the theme local and individual, giving it time and place, in the present, at East Coker:

> *Now* the light falls . . .
> *Where* you lean against a bank. . . .
>
> (ll. 14 & 17);

Part three joins this local present to a personal and historical past, as the poet participates in his own ancestry at the junction moment of midnight—neither one day nor the next, but simultaneously both:

> In that open field
> If you do not come too close, if you do not come too close,
> On a Summer midnight, you can hear the music. . . .
> (ll. 23-25)

And in part four we move to a new beginning:

> Dawn points, and another day
> Prepares for heat and silence. Out at sea the dawn wind
> Wrinkles and slides. I am here
> Or there, or elsewhere. In my beginning.   (ll. 47-50)

In this fusion of experiences, the poet and reader exist, with the poem, simultaneously in several realms of consciousness. "I am here," in the present East Coker of part two, "or there," in the generational and traditional past East Coker of part three, "or elsewhere," at the "still point," where present and past are resolved, through the patterns of nature from part one, into "never and always." The self stands perfectly poised at the conclusion, in its timeless moment, the individual completely self-possessed "in my [eternal] beginning," pregnant with the seeds of the ancestral past.

With the past thus reaching through the present into the future, "here" and "now" take on themselves a new significance, the significance of incarnation:

> Here the impossible union
> Of spheres of existence is actual,
> Here the past and future
> Are conquered and reconciled. . . .
> (DS, v, 33-36)

> History is now and England.   (LG, v, 24)

> And all is always now.   (BN, v, 13)

289

> . . . this intersection time
> Of meeting nowhere, no before and after. . . .
>
> (LG, II, 52-53)

> Here, the intersection of the timeless moment
> Is England and nowhere. Never and always.
>
> (LG, I, 52)

Observe that if, in these last two passages, we divide "no-where" one way, we get "no where"; if we divide it another way, it becomes "now here." The pun, as the poem mulls it, is characteristic and much more than idle or fortuitous: it touches on the nature of the "still point," which is both "no where" and "now, here," and thus touches on the essential quality of consciousness in the *Quartets*. One might say of the phrase-motif, in a paraphrase of Eliot, that we are here on "frontiers of consciousness beyond which words equivocate, though meanings still proliferate."

gate

The image of a gate opening into a first, Alice-in-Wonderland world is described in "Little Gidding" as both "unknown" and "remembered." Why should we both remember it and yet not know it? The paradox is perfectly accounted for and resolved if we examine the image-motif in its earlier occurrences. At birth, the individual is nearly all potential, almost nothing actual. The process of life is realization or actualization of possibilities. But for each individual, of course, there must have been many more possibilities than could ever be realized: he had, at every point, to choose possibilities, to select one door or one gate rather than another. There were many past possibilities, but there is only one present reality. What we might have done is as surely a part of present consciousness, i.e., present reality as it makes itself known to us, as what we actually did. Choosing to go through a certain gate has led to the present; choosing not to go through another gate has also led to the present. We remember choosing one, and we remember not choosing the other. Hence,

> What might have been and what has been
> Point to one end, which is always present.
>
> (BN, I, 45-46)

Hence, also, the "unknown, remembered gate," as an image at the end of the *Quartets*, must include both "the door we never opened / Into the rose-garden" (BN, I, 13-14) and "the first gate into our first world" (BN, I, 20-21). The poem, through this image, suggests further that memory is a special and distinct kind of knowing experience. We never, perhaps, knew the particular "rose-garden" as an actual place and fact, but we may still call it up in memory as a possibility and so as a perpetual reality in present consciousness.

tongues of flame

The metaphor in "tongues of flame" (which comes to hand ready-made from the Book of Acts: see below) is a double one. Metaphor is always a two-way process of meaning anyhow, but in "tongues of flame" we have not only the external reference present in all metaphor, but an internal identification or equivalence as well. Internally, as we become aware in the course of the *Quartets*, "flame" and "tongues" are equivalents: tongues burn throughout the poem like fire, and flame regularly assumes the power of speech. And beyond this internal give-and-take, the "tongues-of-flame," as a single, tightly bound metaphor, refers the reader outside to its own unnamed equivalent. Thus:

$$\text{burning tongue} \mp \text{speaking flame} = X$$

where X is the unknown that becomes known to us in our experience of the entire poem.

The fourth section of "East Coker" contributes to our understanding of the metaphor as it meditates on the conditions, absurd in human terms, which are associated with Christian salvation.

> If to be warmed, then I must freeze
> And quake in frigid purgatorial fires
> Of which the flame is roses, and the smoke is briars.
>
> (ll. 18-20)

Purgation is a fiery paradox, being, from our side, both human suffering and divine love. Turned over, the coin reveals the face of God in his human form ("briars"—i.e., rose thorns), willingly suffering for the redemption of his fallen creature. A similar flame of grace pierces through time in the spiritual spring-in-winter of "Little Gidding" to illuminate and order a scene of human confusion and uncertainty:

> When the short day is brightest, with frost and fire,
> The brief sun flames the ice, on pond and ditches,
> In windless cold that is the heart's heat. . . .
>
> (I, 4-6)

As in "East Coker," the flame descends with a divine significance into the human realm, and that which is a paradox in the human view is accepted as a necessity from the divine purview. Like sin, the flame, because it contributes to providential meaning, is "behovely."

In the second and fourth sections of "Little Gidding" we see the heavenly messenger in modern war-dress, "the dark dove with the flickering tongue" (II, 28) descending once more with speech to terrify and to redeem:

> The dove descending breaks the air
> With flame of incandescent terror
> Of which the tongues declare
> The one discharge from sin and error.
>
> (IV, 1-4)

Here in the streets of London, metaphysically transfigured by divine grace, the flame speaks and the tongues burn, as they do also at Little Gidding itself where the transfiguration is effected by the living presence of the entire dead past, burning and speaking, communicating their meaning to and through the present:

> And what the dead had no speech for, when living,
> They can tell you, being dead: the communication
> Of the dead is tongued with fire beyond the language of the
> living.
>
> (I, 49-51)

Like Milton and Charles I, the dead and the living, the human past and present, "are folded in a single party" (LG, III, 42), or "are in-folded / Into the crowned knot of fire" (LG, V, 44-45), which becomes the human realization of the Holy Spirit and a manifestation of the divine pattern in natural, temporal, and human forms. In the source of Eliot's metaphor, Christ tells his disciples that "John truly baptized with water; but ye shall be baptized with the Holy Ghost not many days hence." In the description of their baptism by fire, the external reference for the double metaphor of the *Quartets* becomes apparent: the burning tongues and speaking flames are spirit-in-body, God-in-man, the Holy Ghost, divine grace operative in and through our lives, creativity both divine and human. We call the power by many names, we dramatize and mythologize and metaphorize it in different ways, but it is always the same.

> And when the day of Pentecost was fully come, they were all with one accord in one place.
> And suddenly there came a sound from heaven as of a rushing mighty wind, and it filled all the house where they were sitting.
> And there appeared unto them cloven tongues like as of fire, and it sat upon each of them..
> And they were all filled with the Holy Ghost, and began to speak with other tongues, as the Spirit gave them utterance.
>
> (Acts 2: 1-4)

293

And the end of all our exploring
Will be to arrive where we started

"In the circle," Heraclitus says, "the beginning and the end are common." The theme recapitulated in Eliot's lines implies that human evolution and transformation is both circular and continuous: if the one, then necessarily the other. This circularity and continuity of human experience identify individual consciousness with godhead. God is the continuous still point at the center of a turning circle. As such, he is necessarily theoretical, for the point is still only so long as not realized. If the point is not theoretical, if it be real and extensive, then it is spatially trammeled; then it becomes not a point and not still, not perfect and not God, but a circle and turning, imperfect and human; for that is what we are to God in the image: circle to center. Logically, then, we are God realized, limited because extended in space and time: he the perfect potential, we the imperfect real—of, however, the same essence. "I am Alpha and Omega, the beginning and the ending";

> Or say that the end precedes the beginning,
> And the end and the beginning were always there
> Before the beginning and after the end.
>
> (BN, V, 10-12)

Or say that there is a meaning made real in human experience, which meaning, however, lies outside that experience. "The solution of the riddle of life in space and time," Wittgenstein says, "lies *outside* space and time."[14] There is that, in Beethoven's sense, which comprehends corporeal existence and can never be comprehended from within that existence. It is the paradox of Eliot's image and theme that the point should comprehend the circle but never the circle the point.

The adaptation of the sestina form that Eliot adopts in the

[14] *Tractatus Logico-Philosophicus*, 6.4312.

second section of "Dry Salvages" suggests the continual circular motion, the constant flux and reflux, the endless going out and return of human, mortal experience. This perpetual coming and going is set against the greater constancy of the sea, but the sea also must be referred outside itself for perfect stability and stasis, for the whole pattern that comprehends it. The rhymes (sometimes repetitions) of these thirty-six lines are like waves—forming, building, breaking; forming, building, breaking—that play over something much more constant but something which is also in a sort of motion; for the sea is subject, not to human time, but to cosmic and universal time, "a time / Older than the time of chronometers" (DS, I, 37-38), the time of the seasons and of nature, of the constellations, of the reconciled boarhound and boar. The sea, too, like all nature—though the motion is not evident in our overclose perspective because we partake of the motion; we are going with the sea, and our motions are the same: forward and westward—is

> Whirled in a vortex that shall bring
> The world to that destructive fire
> Which burns before the ice-cap reigns.
>   (EC, II, 15-17)[15]

But for us, while we are in the grip of mortality, the sea is the element out of which all life comes and to which all life returns. In the symbolic language of the depth psychologist, the sea is the great unconscious from which consciousness comes to momentary, individual realization, returning in the end to the unconscious again.

---

15 The idea and the imagery are again Heraclitean: "Fire lives in the death of earth, air in the death of fire, water in the death of air, and earth in the death of water" (Fragment 34). And cf. G. S. Kirk and J. E. Raven, *The Presocratic Philosophers* (Cambridge: Cambridge Univ. Press, 1966), pp. 128 and 152-53, on the "vortex-action" that, according to some pre-Socratic philosophers, may be responsible for the cosmos.

In my beginning is my end. . . .
>   In my end is my beginning.
>   (EC, I, I; EC, V, 38)

Like the sacred river Alph, the river of human consciousness
in *Four Quartets* flows in a mystical circle, from and to the
sea that gathers it up at either end. All the points on the circumference are touched, and in the end the circle is drawn up
into its own center.

And the FIRE and the ROSE are one

Eliot's own remark about his roses (which applies also,
mutatis mutandis, to his fires), in a letter to Bonamy Dobrée,
only comes as confirmation of what is anyhow discoverable
in the poem itself (though Dobrée rather peculiarly remarks,
apropos of Eliot's hint, "I must confess that I was not much
illuminated"): "There are really three roses in the set of poems; the sensuous rose, the socio-political Rose (always with
a capital letter) and the spiritual rose: and the three have got
to be in some way identified as one."[16] The roses are made
one in the most literal sense in the final line of "Little Gidding"
where not only do all the various roses become "*the* rose," but
this inclusive rose is further brought into union with the fires
—now, likewise, become "*the* fire"—which recur throughout
the poems.

Eliot's way of bringing the various roses into one rose suggests an act of love in the Platonic sense, as Diotima explains
to Socrates: it is love, love of the beautiful and eventually the
good, that moves us in this world ("desire," the poem calls it)
and that brings us, as if up a ladder, from the sensory experience of one beauty among many to the more universal experience of beauty in several similar objects, and finally to
knowledge of and participation in Beauty Itself. And this
last is a pure spiritual state.

[16] *Sewanee Review*, LXXIV (Winter 1966), 106.

296

Personal	: :	sensuous rose (desire/eros)
National	: :	sociopolitical Rose (patriotism)
Universal	: :	spiritual rose (Love/Agape)

This movement in rose symbolism from eros to Agape, with a halfway house where we identify ourselves with the heritage of our past, is an exercise in the depersonalizing of emotion: placing the individual emotion in an impersonal pattern, we may catch a glimpse of the essence which motivates and informs both the personal and the more-than-personal, but still human and natural. From this human-personal and human-suprapersonal we abstract the common essence, if we can, and that, as St. Augustine and Duns Scotus say, is God: "Bonum hoc et bonum illud: tolle hoc et illud, et vide ipsum bonum si potes: ita Deum videbis."

The roses of "Burnt Norton" are, for the most part, sensuous roses recalling past, personal experience, either potential or actual, "Disturbing the dust on a bowl of rose-leaves" (BN, I, 16). The sociopolitical Rose—the "Royal Rose" (DS, III, 3) and the "spectre of a Rose" (LG, III, 35)—represents a different level of detachment. It points to a corporate experience, in family or nation, leading down to and momentarily living in the present: the relation of "tradition and the individual talent."[17] The spiritual rose—for example, "The moment of the rose and the moment of the yew-tree / Are of equal duration" (LG, V, 19)—goes entirely beyond, even if through, the sensuous and the sociopolitical roses. At this level, we know that "the moment of the rose," the moment in and out of time, of transcendent ecstasy, of incarnation, "and the moment of the yew-tree," the mortal-immortal moment that

[17] Cf. R. M. Rilke, *Letters to a Young Poet* (New York: W. W. Norton & Co., 1934), pp. 49-50: "Even with the trivial, with the insignificant (if it but happens out of love) do we . . . begin him whom we shall not live to know, even as our forbears could not live to know us. And yet they, who are long gone, are in us, as predisposition, as a charge upon our destiny, as blood that stirs, and as gesture that rises up out of the depths of time."

297

ends this life, "are of equal duration": we assume for eternity, which is also every quick moment of self-possession, the spiritual condition achieved or attained in the moment of death.

The fires of *Four Quartets*, too, like the roses, can be classified as sensuous, sociopolitical, spiritual. Or, perhaps better, we can see them as human (the fires of lust or desire); as natural (the cyclical return of nature to its essential state of fire: "nature," as Hopkins says, "is a Heraclitean fire"); and as supernatural (purgatorial fire that purifies as it punishes and lovingly draws the human to the divine).

And the fire and the rose are one.

Already in the fire, man and God are joined; already in the rose, man and God are joined. When these unities are united what more can there be? Is it not unity atoned with itself and perfection infinitely perfected?

To attempt to draw together all the places in *Four Quartets* where "one" occurs as word, image, or theme is too great a task, for the poem is everywhere and essentially *about* oneness: the oneness of self and the unity of consciousness; the reconciliation of warring opposites, and the integration of past and present, in a single, significant pattern; the atonement of human wills with the divine will; union among men and communion with God; the communication of humans and communication between man and God. Eliot compacts his meaning, gradually achieved in accretion, in the narrowing pattern of the end of the set of poems. One has the sense that "Little Gidding" is the significant climax of the four poems; that the last twenty lines hold the essence of "Little Gidding"; that each successive unit draws up behind itself the accumulated meaning of the entire preceding poem; that the last line, if we gather and follow meaning thus far, holds, as the center of a circle contains its circumference, the whole potential form and meaning of *Four Quartets*, now recreated and become actual; that the last word, which is "one," is all. But in going this far we have gone well beyond the limits of language as a tool of the conscious mind. With an effort we try to focus meaning in verbal, rational, discussible concepts only to miss the poem and its effect time and again. "Things fall apart, the center will not hold"—but it is the center of consciousness, not of the poem, that gives way: the more we exercise our will to bring the poem back to that conscious center and to rational clarity, the more we miss all the indistinct, ever-expanding, and very real circumference of the circle. In this way at least, and in other ways too, I think, Eliot's poem is very much like God and the self in C. G. Jung: "a circle whose center is everywhere and circumference truly nowhere."

3. "folded in a single party"

Any reader of Eliot will recognize that to call the *Four Quartets* autobiographic poetry requires some considerable explanation and qualification. It would unquestionably be an easier thing to establish the autobiographic elements of, for example, the *Prelude* or Yeats's Tower poems than of *Four Quartets*. But in the very ease with which we can identify Wordsworth's conscious life with his poem there is the temptation to rest content with natural geography and chronology, with poetic pictures neatly illustrating an educational text in moral development, and to suppose that these represent the subject of the poem; to suppose that what Wordsworth knows about himself and can tell us, with clear psychological comprehension and at great explanatory length, will serve well enough for the "bios" in autobiography. Or if one were to take Yeats's poems, which probably represent a richer material in self-expression than either the *Prelude* or the *Quartets*, there is the danger of being distracted by the poet's flair, by what he said and did in the world of men, by his "circus animals" and his troop of friends put on display regularly as partial symbols for the whole poet himself; there is the danger of listening too much to Yeats's own description of himself and his soul, delivered brilliantly both in and out of the poems, and of listening with such delighted fascination that we are distracted from the poetic self that is only in the poem and that is the only self relevant in discussing autobiographic art.

> There was a Boy: ye knew him well, ye cliffs
> And islands of Winander!—many a time
> At evening. . . .   (*Prelude*, v, 364-66)

One never gets this sort of Wordsworthian natural geography and exterior biography in Eliot; nor does Eliot refer freely to his offices in Russell Square as Yeats does lavishly to his Tower near Gort and to its winding stair, its broken battlements, and the stream flowing by. What sparse personal reference there is and what little geography (the four place names, for example), or what few events figure in the *Quartets*, are plainly, on first occurrence, supernatural or extramundane and do not require to be transformed from the natural realm either by the poet's explanation or the reader's symbolizing imagination. It may be, however, that this lack, this absence of the persons, the possessions, the places, and the happenings of a particular life, motivated apparently both by personal reticence and poetic strategy, will prove in the end, for our purposes, a virtue rather than a defect; that if we must go very carefully in seeking Eliot's subject, the care will provide its own critical reward. I have never seen, but can well imagine, an illustrated *Prelude*, and photographs of Yeats country and of his symbols are easy enough to come by; but I cannot quite conceive of any photographic images that might usefully accompany the *Quartets*. The chapel at Little Gidding is no doubt interesting, but a picture of it would help very little in reading that poem. I am not sure that this is all to the bad. In any case, when one says that the *Quartets* are "autobiographic," that does not at all mean that in them will be found datable, placeable, perhaps photographable, events.

Four Quartets is not, however we look at it, an imitation of events but, if an imitation at all, then of something quite different: perhaps an imitation of a process. Poetry that is expressive and autobiographic in a deeper than personalistic or historic sense draws metaphors, or accepts and adopts them, from the self as it is becoming, and then displays all the world to the reader through the glass of these metaphors. It does not submit to the fixed and, as we call them, objective forms of a pre-existent universe, but, insofar as it treats these external lineaments, transforms them into expressive vehicles of subjective emotions and private consciousness. In a general way, this is the mode of the *Quartets*, and their one great subject, lying well below the surface of the poem and hardly remarked in most critical writing on it, subsuming and informing all secondary interests (e.g., poetry, history, philosophy, religion), is the evolving self: that self which is the determining subject, or subjective center, of all creativity, and is the great subject-object of the creations of Jung and Montaigne as well as of Eliot.

Four Quartets has been called "philosophic poetry," and I think that, with necessary definitions, one might accept this as a working description. This is not at all, however, the same thing as saying that, as one commentator puts it, "Eliot has sought to vindicate the ways of God to man. The *Quartets*, a new *Essay on Man*, are the poetic jottings of a philosophy holding that the world is an organ of the divine purpose."[18] Eliot may very well have believed this about the world; who can say? But I am sure that his poem has no resemblance at all

[18] Grover Smith, *T. S. Eliot's Poetry and Plays* (Chicago: Univ. of Chicago Press, 1960), p. 297.

to the *Essay on Man*, nor is it "poetic jottings" of any kind, nor does it contain anything like a philosophy. "Philosophic" is merely an adjective, suggesting some of the characteristic interests of the poem: but the proper substantive is "poetry." To assume that the poem aspires to the discipline of philosophy but fails and so collapses into "poetic jottings" is to take hold of the wrong end of the stick and beat the poem with it. Moreover, if we thus consider the poem to be philosophy *manqué*, we not only do the poem an injustice but ourselves as well, for in so doing we shut ourselves out, as readers, from what is there in fact and of great value. I. A. Richards, speaking both as a friend of the poet and as a critic of the poetry, comes much closer to the true essence of the *Quartets*: "Few minds," he says of Eliot, "have more enjoyed the process of pondering a discrimination: pondering it rather than formulating it or maintaining it."[19] The discriminations that Eliot ponders in the *Four Quartets* are mostly to be described as "philosophic," but the poetry is in the intensity with which Eliot realizes the pondering not in the neatness or finality with which he arranges his philosophy. One might say that pondering is not only the mode but, in a sense, the subject as well of the poem. In any case, the pondering proves to be a circular process that does not issue in an answer but turns in upon itself for substance, and Eliot never, speaking in his own voice, formulates a philosophy or maintains a conclusion. Indeed, I am not sure that we can say that Eliot ever speaks in his own voice in *Four Quartets*, and if he does not, then that fact is of great importance.

If we consider such a passage as this, which has the same feeling about it as a good many passages in the poem,

> Whisper of running streams, and winter lightning.
> The wild thyme unseen and the wild strawberry,
> The laughter in the garden, echoed ecstasy. . . .
>
> (EC, III, 29-31)

[19] *Sewanee Review*, LXXIV (Winter 1966), 22.

there can be no question that *Four Quartets* is, in an important way, an expression of personal emotion; that it is, in other words, lyric poetry. But to whom, one must ask, is the emotion "personal"? Who is the "person" of the poem? Again, it is reasonable to say that it is, in part, "meditative verse" as Eliot describes that: "the voice of the poet talking to himself—or to nobody" (*On Poetry and Poets*, p. 106). But is it exactly or only the poet who is talking in the *Four Quartets*? I would suggest that the poem presents us with something different and something more; that it is a dramatized meditation pursued by one who is both Eliot and other than Eliot, and that in being so it avails itself of many of the virtues of dramatic poetry without surrendering those of meditative verse.

Let me give an example: in the second section of "Little Gidding" the speaker of the poem and "a familiar compound ghost / Both intimate and unidentifiable" meet and tread "the pavement in a dead patrol," talking philosophically of things past, passing, and to come. The identity of this ghost has naturally vexed Eliot criticism a great deal: it is said to be Yeats and Joyce, both dead a few years since, their bodies "left . . . on a distant shore"—or even Shelley, by the same evidence; but the ghost has also been identified as partly Pound, not at all dead of course, and partly Swift, with a considerable admixture of Milton and Dante and an important phrase from Mallarmé. Undoubtedly there are others dancing together in this complete consort of a ghost as well. But might one not also, and perhaps more fruitfully, consider it to be past Eliots; for is that not what a compound ghost would be—a congeries of spirits standing for our heritage and our ancestral significant moments; a collection of disembodied souls representing our personal, professional, national, human past and informing our individual present? "So I assumed a double part," the voice of the poem says,

303

> . . . and cried
> And heard another's voice cry: "What! are *you* here?"
> Although we were not. I was still the same,
> Knowing myself yet being someone other. . . .

Is this Eliot speaking? Well, yes, in a sense; but not Eliot
alone, or not only the Eliot of the present historic moment.
It is what Eliot has been in the past and what he is becoming
into the future, speaking in "another's voice" and surprised
to hear his own speech. Likewise, the ghost is known and unknown, figures from the past and a figure becoming for the
future, himself and another:

> And he a face still forming; yet the words sufficed
> To compel the recognition they preceded.
> And so, compliant to the common wind,
> Too strange to each other for misunderstanding,
> In concord at this intersection time
> Of meeting nowhere, no before and after,
> We trod the pavement in a dead patrol.

The speaker in this section, and this is more or less true
throughout the *Quartets*, is Eliot and not Eliot, the ghost is
Eliot and more than Eliot, the street is in London, in history,
and in purgatory, and the action is a fully dramatized meditation in a supernatural, transfigured setting of an "intersection
time" when chronological relation is replaced by significant
relation and geographic location by nonspatial intensity.

In search of the "person" or the "voice" of *Four Quartets*,
it seems to me that Eliot, insofar as he is the speaker of the poem, could be said to be almost an anonymous lyric poet and
the poem an expression of depersonalized or transpersonalized
personal emotion. It seems, indeed, natural, in discussion of
the *Quartets*, to refer to "the poet" rather than to "Eliot,"
which is evidence of his success in making the emotional experience of the poem anonymous. A suggestive analogy might
be made with certain Middle English lyrics (e.g., "Alison"

or "Lenten ys come with love to toune") where the voice, by historical chance but also in tone and treatment, is in fact anonymous, and the emotion of seasonal revitalization rendered in the poem becomes, by that fact, both specifically individual and anonymously, comprehensively human. Likewise, the speaker of *Four Quartets*: without ever ceasing to be individual—indeed, becoming individual by the process of the poem—he enacts a representative drama, very much like Montaigne's drama, of spiritual man in meditation. Through this "anonymification," *Four Quartets* succeeds in being both more and less personal than earlier poems such as "Prufrock" or "Gerontion" in which Eliot created "type" figures—i.e., individually coherent personae not to be totally identified with, but also not to be totally separated from, the poet speaking through them. In the *Quartets*, however, the poet has submerged his self sufficiently in the general experience of mankind that he may return to the personal "I" and "we" and find therein not the historic and typical but the representative and symbolic.

If one calls *Four Quartets* "philosophic poetry," then one should be very careful at the same time to recognize that the poem is not at all an ordered (or worse, disordered), single-minded presentation of *a* philosophy; and as long as we see it as a dramatic poem of the self we shall, as we must, avoid confusing it with a poeticized philosophy like the *Essay on Man*. The "truths" that are pondered in the enacted communication of section II of "Little Gidding" are not absolute and objective but relative and subjective: truths that take their coherence and effectiveness from the intensity of the artist's imagination and realization of them rather than from their own inherent validity as a discursive explanation of the external universe. "A philosophical theory," Eliot wrote in 1921, "which has entered into poetry is established, for its truth or falsity in one sense ceases to matter, and its truth in another

305

sense is proved."[20] What he means, of course, is that the theory
is established as drama and as poetry without regard for its
truth or falsity as philosophy; the poem is validated in the
reader's imagination not in the external world. *Four Quartets*
goes even further than this as dramatic poetry, subjectively
centered in the artist's and the reader's imagination: the embodied conflict of the *Quartets'* drama engages thoughts and
emotions rather than ideas and characters; it enacts a pondering rather than a theory. Thoughts, unlike ideas and theory,
cannot be separated from the mind that thinks them, and the
poem concerns itself with the working of the mind, not with
its separable, formulated products; with the process of the
psyche, not with ideas or theory as such. Putting the matter
in Jung's language, one might say that *Four Quartets* is the
autobiography not of ego-consciousness alone, though of
course the portrait includes that, nor of the external person
and his acts, but of the whole psyche and self. The feelings
of the *Four Quartets* are too complex for simply rational
language, and the thoughts of the poem do often lie too deep,
if not for tears, at least for intellectual articulation.

"I am certain," Keats says, speaking as an artist, "of nothing but of the holiness of the Heart's affections and the truth
of Imagination—What the imagination seizes as Beauty must
be truth—whether it existed before or not." Eliot claimed,
with what I take to be a sort of prim, intellectual humility,
not to understand the end of the "Ode on a Grecian Urn,"
and one cannot be sure that he would have been any warmer in
his enthusiasm for what Keats says here; but it is the "truth
of Imagination" that *Four Quartets* establishes, and the poem
depends upon the creative powers of the imagination for realizing its own proper object. That object—"Beauty," as Keats
calls it—will *be* as intensely as the poet and reader can make
it be, "whether it existed before or not." Speaking of religious

[20] "The Metaphysical Poets," *Selected Essays*, pp. 288-89.

belief, but also as an artist rather than a priest, Tolstoy says much the same thing as Keats: "As my body has descended to me from God, so also has my reason and my understanding of life, and consequently the various stages of the development of that understanding of life cannot be false. All that people sincerely believe in must be true; it may be differently expressed but it cannot be a lie, and therefore if it presents itself to me as a lie, that only means that I have not understood it."[21] "All that people sincerely believe in must be true": it is characteristic of Tolstoy that his expression should be a bit strong for many tastes and that some readers who might otherwise be friendly enough to his brand of solipsism would shy away from the extremity of this remark. But let us consider whether, given his premises, which may not prove so outrageous or unusual, Tolstoy might not be more perceptive and exact in his statement than we would ordinarily want to admit; and whether Tolstoy's premises are not, in fact, rather close to Eliot's as the author of the *Quartets*. If, as Tolstoy said in a hundred different ways, we are all of us instances of Godhead incarnate; if, in our consciousness, and only there so far as the created universe is concerned, the divine realizes itself; if what we "sincerely believe" is our deepest imagination and our best apprehension of that realized divinity that we experience as a personal, subjective state—then it is not hyperbole but in fact the merest tautology to say that "All that people sincerely believe in must be true." How could it *not* be true? It is God believing in himself and causing himself to be as sincerely and as intensely as he can, given the imaginative, believing limitations of the individual through whom the belief is effected. I do not suppose that the Eliot who was "classicist in literature, royalist in politics, and anglo-catholic in religion," and who exercised himself so vehemently against

21 *A Confession*, Oxford Classics (London: Oxford Univ. Press, 1940), p. 68.

the "Inner Light" ("the most untrustworthy and deceitful guide that ever offered itself to wandering humanity") and against the *"personal view of life"*[22] that, he claimed, constituted the heresy of modern writers and modern literature, would care to go that way with Tolstoy—who, after all, was romantic-realist in literature, anarchist in politics, and excommunicated heretic in religion, and who never followed anything *but* his Inner Light. Yet, the fact I think is that the Eliot who wrote *Four Quartets* did go that way in the poem; or at least the poem goes that way for the reader whatever Eliot, the man of prose and of religious and literary orthodoxy, might have desired.

What Tolstoy says about belief makes of religion, as of philosophy and psychology, a creative act in self-knowledge. For the artist, I should think, this is more apparently and more indisputably the case than for the theologian. Absolute standards of truth or falsity against which to measure the artist's creation do not exist, for it is his creation, made out of his subjective experience. When the poem not only begins, like all poetry, in the poet's "own emotions" but, as I believe to

[22] The emphatic italics are Eliot's: *After Strange Gods* (London: Faber & Faber, 1934), p. 59; "classicist," etc., is from the preface to *For Lancelot Andrewes* (London: Faber & Gwyer, 1928), p. ix. Cf. Baron von Hügel, who may have touched on "modernism" but undoubtedly remained orthodox, on the concept of a Tolstoyan "Personal God": "Yet it is only self-conscious spirit that we know well, since it alone do we know from within. Self-conscious spirit is immensely rich in content; and self-conscious spirit is by far the widest and yet deepest reality known to us at all. . . . But there is nothing intrinsically unreasonable in thinking of the ultimate Cause, Ground and End of the world as certainly not less than, as somehow not all unlike, what we know our own self-conscious mind, feeling and will to be. . . . In so thinking we find in, or attribute to, the supreme Reality what we ourselves possess that is richest in content, that is best known to us, and that is most perfect within our own little yet real experience—and we have done what we could; and life and history abound with warnings how easy it is here to go apparently further and to fare in fact very much worse ("Religion and Reality," *Essays and Addresses on the Philosophy of Religion*, 2 vols. [London: J. M. Dent & Sons, 1921], 1, 50).

be the case with the *Four Quartets*, turns inside out and embraces that private experience in awareness as its very subject or object, then even relative standards of truth and falsity are somewhat beside the point in reading and judging the poem. Here again, in this turn and return on the self, the difference between the *Essay on Man* and the *Four Quartets* is crucial. As readers without a yardstick and a poem that anyhow refuses to stay to be measured, we can only look within: we must judge the poem by how adequately it answers, not to the external universe, not even to the poet's experience—since we have no knowledge of that—but to our own experience; not the surface experience of everyday activities either, but the deepest experience of what it means to us to be human beings and to be ourselves.

"Why, for all of us," Eliot asks, "out of all that we have heard, seen, felt, in a lifetime, do certain images recur, charged with emotion, rather than others?" He mentions several such mysterious and significant-feeling images, apparently from personal experience—"the leap of one fish . . . the scent of one flower, an old woman on a German mountain path," etc. —and then continues: "such memories may have symbolic value, but of what we cannot tell, for they come to represent the depths of feeling into which we cannot peer."[23] Describing here the image-material of poetry, Eliot adopts a figurative language strikingly similar to the myths and metaphors that depth psychology employs when that "science" tries to evoke some sense of psychic process; he, like the psychiatric workers of that deep mine, speaks of reaching darkly into the depths of emotional experience where conscious mind cannot go but whence images, rhythms, auditory excitations, all the by-products and expressions of an organic being in operation, are thrown up to affect and to be remarked, to

[23] *The Use of Poetry and the Use of Criticism* (London: Faber & Faber, 1964), p. 148.

309

serve as symbols and metaphors, but never to be held or described or rationally known. Again, in the same book and the same vein, Eliot describes the "auditory imagination" as a "feeling for syllable and rhythm, penetrating far below the conscious levels of thought and feeling, invigorating every word; sinking to the most primitive and forgotten, returning to the origin and bringing something back, seeking the beginning and the end." This imagination, he says, as it works in poetry and elsewhere, "fuses the old and obliterated and the trite, the current, and the new and surprising, the most ancient and the most civilized mentality" (pp. 118-19). Eliot does not say what it is, or give a name for it, this elusive *je ne sais quoi* that the "auditory imagination" gropes for and would bring to light, that it hears and tries to describe and misses, hears again, gives over trying to describe, and then captures in a rhythm, an image, a recurrent phrase. One name for it, out of the many that have been elaborated by men, might be "Anima Mundi in anima hominis"; for is not this ineffable, unifying something, with which the auditory imagination has contact but which it cannot hold, the unconscious itself, whereby each of us succeeds to the entire estate of man? Consciousness evolves slowly and uncertainly for the poet, making its way with frequent difficulty and occasional felicity into language in the poem; but as it evolves, consciousness does not forget, though it can never contain, the unconscious from which it comes, nor does it refuse to that great source of energy its needful metaphoric and rhythmic expression. It is a fine thing for consciousness to create itself by the rational language in which it communicates, but it is finer by far if that rational language be adapted rhythmically to the expression, and so to the creation, of unconscious psyche too.

Out of his own incommunicable emotional experience, Eliot creates something in the *Four Quartets* that goes beneath that experience to the shared, the common, and the universal, and beyond that experience to the transcendent and superhuman. He moves away from the limitedly private in either direction to where communication is possible in the forms of art. The poem unquestionably contains, reflects, and expresses a self, but a whole self, rhythmic and rational like the language, not a partial self; and it is symbolic or representative: not the private self of T. S. Eliot, yet raised out of, through, and beyond that self. Whatever Eliot may have been as a man, the limitation of wholeness implied in psychological "typing" seems not to obtain for the poet in his work: he, or the voice of the poem, is simultaneously introverted and extroverted, adapted alike to the world of the senses and the realm of intuition, equally sensitive in thought and in feeling, conscious of everything in the world and of nothing more than of the self as it becomes conscious.

Eliot's poem makes the same ascent as music: "from rhythm in sense to the immortal rhythm which is in truth."[24] Notice that in St. Augustine's notion of music as mathematics ideas do not bring us to the desired union, for those products of the mind mostly separate in individual consciousness; but rhythms, he maintains, carry us back and up, unite us with our ancestors in ourselves, reveal the spiritual essence that infuses the created world, and reflect the source of all being. So too for the poet, rhythms hint at an energy indescribable and untouchable but real and powerful; they demonstrate that there is something lying beneath human consciousness and something, the same thing, at the top of the Platonic ladder—if, that is, as we read the poem, we are sufficiently creative artists to imagine it there and so to make it be.

And at the other extreme from the musical ascent by

[24] The "argument" to the sixth book of St. Augustine's *De Musica*: "In quo ex mutabilium numerorum in inferioribus rebus consideratione evehitur animus ad immutabiles numeros, qui in ipsa sunt immutabili veritate." The abbreviated translation is from W. F. Jackson Knight's "Synopsis" of the *De Musica* (London: Orthological Institute, 1949).

311

rhythms, it was Balzac, as realistic a novelist as the world has ever seen, dedicated to the search for reality inherent in external appearance, who said (in the person of his archetypal artist Frenhofer in *Le Chef-d'oeuvre inconnu*), "La mission de l'art n'est pas de copier la nature mais de l'exprimer." The nature that Balzac's own art expressed in the hundreds of characters he created was, of course, that human nature that he knew, in all its diversity, literally from within: the *Comédie humaine*, like Shakespeare's plays, represents a massive self-expression through the varied forms of human nature. In a rhythmic variation on a passage quoted earlier—

> The distraction fit, lost in a shaft of sunlight,
> The wild thyme unseen, or the winter lightning
> Or the waterfall, or music heard so deeply
> That it is not heard at all, but you are the music
> While the music lasts.—   (DS, v, 25-29)

Eliot finds in the sensory forms of nature sufficient expression for subjective states, in particular for those moments of completion and of ecstasy when the self is reborn anew. In the subtle, pervasive smell of thyme and the implied taste of the herb, in the warm feel of sunlight and the chilly sight of winter lightning, in the sound of the waterfall, in all of these, alone and together, the self finds its metaphors. While they are all there, of course, in nature and now in the poem, they mean nothing until we bring their meaning to them, until in our awareness they complete and represent our whole being and so lift that being out of itself into another pattern and onto another level of existence and significance. In music and poetry there is something added that the natural forms do not, in themselves and alone, necessarily possess—rhythmic organization: the pattern that the poet finds in himself and projects over nature and then, finding it in nature, uses to express the self that has thereby come into being. So too the reader: after we read and become, in our moment, the poem, then we imagine the natural forms always to have had the pattern and the rhythms we now discover; but that is only because we see nature through the metaphoric glass and by the senses of the self artistically transformed. We are the poem as we read it, as the words, the images, and the rhythms pervade and become our being; the poem stands for us, and not for us a moment since or a moment hence but now as the images lie in the mind's eye and penetrate the mind's ear, as the subtle rhythms go below the conscious mind to recreate for us the same new-born self that they express. As that self is the poet's and not the poet's, so it is ours and not ours; perhaps it is most properly to be called the self of the poem—requiring both poet and reader, as they require it, to come into unified being. Thus it is that in "analyzing" *Four Quartets*, one is not taking apart an external thing; "analysis" here is much more like fingering the springs of one's own being—that being that only exists as it becomes with the process of the poem.

The *Quartets* have in common with the *Essays* of Montaigne this great capacity: to be new and different in every moment that the reader responds to them. For the voice of the *Quartets*, for the "I" of the *Essays*, and for the reader, the consciousness that lies behind and around the creation, that seeks and finds words and sounds and metaphors for experience, is a constantly renewed thing, a quality continually "aborning," a state different at every point, and especially at the end (if there is an end), from what it was the moment before. It is no exaggeration to say—indeed, I think Eliot's poem every minute proves—that these expressive discoveries are as new and surprising for the poet as for his reader; and, which is to say the same thing, that they are entirely new and surprising each time one really returns to the poem, with all one is and not just with the eye. Not that our consciousness takes on philosophic substance but that it formally expands in its questioning and meditating and discovering. It is precisely this expanding, evolving consciousness that the poem both contains and expresses, both is and means. The poet, finding metaphors that increase awareness as they express it, formalizes the reader's experience equally with his own and brings coherence to both. Because this coming to consciousness has not happened but is happening in us, the poem never presents us with ordinary autobiographic description. How could it? Instead of resurrecting old counters from past experience and moving them around a new board, the poem performs, for its creator and its re-creator, the very imaginative, self-explorative process that it is about. Thus, the mode of the *Quartets* is not to discover truth and to present it, but to pursue and to create it, and not to create it outside the pursuit but within it. And in his re-creation, the reader, in effect, becomes the pursuit, the pondering, the process, the poem.

"This," in the *Quartets*, "is the use of memory": to free ourselves from the limitations of egotism by revealing the whole pattern of history in which the whole pattern of the self has been and is involved. Finding in our own actions the instincts and the necessities of humanity, we move from selfish attachment through the detachment of historic perspective, finally back to the central self that has succeeded in ordering history in its own image; that self being reintegrated now according to its newly created pattern.

> See, now they vanish,
> The faces and places, with the self which, as it could, loved them,
> To become renewed, transfigured, in another pattern.
>
> (LG, III, 14-16)

Thus the creative moment, whether God in his world, the poet in his poem, or the individual in his self, is the great, continuing act of love that produces something never to be lost from the sum of the universe. We may not, in our divided state, see its eternity, but any creation, divine, artistic, or individual, as Los informs us in Blake's *Milton*, is forever:

314

The generations of men run on in the tide of Time,
But leave their destin'd lineaments permanent for ever & ever.[25]

Again like Montaigne, the speaker or philosophizer of *Four Quartets*, who is also us, embodies and proves a dramatic truth but only questions philosophic truth. As readers of the *Essays* or the *Quartets*, we have no more knowledge at the end than at the beginning; but we see things differently and we relate things in different ways not because they have at all changed but because we have, and because there exists now a new metaphor for our self. The *Four Quartets* present as little of "a philosophy" as the *Essays*. "The poet who 'thinks,'" Eliot says in an essay of 1927, "is merely the poet who can express the emotional equivalent of thought."[26] *Four Quartets* is an intense evocation of how it feels to pursue such thought as we call philosophic, an intensely realized metaphor and dramatization of what it is like to meditate. "The term, Philosophy," according to Coleridge, who was speaking of his own activities, but he describes equally well the practice of either Montaigne or Eliot, "defines itself as an affectionate seeking after the truth; but Truth is the correlative of Being."[27] In this way the material of *Four Quartets*, even "what the poet starts from" and what he ends with, is not Truth in an absolute, capitalized sense, but "an affectionate seeking after the truth," which is a lower-case word, a subjective fact, and a relative experience. In the process of becoming aware and of expanding consciousness, the poet, with his reader, comes into a unified state of being in the poem; and the correlative of being (perhaps not an "objective correlative" but a subjective one), as Coleridge says, is truth, which will be as intensely there in the poem—the truth of the poem, nothing else—as the self or the being brought to consciousness.

[25] *Milton*, Book the First, section 24: *Poetry and Prose*, p. 401.
[26] "Shakespeare and the Stoicism of Seneca," *Selected Essays*, p. 135.
[27] *Biographia Literaria*, ed. J. Shawcross, 2 vols. (London: Oxford Univ. Press, 1907), 1, chap. 9, 94.

It is odd and interesting, also I think significant, that three men as distinct and different in their conscious and public personalities and in their "works and days" as T. S. Eliot, Michel de Montaigne, and C. G. Jung, should have found, beyond the reach of discursive language but not beyond the evocative powers of metaphor, style, and myth, the same essential subject: the whole self-in-becoming. Of the *Four Quartets* one might say yet more: that in them the poet combines the intuitive depth of the mystic's vision with the sensory delicacy of the scientist's observation and the structural inevitability of the logician's syllogism, the complete consort dancing together to the rhythm of the emotions and of the unconscious, to realize the complete pattern of self. And how—being moved by that rhythm, being caught up in that pattern—how *shall* we know the dancer from the dance?

six : Synthesis

the correlative of Being

From the argument about autobiography and poetry in the foregoing pages certain conclusions begin to emerge—conclusions not confined to autobiographical literature or to poetry but touching as well on the other characteristically human endeavors of philosophy and psychology, and bearing, indeed, on the one subject, the one motive, behind all human endeavors in whatever field: the experience, precisely, of being human. When one reflects on the "meaning" of the lives and the works and the autobiographies of Fox and Darwin, Mill and Newman, and when one considers the significance of what Montaigne offers us in his *Essays*, Jung in his *Memories*, and Eliot in his *Quartets*, then certain ideas seem to assume a shape, as it were on their own, from the mere conjunction of different works and different men, all nonetheless engaged in the business of living and writing about it—ideas that are at first vague and tentative, then gradually clearer and more precise, and eventually both inevitable and far-reaching in their implications. I have in mind such conclusions as these:

that the ideal of Symbolic Man might be abstractly and synthetically composed from the typical or extreme psychologies of "one-sided" men; that to add together four distinct and perhaps eccentric fourths is to conceive the one and ideal, concentric whole;

that philosophy and psychology are not, or should not be, preceptual, nor are they objective or divine, but are lived, subjective, human "sciences," proper and peculiar to man, essays in truth or experiments in being;

that the opposites, the partials, and the contradictions presented to us in experience—and life itself seems to be generated in the interplay of such opposites—are all reconciled and resolved in the act of self-realization;

that, as one can conceive of an ideal psychic being, which would no longer represent a limited "type" but would stand for the symbolic whole, and as one can realize self, so there is also an ideal act of autobiography which creates in metaphor and recreates in the reader's experience that ideal psychic being and realized self; and that we sometimes call this ideal act autobiography, we other times call it poetry, but it is always art.

Christianity tells us that man, before he fell, was entire to himself, complete and whole, lacking in nothing, essentially the same perfect being as the Platonic Idea of Man or the Adam Kadmon of the Kabbala; and Christianity also promises, on certain conditions of faith and practice, a postrestoration vision equal in wholeness and splendor to that prelapsarian one. It may be, however, that in this in-between state of fall and aspiration in which we find ourselves, where wholeness is more a notion than a condition, we can conceive of wholeness, or realize it, only synthetically and symbolically. For synthesizing Symbolic Man there can be, I should think, no better source and substance than the autobiographies of men who went their own, undoubtedly limited, ways, lived their lives as best they could, became themselves as fully as possible from the capacities that were potentially theirs at birth. The Platonic ladder that reaches to the Idea of Man is constructed of materials that one takes from quite different and even opposed sources—one rung formed of Mill's experience, another of Darwin's, Newman making one side of the ladder, Fox the other—materials alike only in that all of them once lived as men. Or in aggregate they might better be seen not as a ladder, where rungs must be higher and lower, but as a wheel with four spokes, at the four points of the compass, a great circle or sphere with its single still point at the theoretical center and a rich human variety on the real, turning circumference. This composite psychological wheel one must conceive of as tensely energetic, as a thing of multiple violence contained in pattern, for the pulls of the four arms would be in all directions at once and as strong as the personalities of the four men. The lion, it may be, will one day lie down peacefully with the lamb, but not Darwin with Fox, not willingly, and not Mill with Newman—except, that is, in our ideal conception.

Fox's way, the pull that he gives to the wheel, was to turn entirely inward, and that was the source both of his triumph and his failure, the source of his very being. While Fox was himself always one and the same, that oneness yet brought a variety of results, for others differed markedly and changed continuously in their reactions to that which was George Fox. To see that men might disagree with Fox and still be good men—which was not always apparent to Fox himself, for he gave as little of his attention to others as to the outside world —one has only to consider what Fox would have meant to any of the other three men, all of them good men, his partners in the psychological wheel. What would Fox have been to Newman, who valued so highly tradition and institutional religion, both of them anathema to Fox? What would he have been to Mill, who was uncharacteristically passionate in his denunciation of those who could be convinced on a priori grounds and by intuitive evidence? Or to Darwin, who found his all and only in a natural, created world accessible to those senses that Fox knew nothing of? For if Fox was in-turned to the Light of God, Darwin, on the contrary, admitted no divinity besides external nature where, he was sure, the law of evolution, general, inexorable, and nonhuman, could be read inductively by the rational observer. And that assumption or

319

that certainty was the source of all that Darwin was and did. Here, at least, Fox and Darwin were alike: from the individual's temperamental bias came both his success and his vulnerability, from it came, in Darwin's case, the scientific achievement and, inevitably, the psychic illness. It is as if Fox, pulling with all his personal force and individual limitation toward the center, were counterbalanced by Darwin, pushing away from that subjective heart, with an equal and opposite strength, after his objective, external goddess.

Mill's was a mind of high abstraction that, in contrast to both Fox and Darwin, turned in neither direction but sustained itself by its own productions. Though he acknowledged the necessity of experience as stimulus to thought, Mill seems capable of working from one thought alone without the necessity of further contact either inside or outside: set moving, his mind could abstract from abstractions almost to infinity. Newman, on the other hand, given his typical psychology, mediates between outer and inner, being a man with some degree of each of the virtues exaggerated in the other three; for it is feeling such as Newman's, operating from the center of being, that judges and values everything that the individual experiences: all the insights of intuition, all the evidence of the senses, all the conclusions of the mind. The profoundly inner and the broadly outer, the highly abstract without a *pied-à-terre* in the concrete-real, and the quick mediator that touches and judges them all, looking in, then out, abstracting from both and considering the value of all—this is the composition of ideal psychic being, and it is, significantly, rather like certain descriptions of all the aspects of the psyche: the unconscious and consciousness, superego and ego.

If one thus combines—which is not, of course, possible in living reality—the mind of John Stuart Mill with the senses of Charles Darwin and the intuition of George Fox, and binds them all into unity with the feeling of John Henry Newman, the result is Symbolic Man, a synthetic creature that one might also call by the symbolic name of, let us say, "Montaigne"; not, however, Montaigne as living, sixteenth-century man, but Montaigne-in-his-*Essays*, or Montaigne as his own metaphor for man, or Montaigne as his own ideal conception of himself. Of the *Four Quartets* one might say much the same, referring, however, to the "Voice of *Four Quartets*" rather than to "Eliot," in order to emphasize the anonymity, the symbolic wholeness, the more than personal experience of metaphorized Man. Again, Jung, if we think of him both as man and his own conception of Man, appears more than life-size, somehow complete in the conjunction of fact and theory. The makers of the *Essays*, the *Quartets*, and the *Memories*, whatever they were committed to as men, are dedicated, as artists, not to science, not to logic, not to a god or to *the* God, but to metaphoric recreation and celebration of the realities of the human condition, individual and universal. They bring together the various separated daimons of partial men into the inclusive one of the symbolic self. One might say that Fox, Darwin, Mill, Newman, each of them embodied truth by his life but could not know it; and that Montaigne, Jung, Eliot, in the great self-consciousness of their works, portray together an embodiment and a simultaneous meaning. These men seem to prove—refuting the letter but not the spirit of Yeats's remark—that it is possible, in metaphoric art of the whole self, to embody truth *and* to know it. But this is so only for art, not for life.

Philosophy, psychology, and poetry thus engage the whole man and all of his experience as logic, natural science, institutional religion, and Puritan evangelism do not. We can distinguish, consequently, two legitimate, but quite different, senses of autobiography: one, that relates to the performance of poetry, of philosophizing and psychologizing, is a continuous action, the philosophy, psychology, and poetry being

321

identical with the autobiography; the other, dealing with such activities as logic, natural science, the evolution of religious opinions, and puritanizing evangelism, comes after those activities and, while shaped by the same personal tendency, neither coincides with nor is identical to those activities. A habit of mind, with Darwin, say, or with Mill, shapes the style, but it is not the subject and object of the book: while methods of working and modes of seeing carry over from the other books of Darwin and Mill to their autobiographies, substance does not. Mill's *Autobiography* is logical, but it is not logic; Darwin's *Autobiography* intends to be as objective as natural science, but it is not natural science. Montaigne's book, on the other hand, is both philosophy and philosophical, a contemplation and an enactment of being; Jung's book is both psychology and psychological, the self in concept and the self in performance; Eliot's poetry is both philosophical and psychological—being a poem, it is also embodied philosophy and dramatized psychology. To interpret any of these latter works, one must go beyond logic—not abandon it, of course —beyond rational intellect and the evidence of the senses; one must live the works and become them, in the same sense in which one says that the authors embodied their being entirely in the creation of the works. Keats suggests that Shakespeare's plays should be seen as a commentary on his symbolic life, a remark that might be turned around to say, in addition, that our lives individually comment on, or draw out the meanings of, Shakespeare or Eliot, Montaigne or Jung; and, to the degree that they do so, our lives too become symbolic.

Scientific theory, though subjectively conditioned in its origin, may be objectively validated in experience or experiments in the external world; philosophy, being of the nature of poetry, is validated in experience in the inner world of thought and emotions, in the understanding of one's self. The predicament of psychology is to fall, or rise, between the two: like all human pursuits it is subjectively based; it proposes, like physics, general and objective laws of behavior; but these laws, since they deal with "as if" states, with conscious-subconscious conditions, with unique being, can be validated, like philosophy, only in the imagination, in the thoughts and emotions, of the individual. Sir James Jeans, in an interesting passage in *Physics and Philosophy*, implies that the difference between his titular subjects is to be found not in the questions they deal with, nor in their testing of theories, but in the success of the two disciplines in solving the problems they propose for themselves. After quoting Anatole France's remark on the crude inadequacy of language as a philosophical tool ("un metaphysicien n'a, pour constituer le système du monde, que le cri perfectionné des singes et des chiens"), Jeans takes the view that philosophy, after thousands of years, continues to fail where physics has at least begun to succeed. "Yet," he says, we should not look down on the philosophers, or think their burden is light, for "the major problems of philosophy are for the most part very difficult; many of them tax the human mind to the utmost limits of its capacity, and have baffled the most acute intellects of our race for thousands of years— indeed it is hardly too much to say that not one of them has been solved yet."[1] In an optimistic conclusion to his book— the last paragraph—Jeans seems to suggest that these "major problems of philosophy" can be and will be solved and so, one by one, ticked off from the list of human work that remains to do. One wonders, however, whether the "major problems of philosophy" are soluble in the same sense as the "major problems of physics" may be. At least one can be quite certain in saying that problems of philosophy do not find their eventual resolution in the "most acute intellects of our

[1] *Physics and Philosophy* (Cambridge: Cambridge Univ. Press, 1942), p. 85.

323

race," or in the least acute: if resolved, they must be so in a whole life, in the whole being of Socrates, not in a schematic, rational answer of the intellect or a logical theory about the nature of things. Considering that this is the only way problems of philosophy can be answered, I should think it no exaggeration to turn the remark around and to say that *all* the major problems of philosophy have been solved—again and again and again: not, perhaps, for the human race, except in exemplary ways, but for the only living unit of the race. Heraclitus, for example, solved a whole host of problems when he said, "You cannot step twice into the same river": he solved them, that is, for the moment and made the question, if not a final answer, available for the reader to solve and resolve in his own life and thought. Plotinus solves a problem bearing on the philosophy of autobiography, and proves that he understood the solution of Heraclitus, when he writes, after a quotation from Heraclitus, that "he seems to teach by metaphor, not concerning himself about making his doctrine clear to us, probably with the idea that it is for us to seek within ourselves as he sought for himself and found."[2] That the problems have been solved once before, or perhaps many times, does not at all mean that they need not be solved any more—quite the contrary. The charge on us as human beings, as the heirs of our fathers and the spiritual inheritors of Montaigne, Jung, Eliot and all "the most acute intellects of our race," is to solve the problems again, as those ancestors did, but in our own way.

Indeed, it is difficult to know exactly what problems Jeans has in mind. The reader of *Four Quartets* who has followed the process of the poem and lived it, right up to the conclusive "one," must feel that the problem of the One and the many is solved and resolved entirely in the last line of the poem.

[2] Fourth *Ennead*, tractate eight, no. 1; trans. Stephen MacKenna and B. S. Page, 3rd ed. (London: Faber & Faber, 1962), p. 357.

The problem of free will and necessity—surely another of philosophy's "major problems"—is solved to the responsive reader's satisfaction in the poem that Yeats lived and wrote as "A Prayer for My Daughter":

> all hatred driven hence
> The soul recovers radical innocence
> And learns at last that it is self-delighting,
> Self-appeasing, self-affrighting,
> And that its own sweet will is heaven's will.

Montaigne solved the same problem in the same way: with his life and in his metaphor. And these problems that have proved so vexing in the history of philosophy—are they not solved for the reader of Eliot, of Yeats, of Montaigne if he *feels* they are? Of course these are all individual and subjective and interim solutions, but one should not imagine that they could be otherwise. Philosophy, which is composed really of questions, attempts, hints, aperçus, does not accumulate answers for all the ages; it lives them in the quick moment of being.

Or perhaps the major problem of philosophy, subsuming all the lesser "major problems," is Truth. If so, then one can only suggest again, with Coleridge, that "Truth is the correlative of Being." The great autobiographers are great precisely because they have never ceased in their "affectionate seeking after truth," so have never ceased coming into being, so have never ceased to realize truth. "Know thyself," I should imagine, is an answer, if we can but realize it, to all the problems of philosophy: an answer which has, in order that it be valid and viable, to be filled and completed in our response to the imperative. It becomes an answer as we obey the command. The degree to which Montaigne was Montaigne, the extent to which he knew and became himself, is the degree to which he solved the problems of philosophy. More than that we could neither ask nor desire. This, of course, is one reason why auto-

325

biography is so valuable, and especially autobiography of the twofold variety where the answer is re-enacted in metaphor even as and while enacted in life.

No biographer—leaving aside for a moment the auto-biographer, who on this point is in a rather peculiar position—can afford to confess that there is no underlying organizational principle, no hidden harmony, no coherent shape and direction discoverable in the life he would write. No biographer has ever said, or ever will say, that the life of his subject, as reflected in his actions, was a mere chaos and confusion. It may be that he imposes the pattern, but if it is not there and apparent in the final *Life*, we assume, as readers, that the biographer has written a meaningless work, or that he is at fault in not finding the clue and drawing it out to reveal the essential unity. If we thus assume, in effect, that every human existence, taken after the fact, has its particular delineation, its distinctive form and direction, its own "teleological unity," do we not thereby imply the notion that every life is realization of a potential that is both generally human and uniquely individual? We imply belief, that is to say, in a coherent and integral self, potential at first and destined, though no one can foredraw the exact shape of destiny, to be realized through many experiences until it shall become this one, and no other, self.

The self of each of us, that one source at which we experience life, is surrounded by a complex and sometimes, no doubt, bewildering series of concentric circles: those greater and greater abstractions derivable from the single concretion and the final reality of individual being. That single and unique being, which is so odd to the individual and, I think, inconceivable to everyone else, is what we designate by the proper name—Michel de Montaigne, John Henry Newman, Thomas Stearns Eliot. And like the peculiar, private consciousness that it signifies, the proper name is something always there and essential to the individual, something that one cannot quite imagine being without: being named (for example) "James," or *being* "James," I cannot conceive what it would be to be "John" or "Byron," what it would be to have another consciousness with another name, or to hear, as one might say, the echo of heartbeats other than my own. We are all, outside this central uniqueness, hedged in by the imperatives of each of our group abstractions or identities, so that the family says that, to bear the name and remain one of them, we must do this, the city tells us we shall do that, the nation makes other claims on us, our humanity urges that we be men. For the mature and integral self, however, the first and last imperatives are probably the ones which finally and only matter; and for the momentarily completed self they seem to be one and the same: to "know thyself" is to "be a man." In that moment, the final abstraction says and becomes the same as the first particularity, and at that point the man is Man symbolically realized.

One speaks of "that moment" when and "that point" at which the self is completed or realized, but these terms should be understood as the metaphors forced by language into a discussion of the transrational that tries still to be rational; for the realized self, as Montaigne, Jung, Eliot, all agree, is quite unaffected by spatio-temporal limitations, and if it is touched by conditions of space and time, it is to that extent incomplete. Being a spark off eternal, ubiquitous divinity, the self, in realizing that source and destiny, becomes again an epitome of its own divine heritage and so transcends the conditions through which paradoxically the realization must be effected. Yet one can only speak in terms of those human conditions, not in terms of the divine realization: there are, for that transcendence, no terms, there is no human language, unless it be poetry. The archetype of wholeness, to put the matter of time and

327

space in Jung's metaphoric language, remains always the same as an instinctual creative base and background of human life as we know it. It remains the same, this potential *donnée*; only we change. But ever and again one attains to that archetypical image, or seems to come to creative, conscious realization of the inherent human pattern; one becomes, in short, what one has always been and been intended to be—and for a moment we are in eternity, outside any restrictions. It would seem that, in realizing the self—which is the moral demand that the given life makes of us—one is perfecting humanity and completing creation in the only way that one can do it: in one's own self. Thus it may be that God needs our help, not exactly in Mill's Manichaean sense to do battle against the evil power (though if evil is the absence of good, these may come to much the same thing), but to achieve creation itself. Perhaps our efforts at consciousness do, in the end, add up to God. At least, it is undoubtedly true that for many men the attempt to comprehend the self and its relation to the universe —an attempt that will be, depending on the individual, primarily intellectual or emotional or intuitive—that this attempt is nothing less than an experience of God. This is what is meant, in part, in saying that *Four Quartets* is philosophic poetry and that it resembles God and the self in Jung: the very process of the poem seems, to the reader who becomes it, like an experience of Deity, and that experience is inevitably internal, personal, private—an experience also in and of the self.

Coming to consciousness and self-consciousness is thus, for many men, like an experience of divinity, or is a way of experiencing divinity, and this is so whether we maintain or deny that such an experience of Deity is also creation of Deity. In any case, taking whichever point of view one likes, it would certainly be true to say that the Deity did not exist in exactly this way, a way that depends so much on psychological

328

conditions and subjective motives, before all the various internal tendencies and external influences conspired to effect this particular effort in consciousness. The point is that it does not seem to matter, when realization of the self is in question, whether we say "only subjective" or whether we say "God": what one experiences is unquestionably "only subjective," but what one experiences—and if this is what one experiences, who can say it is not?—is, undeniably, "God." This is but a step from saying, what is also true, that realization of the self is divine, and that, in our moment, in perfecting his creation, we return the favor of God and create him in our own best image. As self-realization reconciles the human and the divine, so also it reconciles—or seems to reconcile, and that is the only thing that anyhow matters—all the other opposites that have beguiled man and plagued him since he became something that could be called human. Realization of the self, for example, as in Yeats's "Prayer for My Daughter," constitutes a reconciliation of the claims of free will and necessity and, as I have already suggested, it resolves the dilemma of the One and the many. It brings into a single process, as being the opposed but cooperative poles of energy that vitalize the process, such opposites as the subject and its objects; the world inside and the world outside; place and infinity; time and eternity; form and the formless; thought and emotion; experience and meaning; art for art's sake and art for the reader's sake, or, in Lawrence's phrase, art for my sake. Trying to say something in this book about the experience of the self, I have found the language of paradox unavoidable: "on the one hand this" and/but "on the other hand that." In reconciling so many opposites and contradictions, the self is seen, perhaps like all reality, to be intensely and ultimately paradoxical. The subjective point of view, which is all one can work from, determines at every instant the way things are seen, and a slight refocus of the subjective vision—as we can

329

refocus the eyes to see in a drawing a new figure where before we had seen quite a different one—makes the contingent inevitable and the conditional absolute. But the profoundest paradox of all, I imagine, is that this very paradox is itself, if one thinks about it, simple and complex: reality, being subjective and objective, is in both aspects both one and many, both univocal and equivocal.

The ideal spirit or psyche that one can synthesize from the various parts proved in various men's partial lives is not, of course, something that any one man has ever enjoyed or ever can enjoy in his life, or if, seemingly, he experiences it for a moment, then not throughout his life. Yet we can, as before, imagine that ideal spirit in which the most acute intellect, the profoundest intuition, the most exact senses, and the surest feeling exist as a oneness of being that renders the faculties inseparable from one another as if each were the expression of the whole being. Beyond these, what more is there, what else of human possibility, to be comprehended in the whole being—except, which we cannot give by either analysis or synthesis, but only from our own life, the creative spark to make the being live. If no one man, however, possesses the ideal spirit, and if synthesis has no life in itself, yet a poem like *Four Quartets*, a work of art about the nature of self-being, makes the spirit symbolically real and brings it to life, as, in fact, we do also in our fullest response to the poem. The experience of *Four Quartets* is not solely emotional or intuitive, nor is it altogether intellectual or sensational, though it partakes richly and at every point of each of these: the various and partial faculties are merged in the effect of the poem as a total being, drawing out a total response. *Four Quartets* renders the feeling of thought, it evokes sensory contemplation and intellectual emotion, it has about it an intuition so deep that this intuition becomes identical with whole being.

330

Poetry, as Coleridge remarked, is a creative act analogous, in its own realm, to the divine *fiat*, bringing into being a symbolic self and with it an entire universe.

Though he may be its creator, the poet, like any man, can exist only in his own universe. The dilemma that physics, according to Max Planck, faces again and again is that experimenters cannot get outside their experiments: the recording apparatus, the experimenter, the subject becomes willy-nilly a part of the phenomenon, the experiment, the object. The assumptions of the experiment become the conditions of its results. This must inevitably be truer yet when, as in autobiography, life itself is the experiment and when the elements of all life, as individually experienced, are the acting and reacting agents: there can be no question of the experimenter, i.e., living man, being either outside the system or in control of its conditions. I do not mean, of course, that the autobiographer cannot fix the limits of his autobiography around a finished action. Fox, Darwin, Mill, and (to a degree) Newman do just that. But even as the autobiographer fixes limits in the past, a new experiment in living, a new experience in consciousness, whether he intends it or not, and a new projection or metaphor of a new self is under way. One cannot write an autobiography without being alive and without also proving the quality of that life in the created metaphor; for to exercise memory, to be conscious and to increase consciousness, to make one's metaphor, is to live. This is why the great poets and the greatest autobiographers figure in their creations as circles within circles: the experimenter observing the experimenter-and-his-experiment and observing himself observing the experimenter-and-his-experiment and observing . . . and so on to infinity, or to that ideal state of full and perfect self-consciousness where there is awareness of the total self, physical and spiritual, instinctive and willed, awareness of all the forces of the surrounding universe, including, as well as one can, other selves, awareness of any controlling, divine spirit. Such a perfect, hypothetical experiment and experience is another name for self-completion and self-realization on the part of a perfected human become divine: it is transcendent self-awareness, the created universe existing as a thought in the totally self-aware mind of—call the being what one will—God.

That universe and its meaning, or that ideal spirit and its real existence, are what one seeks, whether synthetically or symbolically. Fox, Darwin, Mill, and Newman provide for us the elements of synthetic realization; Montaigne, Jung, and Eliot, the whole symbolic realization. They were all great men, and in no way more than this: that each, in the only way he could and as only he could, testified to his own humanity. Life—their lives and works and symbols seem to say—has no explanation, but it may have a meaning. And that meaning will be discovered by us, if at all, as it was discovered by these men, if at all, as the correlative to one's own being, a metaphor of one's own self.

Index

333